WARWICKSHIRE
TOWNS & VILLAGES

Geoff Allen

Series Editor: Terry Marsh

Published by Sigma Leisure – an imprint of
Sigma Press, 1 South Oak Lane, Wilmslow, Cheshire SK9 6AR, England.

British Library Cataloguing in Publication Data
A CIP record for this book is available from the British Library.

ISBN: 1-85058-642-X

Series Editor: Terry Marsh

Typesetting and Design by: Sigma Press, Wilmslow, Cheshire.

Cover Design: MFP Design & Print

Cover photographs: main picture – Malt Mill Lane, Alcester; smaller pictures, from top – the village green, Sambourne; the Barley Mow, Studley; Church Cottage and All Saints' Church, Ladbroke.

Photographs: by the author

Map: Morag Perrott

Printed by: MFP Design & Print

Contents

WARWICKSHIRE

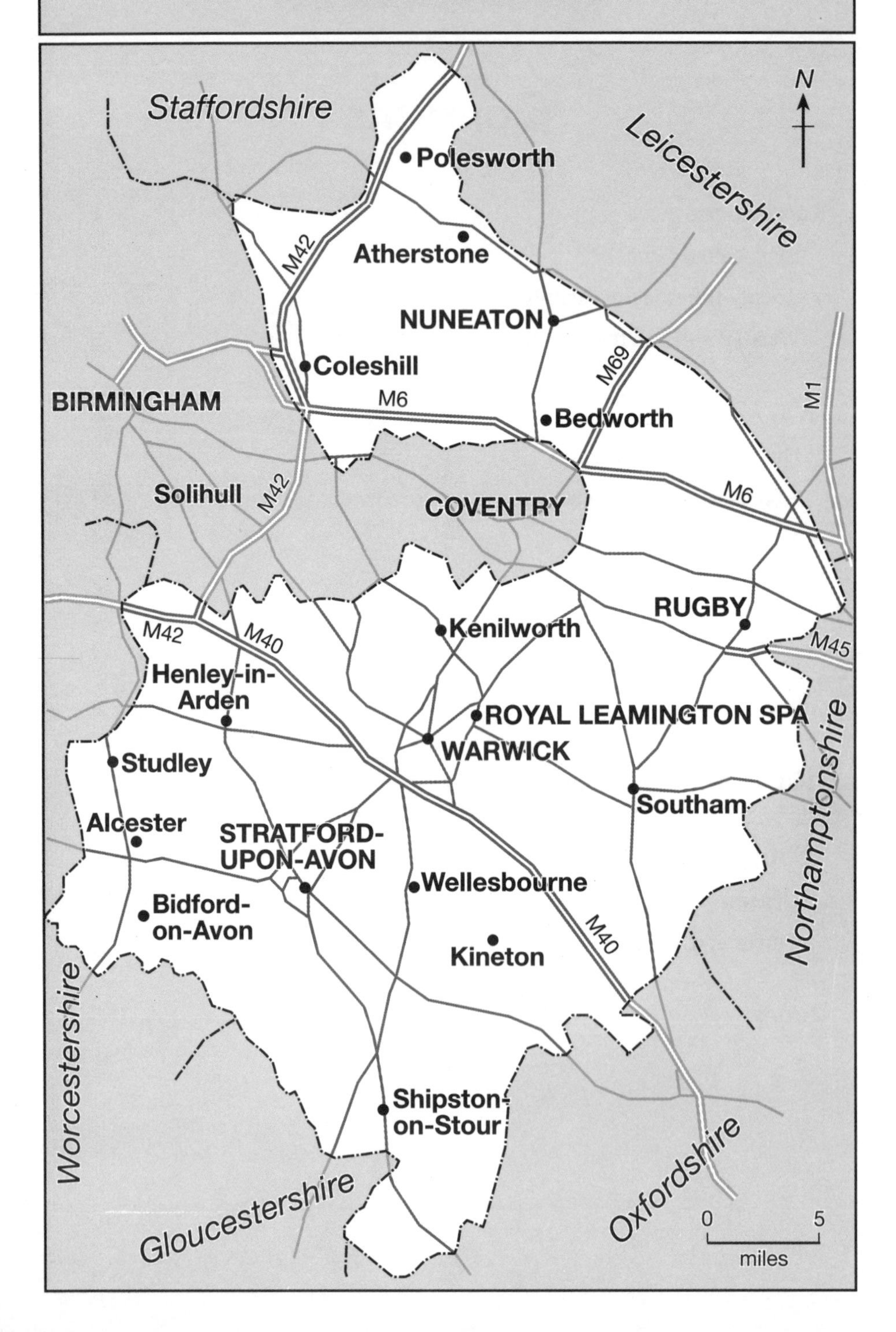

POSTSCRIPT
BOOKS BY MAIL

DESPATCH/ADVICE NOTE

24 LANGROYD ROAD
LONDON
SW17 7PL UK
TEL: +44 (0)20 8767 7421
FAX: +44 (0)20 8682 0280
e-mail: enquiries@psbooks.co.uk
www.psbooks.co.uk

PAGE 1 OF

DELIVER TO:

Mr Hailwood
23 Churchill Crescent
Alrewas
Burton-On-Trent, Staffordshire
DE13 7EH

DATE:

DELIVERY METHOD:
30/06/2005
UK Business Express
2039320

If undelivered,
please return to:
POSTSCRIPT
24 Langroyd Road
London SW17 7PL
UK

ORDERED BY: Mr Hailwood 255260

ORDER No:
YOUR REF:

CUSTOMER ACCOUNT No: 255260
OUR REFERENCE: 2039320

*** See our complete range of titles online at www.psbooks.co.uk ***

WAREHOUSE LOCATION	CODE	QTY	DESCRIPTION	UNIT PRICE	TOTAL
D14B	31114	1	Alphabet Abecedarium	3.99	3.99
D02A	30999	1	Britain: Then & Now	5.99	5.99
R14C	29876	1	Nine Against the Unknown £ =	2.99	2.99
R05C	29807	1	North Yorkshire - Strange but True	4.99	4.99
P14C	27808	1	Warwickshire Towns & Villages SL-	3.99	3.99
1CAT	ZZWEB	1	ZZZ Catalogue (BBWEB)	0.00	

Payment Received With Thanks:-

VI/M Visa/Mastercard 24.95

		6		WEIGHT	2.56	GOODS TOTAL	21.95
NOTES						POST & PACKING	3.00
PICKED BY:		PACKED BY:				TOTAL	£ 24.95

Introduction

The 'Town and Villages of Britain' is a series of titles detailing a county-by-county approach to the many delights and fascinations of our country's cities, towns, villages and hamlets. There is much of interest and value throughout our towns and villages, but not all of it is widely documented, and some of it, particularly local customs, folklore and traditions, is in danger of being lost forever. By bringing all this information together, county-by-county, it becomes possible to build a unique and substantially comprehensive library of knowledge.

All of the books in the series are compiled to the same specification and in gazetteer format, and include information about the way or the reason a town or village evolved; references to anything associated with the preservation of the past, such as museums, heritage centres, historic or prehistoric sites, battle sites, places of worship and other locally or architecturally important buildings. Landscape features are also detailed, including important natural history sites, geological sites, water features, etc. as is information about important local people, and details of events or traditions, such as well-dressings and rush-bearing ceremonies. There are also notes about any significant present-day informal amenity/recreational features, like country parks, open access land, Areas of Outstanding Natural Beauty, nature reserves, and Sites of Special Scientific Interest. Finally, information is given on any significant Roman or prehistory context, and any anecdotal or endemic folklore references associated with the town or village which might illustrate a particular way of life or social development. The books are therefore eminently suitable for anyone interested in their own locality or in local history; students of history, folklore and related subjects; professional journalists wanting up-to-date and comprehensive information; public relations and similar businesses; photographers and artists, and, of course, the tourists and visitors to the counties.

Explanatory Notes

It has been suggested that to qualify as a village, a 'community' must possess a school, a pub, a post office and a church. Such a requirement, however, excludes a large number of places that are of immense interest, many having important historical associations, and which have played a vital part in the development of the county and its people. So, for the purposes of the books in this series, the criteria for inclusion have been kept deliberately simple: there must be something of interest about the place; or it must have associations with events and people of countywide or wider significance.

Often, the 'something of interest' will simply be the village church (its history, contents or architecture), or its green or a river bridge. In addition, the village may be important to the heritage of the county because it maintains the traditions, ways and beliefs of local culture, or has played a key role in the social, economic or political history of the county or the country as a whole.

Only occasionally, however, is the village pub of special interest in this context, and often the development of large supermarkets within easy travelling distance of the villages has, sadly, signalled the demise of the traditional village shop. Local schools have often been swallowed up by larger schools, and far too many post offices are proving difficult to sustain as viable concerns. So, while that 'classic' definition of a village has much to commend it, in reality it is today too restrictive.

Quite what makes a town is another, arguable, matter. But the precise definition is not too important here; it's the place and its people, not its status, that matters. As a very broad distinction, that no-one should take seriously, a 'hamlet' (a few of which appear in these books) is a distinct community, while a 'village' could be said to be a hamlet with a church, and a 'town' is a village with a market.

In many cases, the historical development of the community, whether a tiny village, a town or a city, is fascinating in itself, and so it is that each entry gradually builds up a picture of the county that is unique. That is what this book endeavours to portray, in a logical and easily accessible way, as well as being a source of reference.

Inevitably, there will be places that have been omitted that others might argue should have been included. But the value each community has to bring to a work of this nature has been carefully weighed; invariably, borderline cases have been given the benefit of the doubt and included.

It is equally clear that, taken to its logical conclusion, this book would be ten times larger, and there has had to be a considerable degree of selective editing to make it of manageable size. One day, perhaps, there could be one book that says everything there is to say about the county, but could we afford to buy it? Could we carry it? Would we want it, when part of the beauty of what does exist is the range of voices and shades of opinion so many different authors can bring?

Following the General Introduction, the book becomes a gazetteer, listing the towns and villages of the county in alphabetical order.

- ⓘ After each town or village name there appears, in square brackets, [ ], the name of the relevant district council (see below).
- ⓘ Next appears a two-letter, four-figure grid reference, which will pinpoint the settlement to within half a mile (one kilometre). This is followed by an approximate distance from some other, usually larger, settlement, together with an equally approximate direction indicator.
- ⓘ Those features or people 'of interest' directly associated with the settlement are highlighted in bold text, while an index lists other features or people only incidentally associated.
- ⓘ Where information is given about events, such as agricultural shows, or facilities, such as museums, details of dates and hours of opening are usually available from any of the Tourist Information Centres listed below.

County Information Centres

Coventry: Tourist Information Centre, Bayley Lane, Coventry, CV1 5RN. Tel: 01203 832303.

Kenilworth: Tourist Information Centre, Kenilworth Library, 11 Smalley Place, Kenilworth, CV8 1QG. Tel: 01926 852595.

Leamington Spa: Tourist Information Centre, The Royal Pump Rooms, The Parade, Leamington Spa. Tel: 01926 742762.

Nuneaton: Tourist Information Centre, The Library, Church Street, Nuneaton, CV11 4DR. Tel: 01203 384027.

Rugby: Tourist Information Centre, 4-5 Lawrence Sheriff Street, Rugby, CV22 5EJ. Tel: 01788 534970.

Stratford-upon-Avon: Tourist Information Centre, Bridgefoot, Stratford-upon-Avon, CV37 6GW. Tel: 01789 293127.

Warwick: Tourist Information Centre, The Court House, Jury Street, Warwick, CV34 4EW. Tel: 01926 492212.

Warwickshire on the Internet

Of the many web sites about the county, two useful ones are: **www.cwn.org.uk** (the official source of news and information on Coventry and Warwickshire) and **www.warwickshire.co.uk** (a well organised guide that includes entertainment and acommodation with drop-down menus for the main regions and towns).

Warwickshire

Landlocked in the very centre of England, Warwickshire is a mainly rural county broken up by more than a dozen towns, many of them sizeable. It no longer includes Birmingham and Coventry, or Solihull and its villages. They were cut adrift in 1974 to form the Metropolitan County of the West Midlands and, despite the demise of that authority, have remained outside the shire. Therefore, this guidebook deals only with the official Warwickshire of today – the area administered by Warwickshire County Council. As testified by the following pages, which contain more than 240 town and village entries, it is full of interest. In addition to the former West Midlands County – which slices into Warwickshire from the west, almost cutting off the two northern boroughs of Nuneaton and Bedworth and North Warwickshire – the county is bordered (clockwise from the north-east) by Leicestershire, Northamptonshire, Oxfordshire, Gloucestershire, Worcestershire and Staffordshire. For administration purposes, it is divided into five parts: the three boroughs of North Warwickshire, Rugby and Nuneaton and Bedworth, and the two district councils of Warwick and Stratford-on-Avon. (Oddly, the Stratford council's name differs slightly from the town's, which is Stratford-upon-Avon.) Of the five, Stratford District is much the largest, covering nearly half the county. A more ancient sub-division is between the Feldon and Arden, areas separated by the River Avon, which flows south-west through Warwickshire. The Feldon ('field-land') is the more southerly of the two and, in contrast to pastoral Arden, was intensively cultivated in medieval times. Though the Forest of Arden, with its Shakespearean echoes, was never entirely tree-covered, it was a more secret place of secluded farms and villages than the open Feldon.

Many rivers feed the Avon, most notably the Leam (pronounced 'leem' to the east and 'lem' to the west of its course). In the north, the River Tame has as its main tributaries the Cole, the Blythe and the Anker. The land they traverse consists mainly of liassic clays and limestone in the Feldon and Keuper marl in Arden. The Cotswold fringe is Jurassic sandstone and ironstone, and there is sand and gravel in the Avon valley to the east and the Tame valley to the north. Coal exists at the county's northern tip and in the Coventry area, but the only remaining mine is Daw Mill near Over Whitacre. Though the county is not noted for hills, the landscape is far from flat and a few modest heights stand out. The ridge at Hartshill Hayes, near Nuneaton, gives an immense outlook over the Leicestershire plain and commands a view of the Peak District, while east of Southam the Napton and Shuckburgh hills rise impressively above the level fields. Brailes Hill and Idlicote Hill are the major tops in lovely rolling countryside around Shipston-on-Stour, but for the county's highest point we must head for the Gloucestershire border, where the Ilmington Downs reach 850ft (261m). Warwickshire's sole natural boundary is with Oxfordshire to the south-east, where the Cotswold escarpment rises. To the north-east, the Roman Watling Street marks the border with Leicestershire for many miles, but the remainder of the county's total perimeter of some 200 miles (320km) is mostly arbitrary and has been subject to change.

History Begins

There were people living in the upper Avon valley and carelessly scattering flints in

Palaeolithic (or Early Stone Age) times, and from about 3000BC Neolithic man was farming in Warwickshire. Important sites included the great earthwork at Wappenbury on the upper Avon, Oldbury Camp on the Hartshill ridge, Meon Hill at the north-east corner of the Cotswolds and Nadbury Camp on Edge Hill. High on the Oxfordshire border, the Rollright Stones survive as a stone circle with outliers – folk-tales have naturally been attached to them. A prehistoric salt way from Droitwich to the East Midlands ran through the county, passing where Alcester and Stratford now stand. The Romans came, establishing the Lunt fort at Baginton, near Coventry. They defeated Queen Boudicca in the Anker valley in AD60, before settling peacefully in the area. Their roads included Watling Street, which linked Letocetum (Wall), near Lichfield in Staffordshire, with Manduessedum (Mancetter), Veronae and Tripontium in Warwickshire. In the west, Icknield (or Ryknild) Street led from Letocetum to Alauna (Alcester), and the Fosse Way (which largely superseded the prehistoric Jurassic Way) struck south-west across the county from Veronae, encouraging the creation of many later settlements nearby. Watling Street and the Fosse Way have developed into modern roads.

Saxons and the Danelaw

Roman Britain ended abruptly with the withdrawal of the legions in AD410, but the native Celts and any incomers from Rome and the Empire who stayed on were not left unmolested for long. From the Germanic regions of Europe the Angles arrived via the rivers Trent, Welland and Nene to settle in the Tame and upper Avon valleys, and the Saxons sailed up the Thames and the Severn to reach the south of the county. By the end of the 6th century they had settled. The area was split into two sections, that to the north-east becoming part of the kingdom of South Mercia and the south-west belonging to the Hwicce tribe. By the mid-7th century the powerful and expanding Mercian kingdom under Penda, its last heathen king, had absorbed the Hwicce. Christianised, Mercia became part of the diocese of Lichfield, though the Hwicce lands were soon transferred to Worcester. Settlements with names ending in 'ton' and 'ley' (meaning 'farm or village' and 'wood or clearing') began to appear, especially in Arden, and the town of Warwick developed from the 8th century as a market centre. That was in the reign of the great King Offa, who ruled Mercia from 757 to 796 and whose name is probably commemorated by the village of Offchurch, near Leamington. There he reputedly had a fortified manor house, Offchurch Bury, and may even have been interred in a Saxon stone coffin preserved in the church. By the mid-9th century the Danes began to arrive and in 886 Watling Street became the border between the Danelaw and a diminished Mercia. The Danes had comparatively little influence on the area and their place-names are rare in Warwickshire, though a few exist to the east. They often end with 'by', meaning a village or homestead. Early in the 11th century, the county ('Waeinewiscscr') was created, consisting of ten 'hundreds', as against the four of later times. In the middle of that century, Earl Leofric of Mercia, husband of Lady Godiva, became one of the most powerful men in England.

Norman Invasion

But times were due to change again, and in 1066, as we all know, the Normans arrived with a bang – or, at least, with a clash of swords and a crucial flight of arrows at the Battle of Hastings. William the Conqueror carved up the kingdom and gave estates to Norman lords in place of Saxon thanes, but Leofric's son Algar and Turchil of Warwick, who had not fought at Hastings, were allowed to keep their lands. The Normans were busy fortress builders. The great castle at Warwick, the magnificent ruin at Kenilworth, the impressive hilltop sites at Beaudesert and Brinklow, and the still lived-in Maxstoke Castle near Coleshill all date from their period. In 1085, when William and his lords were well established, the king wanted to know exactly what this England he had conquered consisted of. He therefore sent out surveyors to collect information, which appeared only a year later in Domesday Book. That unique record has about 300 entries for Warwickshire, though there are curious omissions – Coventry, for example. Warwick is the only town recorded, but some places that are now fairly small, such as Brailes, are shown to have been large for that time and more important than now. The inhabitants of the cultivated Feldon were wealthier than those of Arden and their area more populous, with perhaps up to sixty people per square mile. Mid-Warwickshire was not so heavily settled or prosperous and the north was poor and sparsely inhabited. Though Saxon England was Christian and had its places of worship, the building of the parish churches that have become such a glory of our countryside mostly began with the Normans. By the early 13th century 254 of them were recorded in Warwickshire, but only fragments remain of the period's architecture. Later ages tended to knock down and rebuild what they inherited, sometimes because it had fallen into decay.

The Middle Ages

In medieval times great houses began to appear. Baddesley Clinton Hall (Pevsner's 'perfect late medieval manor house') from the 15th century is among the oldest surviving. It is one of six great Warwickshire houses belonging to the National Trust, out of a dozen or more dating from the 18th century or earlier. In addition, Kenilworth Castle is in the care of English Heritage. The county's central position meant that it was often at the heart of events that shook the nation. This book makes frequent references to the Civil War (or wars) of the 1640s and to the Gunpowder Plot of 1605, which was hatched and largely staffed in Warwickshire. Indeed, the name of Robert Catesby, its instigator and a Warwickshire man, rather than that of Guy Fawkes, should be the first on people's lips when they speak of that unforgettable event. Most of the towns we know today grew from settlements that were granted markets in the Middle Ages. Stratford-upon-Avon was among the earliest of about forty Warwickshire markets established between the Conquest and the mid-15th century. Conversely, there are many sites of deserted villages, whose populations disappeared or moved to other sites for various reasons. The two most common were the long decline in the economy after the Black Death of 1349, which took a third of England's population, and clearances by landowners (including the monks of Combe and Stoneleigh abbeys) in order to establish downland for profitable sheep pastures. The south and east of the county were particularly hard hit by depopulation. Examples are Chesterton, still an eerie place to visit, and Wormleighton, on the fringe of Warwickshire's most desolate stretch of countryside. The late Princess of Wales's family, the Spencers of Althorp in Northamptonshire, and their predecessor William Cope, were responsible for the emptying of that vast area. Another notorious dispossessor was Sir Edward Belknap, who cleared land by the Avon at Whitchurch, near Stratford, and on the Burton Dassett Hills. Welsh drovers bound for London's Smithfield market with their cattle made an interesting addition to Warwickshire's road system in the Middle Ages. They established Welsh Road, which still exists as a lane between Cubbington and Offchurch.

The Coming of Industry

From 1723 efforts were made to improve

the miry county road system by establishing turnpikes, and with the beginning of the Industrial Revolution about 1770 the construction of canals began. Within Warwickshire are sections of the Stratford-upon-Avon, Coventry, Oxford and Ashby-de-la-Zouch Canals, plus the Grand Union, a 1929 amalgamation of several waterways. The county has a major reservoir at Draycote Water, near Rugby, and smaller ones at Shustoke. Earlswood Lakes consist of three scenic, wood-bound pools that feed the Stratford-upon-Avon Canal, and a former sand and gravel extraction area near the Staffordshire boundary has resulted in numerous pools, many of which have been landscaped to make up Kingsbury Water Park. Warwickshire had a railway as early as 1826, when horse-drawn carriages began to trundle along the 16-mile track between Stratford-upon-Avon and Moreton-in-Marsh, Gloucestershire. Today, though many dismantled lines exist in the county, services link Birmingham with Coventry, Warwick, Leamington and Stratford, and Coventry with Leamington, Warwick and Stratford. Bedworth and Nuneaton have stations on the Coventry to Tamworth line. The county is at the hub of the motorway system, with the M6, M45, M40, M42 and M69 all within it and the M1 just outside. Thus, as in the days when prehistoric trackways, the canals or the railways were the main means of communication, Warwickshire is at the centre of a web linking it to other parts of the country.

Exploring the County

Those who believe that the best way to explore a county and its towns and villages is on foot are twice-blessed in Warwickshire. Two 100-mile (160km) long-distance footpaths, the Centenary Way and the Heart of England Way, pass through it and take in many of the villages and some of the towns. The first, established by the county council to celebrate its hundredth anniversary in 1989, links Kingsbury Water Park in the north with Upper Quinton, near Meon Hill, in the south, via a route looping east of Coventry. The other – an example of private enterprise, opened in 1979 and leading from Cannock Chase to the Cotswolds – is the product of the Heart of England Way Association. It enters Warwickshire near Kingsbury Water Park and takes a more westerly route than the Centenary Way, but exits near Meon Hill. Thus, using the two trails, it is possible to make a grand circular tour of the county on foot. Guidebooks (see Bibliography) are available for both these ways and for the Warwickshire Villages Trail, a 143-mile (230km) U-shaped route, devised by Gerald Lawrence, that visits 71 villages or hamlets in the southern half of the county.

The Changing Village

Of particular interest to the writer have been the changing faces of the towns and villages. Non-conformist churches in particular have been subject to closure or alteration of use in the last decades of the 20th century, and this book records many of them. Parish churches, too, are not immune – several have become redundant and two, at least, are now houses. The changing scene reflects a changing population, from one that had its roots in the village to one that treats it literally as a dormitory. Warwickshire's villages are probably prettier today than ever before, but are quieter too. Their populations are largely absent on weekdays and their beauty may distract the eye from observing that most of them suffer from declining facilities – schools close, pupils are bussed out, shops and post offices disappear. Even pubs draw their last pints. Thus, when you visit a beautiful village, you are looking at a living, changing thing that is not quite what it was a generation or two ago. We can only speculate about what it will be like when our successors call.

The Towns and Villages

ADMINGTON [Stratford-on-Avon]

SP1945: 5 miles (8km) NW of Shipston-on-Stour

The hamlet straggles along a remote lane in the Feldon, near the Gloucestershire boundary. Its main building – stone-built **Admington Hall**, with mullioned windows and gables – dates from the 17th century, though the front was added a hundred years later. At the same time a gabled **dovecote** was built in the grounds. The house was the home of the Overburys (see ILMINGTON) and later of the Corbetts, whose memorials are in the church at Lower Quinton. The lovely, thatched, black and white **Corner Cottage** (timber-framed, with brick infilling) stands to the north. Southwards, where the Cotswolds rise, is **Lower Lark Stoke**, a stone-walled and mullioned house built about 1600 by Richard Brent, who became Sheriff of Gloucestershire. A later Brent, Giles, emigrated to the American colonies in 1648 and set up a transatlantic branch of the family. The Brent arms and memorial tablets can be seen in Ilmington Church.

ALCESTER [Stratford-on-Avon]

SP0957: 7 miles (11km) W of Stratford-upon-Avon

Alcester is a town with many fine Tudor and Georgian buildings, but the first settlement was the Romans' Alauna, established where their Ryknild Street crossed a salt way from Droitwich and the rivers Arrow and Alne meet. To the west, the ancient Ridgeway marks the boundary with Worcestershire. The name, meaning 'fortress on the Alne', is Saxon, yet there is no mention of it in Domesday Book. The Court Leet is still held in the town hall under the High Bailiff of Alcester. Originating in the 13th century, its officers include an Ale Taster and a Bread Weigher. Like nearby Studley and Redditch, Alcester was a centre of the needle-making industry in the early 19th century.

St Nicholas's Church gazes down the busy High Street, its clock face set askew to face the shoppers. In 1975 an electric motor replaced the mechanism of 1682, now exhibited in the nave. The tower is 14th century, the nave was rebuilt in 1729 and the chancel is mid-Victorian Gothic. An unusual benefaction board of 1683, displaying immense handwritten sheets, has quaint paintings on the covering doors. Monuments include Sir Fulke Greville (died 1559) and his wife Elizabeth, who brought him the lordship of the manor. Their grandson became the first Baron Brooke of Warwick Castle. The memorial has 15 figures of children round its base, two of them shrouded to indicate stillbirths. Despite its late date, the style is pre-Renaissance. The altar rail commemorates the locally born explorer **Major Frederick George Jackson,** who commanded the Jackson-Harmsworth polar expedition of 1894-97. A sculpture by Chantrey of the 2nd Marquis of Hertford depicts him reclining, his finger marking his place in a book.

At 19 Butter Street (the handsome former **Rectory** of 1796), the 11th-century Alcester Ivory was dug up in 1903. Now in the British Museum, it was probably the abbot's crozier from Alcester Abbey (1140-1469). **Alcester Town Hall** was rebuilt in 1641 and purchased by public subscription in 1919 as a war memorial. Nearby stands a white-walled Italianate **Baptist church** of 1859. The town's oldest building is the house of cruck construction, perhaps dating from about 1350, at **19**

Henley Street. The traffic-free **Malt Mill Lane** has timber cottages with overhanging upper floors. At its corner with Church Street is **The Malthouse**, timber-framed and built about 1500.

Out at King's Coughton, **Beauchamp Court** is a mid-19th century farmhouse on the site of Sir Fulke Greville's manor house, which was demolished in the 17th century.

ALDERMINSTER [Stratford-on-Avon]

SP2348: 4 miles (7km) SE of Stratford-upon-Avon

The village – on the Stratford to Oxford road and in the Stour valley – is one of Warwickshire's oldest. The early settlement of Aeldrehame stood a mile to the north and had a church in the 6th century. It became the shrine of St Aegis, but was suppressed by the Archbishop of Canterbury in 673. Aeldrehame lasted until the Black Death wiped it out in 1349, though in 843 the parish of Aeldredstureminster was established where the church now stands. A horse-drawn tramway linking Stratford and Moreton-in-Marsh ran through the village from 1826 to 1869. Its line can be seen where a grass verge borders the main road.

The **church of St Mary and the Holy Cross** has a broad central tower and dates from about 1200, but was heavily restored in 1884. Thus the south 'Norman' doorway is 19th century, but the north one is original. The ticking of the hand-wound clock pervades the interior, where the nave is tall and narrow, without aisles, and the altar stands under the central crossing. The chancel beyond was for some 250 years from 1286 the Conventual Church of Our Lady for the monks of Pershore Abbey in Worcestershire. A stone altar in the south transept was found buried beneath the chancel floor in 1935. It may be the original High Altar consecrated on 14th July 1286. The churchyard is managed according to a plan produced by Warwickshire Wildlife Trust.

Neighbouring **Alderminster Lodge**, in early 19th-century Tudor-style, has barge-boards and an ogee-arched porch. Beyond it, a former coaching establishment, the Georgian **Bell Inn**, is primarily a restaurant, but retains a small bar. **Quince Cottage** is a splendid brick and half-timbered building with a high thatched roof, though it may once have been a humble alehouse. In the 1960s, the bricked-up body of a Roundhead soldier was found there. Its breastplate is in the British Museum. Opposite stands **The Old School** (red-brick, gabled and bellcoted) that served from 1872 until 1971. In a now bypassed section of the main road, between estate cottages of Alscot Park and others with canopied doorways, is **Howard's End**. A large white clock on its red-brick front is said to have come from Euston Station. The time is permanently set at 9.10.

ALVESTON [Stratford-on-Avon]

SP2356: 2 miles (3km) NE of Stratford-upon-Avon

The village, part of Stratford-upon-Avon parish, lies off the Wellesbourne road and within a loop of the River Avon. The large, towered, early Victorian church - **St James's** (1839) – has a single-span roof modelled on Westminster Hall and an elaborate, early 20th-century Arts and Crafts screen. A wall-tablet commemorates Mary Stanley, who died aged 86, together with her daughter and maidservant, following suffocation by a coke fire on Christmas night 1835.

Of the **Old Church**, on a site in Mill Lane, there remains only the chancel in whitewashed brick on a stone base. It contains a carved Norman tympanum and a recumbent effigy (1595) of Nicholas Lane that seems to have been meant to stand upright. Its neighbour, **The Old Vicarage**, is a lovely small cottage with vertical half-timbering and a tiled roof. Across fields stands chequered-brick **Alveston House** of 1689, with hipped roof and dormers, and near its gate the red-brick **Alveston Lodge** was refaced in early Victorian Gothic style.

In the village centre, the Ferry Inn is a reminder of the ferry link with Hampton Lucy, which ended about 1970. Nearby, **The Lodge** (c1840) is white-fronted, with Gothic tracery and crosses on its gables. **Kissing Tree House** was the home of the writer **J.B. Priestley** (1894-1984) and his wife, the archaeologist **Jacquetta Hawkes** (1910-96), for many years up to his death. The sparkling palatial white house has been greatly expanded since Priestley's time. **The Vicarage** of about 1908 stands on the main road, as does the large, Georgian **Hemmingford House**, the Stratford-upon-Avon youth hostel. Outlying **Alveston Pastures**, a Georgian farmhouse, includes some earlier cruck-timberwork and has a yew maze, planted in 1989, based on that at Hever Castle in Kent.

ANSLEY COMMON [North Warwickshire]

SP3193: 3 miles (5km) NW of Nuneaton

A mixture of miners' cottages and modern houses, this former colliery village on the outskirts of Nuneaton straggles along the Coleshill road. The **United Reformed church** (formerly Congregational) at Chapel End was founded in 1800 and rebuilt in 1860. The style is classical, with tall, slim, round-headed windows. To the west, **Ansley Hall**, once described as 'very picturesque', is a sad ruin. An Elizabethan house with 18th-century additions, it was used for some years by the National Coal Board as offices.

The large Norman **parish church of St Laurence** is at Church End, two miles west of the village. Though its noticeboard gives a foundation date of 1200, it has traditionally been linked with Lady Godiva in the 11th century. Its Perpendicular tower is tall and pinnacled, and a Norman north doorway is set above the present ground level. A Georgian sanctuary, added to the chancel in 1760, has a pedimented end with a small round window and a blocked ogee-headed side door. In the chancel are 17th- and 18th-century floor slabs and monuments to the Ludfords of Ansley Hall. The large base of a 15th-century cross stands in the churchyard, as does the sarcophagus of the mine owner William Garside Phillips (see HARTSHILL), who died in 1929. He was the builder in 1880 of a small **pump house** visible from the Centenary Way near Common Farm. It has a 90ft (27m) shaft and supplied the village with pure water, which the farmer still draws.

ANSTY [Rugby]

SP3983: 5 miles (8km) NE of Coventry

The village grew up in a curve of the Oxford Canal, which creates an agreeable setting for its older part, north of the bridge. Here stand the Rose and Castle Inn and several attractive cottages, one of them thatched. South of the bridge, where The Row runs parallel to the main road, are more 19th-century cottages, including a pottery. Pleasant towpath walking extends in either direction, forming part of the Centenary Way. Domesday Book refers to Ansty and Foleshill in Brinklow Hundred. Its value was £12 and the landowner Lady Godiva.

The Gothic-spired **St James's Church** is mainly the work of Sir George Gilbert Scott in 1856, though it includes a 14th-century north arcade and 13th-century sandstone chancel. There are carved late 18th- and early 19th-century gravestones of distinction. Rob and Ann Reader's has a sad postscript: 'Likewise five of their children who died in their infancy,' and William Bradford's tells us that he 'changed Time for Eternity' in 1815.

The outlines of an old ridge and furrow system survive in a neighbouring meadow. **Ansty Hall** is now a hotel. The substantial, three-storeyed, pedimented house in red brick was built in 1678 for a former Roundhead, Richard Taylor. The upper floor was added in 1800.

ARLESCOTE [Stratford-on-Avon]

SP3948: 4 miles (6km) SE of Kineton

This tiny hamlet, recorded in Domesday Book and now part of Warmington parish, lies on a quiet lane beneath a flank of Edge Hill, its slopes marked by old ridge and furrow systems. The Centenary Way passes through. The few buildings include a lovely Tudor **Manor House** of brown stone, which faces a green. It was reconstructed in the 17th century, reputedly by the architect Inigo Jones, and has quaint, ogee-roofed pavilions. Before the Battle of Edge Hill (1642), the boy princes (the future Charles II and James II) stayed there with their tutor Dr William Harvey, discoverer of the circulation of the blood. Charles I surveyed the Parliamentarian position through a telescope from Knowle End on the ridge above, where **Nadbury Camp** has stood since the Bronze Age. The 7-hectare (17-acre) enclosure has a single bank and ditch.

The 19th-century diarist **John Loveday**, who wrote about the locality and of his travels in England, Wales and Ireland, was a member of the family that owned **Home Farm** until 1990. The building is contemporary with the Manor House.

ARLEY [North Warwickshire]

SP2890: 5 miles (8km) W of Nuneaton

Arley – Old and New – is a former mining village on high ground, though it existed long before the colliery opened and is mentioned in a charter of 1001. The medieval manor house stood in nearby Arley Wood, but the present house is modern. At Old Arley, red-brick miners' cottages recall the years from 1901 to 1968 during which the mine was worked.

The Wagon Load of Lime, a handsome, gabled and dormer-windowed inn, stands at the top of the hill, its name suggesting some long-gone lime-workings. Opposite is the red-brick and lancet-windowed **Arley Methodist Church** of 1920. Below, **The Old School House** has a polychromatic gable, and the nearby **Corner Cottage**, sideways to the road, displays upper half-timbering. The small **Verger's Cottage** and the Decorated tower of **St Wilfrid's Church** behind it make a striking picture. Dugdale, who knew Arley when the tower rose above the forest, called it 'the Lanthorne of Arden'. The churchyard is entered through an archway of old yews. There is a sundial above the black and white porch and an ogee-arched priest's door in the ancient stonework of the chancel. Within, a priest of about 1350 rests on a stone pillow. An adjacent brick barn has become the church hall.

At New Arley, the brick-built **St Michael's Church** is in 1927 Arts and Crafts style, its west porch rising to roof height and capped by an open bellcote. Red-brick former miners' cottages stretch along the road.

ARMSCOTE [Stratford-on-Avon]

SP2444: 3 miles (4km) N of Shipston-on-Stour

The small village developed near the Fosse Way in Saxon times and is part of the large Tredington parish. Features include The Armscote Inn (formerly the Wagon Wheel) and many old cottages, though the impressive thatched row facing the inn down a short by-road is modern. The gables, roof and mullioned windows of the mid-17th-century **Manor House** rise above a stone wall. Within is a priest's hole from the time when the Catholic religion was proscribed. The building has its twin in **Armscote Manor**, also from the 17th cen-

Friends' Meeting House, Armscote

tury and enclosed by a stone wall. The entrance, in a long, thatched stone barn, has a half-timbered gable above. The **Friends' Meeting House**, fronted by a lawn, is a small stone building, with a 19th-century lean-to verandah. Constructed (or converted from a barn) sometime between 1674 and 1705, it is now used only for an annual meeting on the first Sunday in August. The founder of the Society of Friends, **George Fox**, was arrested following a visit to Armscote in 1673 and spent over a year in Worcester gaol.

ARROW [Stratford-on-Avon]

SP0856: 1 mile (2km) SW of Alcester

This is a tiny village, named from the river meandering nearby. Farmworkers' cottages of the 16th and 17th centuries display the dormer windows common to the area and a Gothic **tollhouse** of 1826 recalls the former status of the Worcester road. The Victorian **school** was long ago converted to offices. Dugdale tells how, in 1477, enemies of the Lord of the Manor, Thomas Burdet, caused him to be 'Arrainged and Convicted of High Treason', and subsequently executed, for showing displeasure after Edward IV shot a white buck on his land.

Holy Trinity Church, reached by a track, has a small Norman south doorway, spared by the heavy restoration of 1865, and a tower (1767) said to have been designed by the author Horace Walpole. The stone coffin of Gerard de Camville dates from 1303 and the 1870 effigy of Sir George Francis Seymour is by his son-in-law Count Gleichen. In the churchyard, guarded by a sculptured angel, lie the Reverend Beauchamp Walter Stannus (died 1908) and his aristocratic wife, the Hon. Mabella Geraldine. They could head a roll-call of unusual names from the gravestones, including Sisam, Beachus and Gittus. Of the Seymours of Ragley Hall, the 8th Marquis of Hertford once remarked, 'The more recent of my ancestors are buried in Arrow church, the more ancient in the Tower, without their heads.'

The neighbouring high-chimneyed **Rectory** is of 16th-century origin, but much altered and added to. **Arrow Mill**, on a Domesday Book site, became a hotel and restaurant in the 1960s, though its wheel still turns. **Coldcomfort Farm** lies north-west, its name acknowledged by Stella Gibbons as having provided the title of her classic comic novel *Cold Comfort Farm*, published in 1932.

On rising ground in a former deer park designed by Capability Brown stands the Palladian **Ragley Hall**, home of the 9th Marquis of Hertford. In 1956 his father took over the family's rundown 2400-hectare (6000-acre) estate and an empty hall in need of restoration after use as a Second World War hospital and became a pioneer of stately home tourism. Designed in 1680 by Robert Hooke, the mansion has 117 rooms and numerous art treasures. James Gibbs's Baroque plasterwork of 1750 in the Great Hall is claimed to be the finest in England, and a mural, *The Temptation* (1969-83) by Graham Rust, is the largest painted in Britain this century. The stables house a collection of carriages.

ASHORNE [Stratford-on-Avon]

SP3057: 2 miles (3km) NE of Wellesbourne

The small village stands along a winding lane below Ashorne Hill and is part of Newbold Pacey parish. There is no Anglican church, and a brick-built **chapel** by the modern village hall was long ago converted to a house, as was **The Old School**, in Victorian red brick, with its gables, clock tower and wooden belfry. In 1998 the Cottage Tavern was also in danger of having to close.

The village centres on a gathering of black and white, thatched **cottages** at a small green. One of them was occupied by **Edward Bissell** (1910-98), for many years the village postmaster. He amassed a remarkable collection of antiquarian books and manuscripts, including rare children's books, that sold for over £110,000 at Sotheby's after his death.

Much the oldest property in Ashorne is **The Old Farmhouse** (formerly Stonehouse Farm), with grey-lias stonework and a high roof, suggesting former thatch. A drive sweeps uphill to a distinctive modern house, **Cover Point**, built in 1965 for Sir Stanley Harley, a Birmingham industrialist. When offered for sale, it was described as having 'an unusual collection of adjoining sections, reminiscent of the sloped Lego pieces, each topped by an unmatched roof slide.' Its name's cricket allusion is appropriate because the local club claims to be unique in that a stream separates the pavilion from the pitch.

Outside the village, **Ashorne Hill College** of 1895-97, in stone and blue-brick, is notable for its neo-Jacobean interiors. It was the home of one of the Bryants of the

The village green, Ashorne

matchmakers Bryant and May, and later became the Second World War headquarters of the iron and steel industry. **Ashorne Hall** is popular for its Nickelodeon Collection and 1-mile miniature railway.

ASHOW [Warwick]

SP3170: 2 miles (3km) SE of Kenilworth

Though so near Kenilworth and the busy bypass, the village remains a backwater within a great loop of the River Avon. The cottages are mainly brick-built and old, often with half-timbering, but there has been some modern infilling. Most of them stand along a neat cul-de-sac that ends with the Village Club and a short path to the church, which has a lovely riverside setting. Its name, **The Assumption of Our Lady**, is an uncommon dedication from the 12th century. The chancel is Norman, as is the nave, though its south side was ashlar-covered about 1800. Odd features of the north side are adjacent filled-in doorways, one Norman and the other Early English. The tower is Perpendicular.

ASTLEY [North Warwickshire]

SP3189: 4 miles (6km) SW of Nuneaton

The small village that grew up round Astley Castle in medieval times can only be viewed today with a mixture of excitement and concern. The first emotion is inspired by the splendid church; the second is for the boarded-up cottages and school, and the crumbling state of the dry-moated castle owned by the Lord Lieutenant of Warwickshire, Lord Daventry of Arbury Hall (see STOCKINGFORD). A licence to crenellate the **castle** was granted in the 13th century, and in 1450 the Greys (whose fortunes received a boost when Sir John Grey's widow, Elizabeth Woodville, married Edward IV) acquired it through marriage. The nine-days' queen, **Lady Jane Grey**, spent part of her brief life here, before it was demolished by order of Mary Tudor (1553-58). Soon rebuilt, the fortified house came to the Newdegates of Arbury Hall in 1654, was extensively altered in the 18th century and Gothicised in 1820. In 1953 the building was leased as a hotel, but a fire in 1978 gutted it.

The small **school** of 1871 stands empty, the initials C.N.N. reminding us that it was built by Charles Newdigate Newdegate.

Nearby cottages lead to the **church of St Mary the Virgin**, which, impressive as it is, must have been overwhelming when built as a collegiate church by Sir Thomas Astley in 1343. The large nave of the present church was only the chancel of that vast edifice. After the Dissolution of the Monasteries in the 1540s the building fell into neglect, and the central tower collapsed about 1600. In 1607-08, Sir Richard Chamberlayne added the present substantial red-sandstone tower and the chancel, both in late-Perpendicular style. High on the tower is a Saxon sundial, and the filled-in original east window rises above the chancel roof. Eighteen collegiate stalls survive, with misericords and paintings on their backs of apostles and prophets. On the walls, strapwork-framed quotations from the Bible, the Lord's Prayer and the Creed are prominent. Three 15th-century alabaster figures of the Greys (one male, two female) lie beneath the tower and a headless brass on the wall dates from about 1400 – one of the county's oldest. The ceiling is decorated with the shields of 21 Midlands' families. Outside are graves of the Garners, relatives of George Eliot, who portrayed them as the Dodsons in *The Mill on the Floss*. The novelist wrote of Astley as 'Knebley'.

Lady Jane Grey's father, **Henry, Duke of Suffolk**, took part in Sir Thomas Wyatt's unsuccessful rebellion, fled to Astley and hid for three days in an oak tree before his keeper betrayed him. A stone monument at Duke's Farm marks the spot, but erroneously dates his execution as 12 February

1554 – the day his daughter was beheaded. Suffolk's head fell eleven days later.

ASTON CANTLOW [Stratford-on-Avon]

SP1359: 3 miles (5km) NE of Alcester

The village takes its name from the Norman family of de Cantelupe, who arrived in 1205 and built the **ring and bailey castle** by the River Alne. Dugdale tells us that it had fallen into ruin by 1392. The village has had its industries, mostly based on a former mill in Mill Lane. Papermaking began in 1748, needles were produced in the 19th century and, later, ball bearings for bicycles. Lias stone was quarried in the nearby Rough Hills and the Alcester Railway skirted the village from 1876, but has long been disused.

The **church of St John Baptist** stands in a green churchyard pleasingly surrounded by old buildings. There are ancient north and south doorways, the former filled-in and with an ogee-shaped opening above containing a fragment of a medieval nativity scene. The tower is Early English, though Perpendicular in its upper part, and the chancel 13th century. The great porch is by Butterfield, who restored the medieval church in the late 1840s and designed the stone screen and communion rail. Uniquely in Warwickshire, one of its incumbents was canonised. The distinction fell to **Thomas de Cantelupe** (1218-82), who served as Lord Chancellor to Henry III and became Bishop of Hereford. There is a strong tradition that Shakespeare's parents were married at the church in 1557, since the home of his mother, Mary Arden, at Wilmcote was then within the parish. Unfortunately, the records do not go back quite so far.

Bordering the churchyard are the small former **school** and **Master's House** of the 1840s by Butterfield – stone-built, but red brick at one end. Overlooking it is the classical **Vicarage**. An old, timber-framed inn, the **King's Head**, stands opposite the splendid, early 16th-century **Guild House**, with vertical timbering. This is now the village hall and has a modern rear extension. Part of it was once a gaol.

There are several hamlets within the large parish, including lonely Newnham where lias was once quarried. Today it has a small green, a few old cottages and two 17th-century farms, Redlands and Tutnells Hill.

ATHERSTONE [North Warwickshire]

SP3097: 5 miles (8km) NW of Nuneaton

This small town, sited where an escarpment drops to the Leicestershire plain, lies between the River Anker and the Coventry Canal at the county boundary. The line of the Roman Watling Street runs through the town, which was also on the London to Holyhead stagecoach route, but the modern A5(T) happily bypasses it.

Atherstone's staple trade has been the manufacture of felt hats, which began in the 17th century. At its height there were seven firms employing 3000 workers, but cheap imports led to a decline in the trade, which ended in 1998. The boisterous Atherstone Ball Game, which celebrated its 800th anniversary in 1999, is played annually in the streets on Shrove Tuesday. In 1997, **Squadron Leader Andy Green** from Atherstone, driving Thrust SSC, set a world land-speed record of 763mph.

St Mary's Church is an 1840s rebuilding in uncoursed stone. Its central octagonal tower probably dates from the late 14th century, when Austin Friars extended the Norman church. A Norman north doorway has a zigzag arch and there is stained glass of the 1890s by Kempe. Views of the church were opened up when the small market square was created in the mid-20th century. Georgian houses look out upon it.

Traffic leaves via **Friars Gate**, a tall 18th-century archway leading to North

The market square and Friars Gate, Atherstone

Street, along which is an **Independent Chapel** of 1827 (now flats), with Ionic columns and a rear Sunday School extension of 1837. In Long Street (on the old Roman road) two neighbouring buildings recall the Battle of Bosworth Field (1485), which took place six miles away in Leicestershire. One, formerly an inn and now a restaurant, is named from the Earl of Richmond, who, as victor, became King Henry VII. Henry is said to have slept there before the battle. The other, the Three Tuns, has the defeated Richard III on its sign.

North Warwickshire Borough Council's red-brick **Old Bank House** is prominently dated 1711, and the **Midland Bank** was designed (1837) in a lightly classical style by J.A. Hansom, who patented the Hansom cab in 1834. The eccentric, red-brick Gothic **Albert Hall** of 1876 is now a casino. Nearby, the staid **Conservative Club** of the late 17th century has a balcony and a hipped roof, while the name of a small inn, **The Hat and Beaver**, recalls the town's traditional trade.

Atherstone's most picturesque building, **The Old Swan**, displays 16th-century half-timbering. The **Queen Elizabeth School** (formerly St Scolastica's Priory) is an impressive mock-Elizabethan pile by J.A. Hansom, mainly of 1837-41, but with extensions of 1857-58 and 1873. The large red-brick and stone-quoined Victorian **railway station**, in Tudor style, was rescued from dereliction and is in commercial use.

ATHERSTONE-ON-STOUR [Stratford-on-Avon]

SP2051: 2½ miles (4km) S of Stratford-upon-Avon

This is a tiny village in the Stour valley, beside the river and just off the Stratford to Oxford road. The rock-faced and steepled **St Mary's Church** was built in 1876 in the Decorated style, though parts of its 14th-century predecessor were recycled. Long redundant, it is now in private ownership. Behind it, the 18th-century and dormered **Atherstone Farm** underwent a late 20th-century restoration. The plain, flat-roofed former **rectory** is early Georgian, brick-built, with giant pilasters and a third floor that may be a later addition.

Opposite, picturesque **Cliff Cottage** is

black and white, with thatch. Also thatched, **Catlin Mill Cottage**, by the river bridge and falling into dereliction, has brickwork and half-timbering on a stone base. Across the fields, **Alscot Park** (see PRESTON-ON-STOUR) is gaunt but impressive. Outlying **Atherstone Hill Farm**, in early 18th-century brick, was built for **Dr William Thomas** (1680-1738), whose continuation of Dugdale's *The antiquities of Warwickshire* was published in 1730.

ATTLEBOROUGH [Nuneaton]

SP3790: ½ mile (1km) SE of Nuneaton

The settlement was Attile's burgh (an enclosure or fortified place) before the Conquest. Today Attleborough is separated from the centre of Nuneaton by the young River Anker and has long been a suburb of the town. The brick-built **Holy Trinity** of 1841-42 is a large Commissioners' church in Early English style, with a tall apse. The squat spire was added later and a modern extension has been grafted on to the north side.

Nearby stands the **Gireh Particular Baptist Church** of 1878 in patterned red brick.

AUSTREY [North Warwickshire]

SK2906: 5½ miles (9km) E of Tamworth

The village stands at the edge of a plain, where the land drops from the Leicestershire border. With lavish modern infilling between the many older buildings, it is large enough to support a shop and post office. Set in a green churchyard, **St Nicholas's** dates from the 14th century. Its tower is Early English, capped by a broach spire, and the spacious nave has slender arches. The building was restored in 1844-45. **The Old Vicarage** is a handsome 18th-century house, to which a porch was added in Regency times.

Austrey Baptist Church, a tall, impressive, brick building of 1808, with arched windows, stands above Main Street. A fine array of Swithland slate headstones borders its car park. The **Bird in Hand** is white-walled and half-timbered, its thatch curving languorously round the upper windows. In front of it, the base of a medieval **cross** supports a top installed in 1897 to commemorate Queen Victoria's Diamond Jubilee. It is said that labourers for hire used to gather there, in a scene reminiscent of Thomas Hardy. The **Parochial School** of 1850, replaced in 1969 by the Church of England First School, is now the village hall. An ivy-covered 18th-century **Manor House** stands with other fine old buildings in Warton Lane, facing the lovely, black and white **Bishops Farm House** of 1521.

AVON DASSETT [Stratford-on-Avon]

SP4150: 4½ miles (7km) E of Kineton

Nestling among the Burton Dassett Hills, the village street climbs from the inn (The Avon, latterly The Prince Rupert) and the Catholic church to the broach-spired **St John Baptist**, embowered in trees. Though still consecrated, St John's is in the care of the Redundant Churches Fund and Stratford-on-Avon District Council manages the churchyard. It is a striking Gothic Revival building of 1868 in Hornton stone. Within is an early 13th-century tonsured effigy from the previous church, said to be of Hugo, a deacon. **The Old Rectory**, also of Hornton stone, has a 13th-century window in the buttressed north wing and a pyramid-roofed dovecote in the garden. **St Joseph's Roman Catholic Church** of 1854 was built in the Early English style, with lancets and a north-west steeple. Adjoining it is the mullion-windowed **St Joseph's Convent** of 1679. **The Old School**, stone-built and gabled, is now a house. Just outside the village lies a late 19th-century country mansion, the two-storeyed **Bitham House**. The Centenary Way passes through.

BADDESLEY CLINTON [Warwick]

SP2072: 4½ miles (7km) W of Kenilworth

The small, mainly modern village lies on the Birmingham to Warwick road and at the county's boundary with Solihull, though the original settlement was probably by the parish church. Domesday Book has no entry for the name, but it may have been included under Hampton-in-Arden. Since Baddesley means 'the pasture or woodland clearing of Baede', it is appropriate that part of the Forest of Arden survives nearby in the large Hay Wood, which Shakespeare is said to have had in mind when writing *As You Like It*. 'Clinton' came from the powerful medieval de Clinton family.

Along Rising Lane, the **Poor Clares' Convent** stands behind a small, plain **school**. Nearby, **St Francis of Assisi Catholic Church**, rebuilt in 1820 in the French Gothic style, has lancet windows and a bell turret. All are in light-coloured Victorian brick.

Secluded **Baddesley Clinton Hall**, a moated 15th-century building of romantic aspect, was owned by the Ferrers family from 1517 to 1940. The National Trust acquired it in 1980. Earlier the Bromes were there. John Brome, Under-Treasurer of England, bought the original house in 1438 and his son Nicholas began the present one. The antiquary Henry Ferrers, Lord of the Manor for 69 years, added the Great Hall in the 1570s. There are three priest holes and a secret staircase from the Ferrers' days as oppressed Catholics.

Nicholas Brome was a double murderer. In 1471 he slew the Earl of Warwick's steward in revenge for his father's death. The penalty was a £50 fine, payable to St Mary's, Warwick, for masses to be said for the souls of both murdered men. Later, finding the minister of Baddesley 'chocking his wife under the chin' (Dugdale), he ran him through. It was an excommunication matter, but Brome obtained pardons from the Pope and Henry VII in return for building the church towers at Baddesley Clinton and Packwood, raising the height of the former building and adding three bells to each. The fiery man died a penitent, ordering his body to be buried upright 'within the church doors ... as the people may tred upon mee when they com into the church.'

That is what we do today when, entering the Perpendicular **St Michael's**, we step on a stone inscribed 'Nicholas Brome 1517' and find ourselves in a small nave. There is an early Norman font, a tomb-chest (1564) of Sir Edward Ferrers and his wife, and a rood screen of 1634. In the lower part of the large east window kneels Nicholas Brome. Before being restored in 1872, the church was dedicated to St James. A list of 'incumbents and parsons' between 1305 and 1619 on the nave wall is in the handwriting of the historian Dugdale. Visitors in early spring enjoy a magnificent display of daffodils beside the path from the hall.

St Michael's church, Baddesley Clinton

BADDESLEY ENSOR [North Warwickshire]

SP2798: 2½ miles (4km) W of Atherstone

The inscription beneath the half-section of a **colliery wheel** installed in 1991 on the high ground of Baddesley Common tells the story of the village in a nutshell – it records that Baddesley Mine closed in 1989 after 300 years of local coal extraction. The wheel stands on the site of the Maypole Shaft, from which a nearby modern inn, The Maypole, takes its name. Uphill on the Baxterley road, another pub, the Red Lion, served the miners. Opencast mining has also disappeared from the area; its ravaged ground is now occupied by Baddesley First School and the St Nicholas Estate, built in the 1950s. Though the village is attractively set among fields, and lovely woods spread towards Baxterley, there is a feeling that, without the mine, the heart has gone out of it.

The settlement was Bedeslei in Domesday Book, meaning a priest's clearing in the forest. Today, **St Nicholas's Church**, at the edge of the village, is approached by a tree-lined avenue. It was built in the 1840s to replace an inconveniently situated medieval building. The architect was Henry Clutton, who designed nearby Merevale Hall. A Norman arch with zigzag moulding is set against an outside south wall. It belonged to the original church and was later incorporated into the Church House Inn, demolished about 1970. The church contains the Latimer Pulpit, from which Bishop Latimer preached in the old church shortly before he was burnt at the stake as a Protestant martyr in 1555. After the church's demolition it went to the Friends' Meeting House and was installed in St Nicholas's in the 1990s. There is a memorial to **William Stratford Dugdale** of Merevale Hall, owner of Baxterley Pit, who died of injuries received there when leading rescue workers after the great explosion of 1882 (see BAXTERLEY).

Colliery wheel, Baddesley Ensor

Two other church buildings, known as 'Top Chapel' and 'Bottom Chapel', stand along Keys Hill, separated by the modern village hall. The first, now a house, was latterly the **Methodist church**, but behind its Victorian red-brick front is a simple Friends' Meeting House of 1772. The other, **Trinty Church**, was formerly the Congregational Chapel, also in Victorian red brick. Downhill, the red-sandstone **Church House** has Gothic arches and a tall lancet from the medieval church.

BAGINTON [Warwick]

SP3474: 4 miles (6km) NE of Kenilworth

This is a mainly modern village on the county boundary, separated from Coventry by busy dual carriageways and the winding River Sowe, which is crossed by a low-parapeted stone bridge. A tall brick mill, where pottery clay was ground, has become the much-extended **Old Mill Hotel**. The mill-wheel survives. Baginton also has an inn, The Oak, near speckled-brick cottages that look on a small green and a magnificent gnarled oak tree.

There was a Bronze Age settlement by the Sowe and the Romans left behind the site of **Lunt Roman Fort**. Built about AD60, when the legionaries were fighting Queen Boudicca, it became a centre for breaking and training horses, and is unique in having a *gyrus*, or cavalry-training ring. The Royal Engineers reconstructed timber buildings in 1971, and there is an Interpretative Centre and Museum of the Roman Army.

Nearby Coventry Airport has the **Midland Air Museum**, where historic aircraft are on display, including early jets at the Sir Frank Whittle Jet Heritage Centre.

Attractive brick cottages, some with half-timbering, lead past the white-walled **School House** and the flat-roofed village hall (formerly the school) to **The Old Rectory**. The building is stone-built and gabled. It faces the small **church of St John Baptist**, with its uncommon central tower and squat spire. The chancel is Norman and the nave 14th or 15th century. Unusually, there are two chancel arches. Within are large brasses of Sir William Bagot (died 1407) and his wife. The tablet to Elen Campion (died 1632, aged 20) is perhaps the earliest purely classical work in Warwickshire, and another of 1742 to Mrs Bromley pre-dates Flaxman's draped female figure (1813) on the Bromley family vault of 1677. In the churchyard rest seven Second World War Polish airmen who crashed nearby in 1940, and a large table-tomb commemorates members of the Peel family who died between 1848 and 1899.

Adjoining the churchyard is the overgrown and fenced site of **Baginton Castle**. The home of the Bagots, it was probably a North Country-style tower house of the late 14th century. It fell into ruin in the 17th century, but the basement and some stonework remain. Henry Bolingbroke, Duke of Hereford, rode from the castle in 1398 to confront Thomas Mowbray, Duke of Norfolk, before Richard II at Gosford Green (now within Coventry). Each accused the other of treason and both were banished, but Bolingbroke returned the following year, forced Richard to surrender and became King Henry IV.

BARCHESTON [Stratford-on-Avon]

SP2639: ½ mile (1km) SE of Shipston-on-Stour

Approached from Shipston by a narrow lane, Barcheston consists of little more than a church and rectory below a sloping green, and a manor house nearby. The village is said to have been depopulated to provide sheep pastures by William Willington, whose family name was taken by a neighbouring village in the parish. An alternative theory is a cholera epidemic.

Willington's alabaster tomb-chest (1555) stands in **St Martin's Church**, consecrated in 1291. Above the high nave, the 14th-century tower leans noticeably. The chancel has a 13th-century priest's doorway. Finials and gargoyles top the walls and, within the stone porch, the moulded south doorway is probably also 13th century. Upper floors of the tower contain 15th-century priest's chambers. Other monuments include a brass of 1530 to a priest, the long-haired Hugh Humfray, and a brass tablet of 1664 to the strikingly named Flammoch Colburn. The 14th-century font features Edward I and Queen Eleanor.

Near the churchyard path, a stone to Joannes Taylor shows an unlikely date of death – June 31st, 1781. Another commemorates Richard Hickes, weaver of the famous Barcheston tapestries, who died in 1621, aged 97. Mary Willington, whose figure appears on her father William's tomb, married William Sheldon, founder of the local tapestry weaving business in 1561. Its products included now valuable tapestry maps of the English counties. The weaving was done at **Manor Farm**, the former manor house, though the present building is mainly 17th century.

BARFORD [Warwick]

SP2760: 3 miles (4km) S of Warwick

The village is the Bereforde (barley-ford) of Domesday Book. Situated on the River Avon, it spreads along Bridge Street (the busy Warwick to Stow road) and the quieter Church Street.

A cottage opposite the church saw the birth in 1826 of Joseph Arch, and his death in 1919. In between, as one of those self-educated, great 19th-century men of working-class origin, he became champion hedge-cutter of England, a Methodist preacher, founder of the first agricultural workers' trade union and a Liberal MP. Arch's address to a large, open-air meeting at nearby Wellesbourne in 1872 led to the founding of the National Agricultural Labourers' Union, forerunner of the National Union of Agricultural Workers.

Joseph Arch's grave, Barford

He lies buried in the churchyard, where the union erected a memorial obelisk in 1922. In 1960, the Red Lion Inn became the Joseph Arch. Barford's other inn is the Granville Arms, named after the family at Wellesbourne Hall.

Apart from its ancient Perpendicular tower, **St Peter's Church** was rebuilt in 1844. The cost was born by Miss Louisa Ann Ryland of Sherbourne Park. Urns of the Mills family stand in the broad nave and the chancel has a large tablet of 1683 to Thomas Dugard. A weatherworn 14th-century female effigy, which used to lie outside, now shelters within. Parliamentary troops marching to Edge Hill in 1642 are said to have damaged the tower by cannon fire.

The timber-built **Barford Lodge** in Church Lane was a tollhouse on the Warwick to Stratford road until a 19th-century American purchaser moved the building to its present setting. Half-hidden behind a wall in Bridge Street stands the Regency **Barford House**, with Ionic columns. Timber-framed and Georgian houses line the street and a great cedar marks the main junction, giving its name to **Cedar House** of about 1700.

The stone **Barford Bridge** was built across the Avon in 1795, at the ford from which the village was named. It gives a fine view of Sherbourne's spired church.

BARTON [Stratford-on-Avon]

SP1051: ¾ mile (1km) SE of Bidford-on-Avon

This hamlet by the River Avon is a little gem. Its **Manor House** of 1663, gabled and mainly stone-built, stands against the road, and the 17th-century Malthouse Barn premises include a quaint, stone **dovecote**.

The Cottage of Content – inn and restaurant – was established in 1827, though it has 17th-century timber-framing. In the wall of a neighbouring thatched cottage is a small Victorian **postbox**.

BARTON-ON-THE-HEATH [Stratford-on-Avon]

SP2532: 5 miles (8km) S of Shipston-on-Stour

Splendidly set on a ridge near the Gloucestershire border, the Cotswold-style village, unsullied by new building since 1961, has strong Shakespearean connections. It is mentioned in *The Taming of the Shrew*, where the drunken tinker asks, 'Am I not Christopher Sly, old Sly's son, of Burton-heath...?' Shakespeare's uncle, Edmund Lambert, lived there when it was also known as Barton-in-Henmarsh. There is still a **Henmarsh House**, a long stone cottage boasting an item of furniture known as 'Shakespeare's settle'.

Another notable resident was **Robert Dover** (1575-1641), creator of the Cotswold Games held annually on Dover's Hill, near Chipping Campden in Gloucestershire. He lived below the small green, next to the stone-built former **schoolhouse** (now the village hall).

On the green stands a domed **well house**, with classical columns and an urn. The date of 1874 may be confusing – it has been attributed to c1700. It is said that Inigo Jones designed **Barton House** in 1612, but parts are certainly Victorian. From the churchyard, the impressive building is seen to be liberally supplied with gables and high chimneys.

St Lawrence's Church is basically 13th century, though a chancel north window has an 11th-century remodelled stone head and there was probably an Anglo-Danish church on the site. The tower is tall and rather slim, with a saddleback top from the early 14th century. A scroll and a pig were carved on the chancel arch before the design was abandoned and the rest left bare. By a floor-brass to Edmund Bury is a stone showing that he died in 1558, but had to await his wife's death forty years later for commemoration.

The upper floors at the rear of **The Old Rectory** look into the churchyard, while its front-bedroom windows peer over trees towards the road. The house dates from Tudor times and was added to in the reign of William and Mary. Its original use is long past, a preparatory school having occupied it from the early 20th century until the Second World War.

A 19th-century resident related to the rector was **Olivia Wilmot**, the self-styled 'Princess Olivia'. A talented watercolour artist who became landscape painter to the Prince of Wales, she claimed to be a daughter of the Duke of Cumberland and niece of George IV.

BAXTERLEY [North Warwickshire]

SP2797: 2 miles (4km) W of Atherstone

A small village, whose involvement with coal mining was only a phase in its long history beginning in Saxon times. It retains a pleasant green, with a pool beloved of waterfowl. The 18th-century Rose Inn overlooks it and a half-segment of a **colliery wheel** recalls the mining era from 1850 to 1989.

Across the road, a fortress-like sandstone **lodge** of former parkland still serves as the Baddesley Colliery Bowling Club, but a long, classical and bellcoted **mine building** stands sadly empty. The colliery site is 'being restored to a mix of development land and nature conservation'.

In 1882 the pit was the scene of a great fire. Eight men, a boy and eleven ponies were trapped underground. The mine owner, William Stratford Dugdale of Merevale Hall, led a rescue, but a series of explosions followed. Thirty victims, including Dugdale, died in the mine or later from their injuries. Some of them are commemorated by a brass in **Baxterley Parish Church**, where, curiously, there is no dedication to a saint.

The building stands more than a mile west of the village, in a churchyard bordered by an old moat. Its chancel dates from about 1200, but the west end is 17th century and the nave was rebuilt about 1875. Hugh Glover, son of one of the Mancetter Martyrs (see MANCETTER), was responsible for the 16th-century pinnacled tower. The lych-gate was provided by the Reverend Hugh Bacon (1828-1907) in memory of his father, Sir James, who served as a judge until he was 88. The son was rector for the last 53 years of his life and is pictured within the church in marble. A crozier head, found in a wall in 1958, is believed to be the oldest wooden church object in England. Outside the gate, a small plain ashlared **schoolroom** is dated 1839 and inscribed 'Feed my Lambs'.

BEARLEY [Stratford-on-Avon]

SP1860: 4 miles (6km) NW of Stratford-upon-Avon

Most of the houses are modern, but they are away from the Conservation Area, where a 17th-century timber-framed **cottage** (once the post office) faces the church across a small green and partly hides the Manor House.

The small **church of St Mary the Virgin** was rebuilt in 1961-62 using masonry from its predecessor. The north doorway is Norman, with thin pillars, and a timber pyramid roof caps the plain brick tower. There are Gothic Revival windows and a 15th-century font.

The walled, red-brick **Manor House** has a Doric porch and is the home of the actor Richard Griffiths. Facing it are Gothic former stables known as **The Coach House**.

Up Church Lane, **The Stone House** (Hall End Farm in a deed of 1660) is a mixture of old timber-framing, stone and brick. The wooden north front is said to have been brought from Stratford.

A great gnarled oak in Old Snitterfield Road is believed to be about 800 years old. To the west, on the ancient Salteresway, **Bearley Grange** is tall, of red brick and the 18th century. The ancient cross at Bearley Cross on the Birmingham to Stratford road disappeared long ago, but the small Golden Cross Inn stands there at a junction with Salters Lane, an old salt way from Droitwich.

Stratford Gliding Club uses a former airfield near Bearley Radio Station, where plans by the BBC World Service to build powerful transmitters and masts up to 300ft (90m) high were defeated in the 1980s.

Edstone Hall, in Langley parish and now a nursing home, was the seat of the Somervilles - including the poet **William Somerville** (1675-1742), who lies in Wootton Wawen church – and of **Sir Francis Galton** (see CLAVERDON), though it has been rebuilt since the poet's time.

BEDWORTH [Nuneaton]

SP3586: 3 miles (5km) S of Nuneaton

A pleasant former coal-mining town in the Borough of Nuneaton and Bedworth, its name dates from Saxon times. Mining began in the 17th century and ended in the 1970s.

In 1769 the southern section of James Brindley's Coventry Canal was opened to the east, where the Ashby-de-la-Zouch Canal meets it at Marston Junction. Since 1959 the M6 has separated the town from Coventry.

Following the revocation of the Edict of Nantes by Louis XIV in 1685, French Huguenots fled to the area and began silk and ribbon weaving. Terraces of **weavers' cottages** (now shops), with large upper-floor windows, still exist in Mill Street. The Reverend Nicholas Chamberlaine founded **Nicholas Chamberlaine's Almshouses** in 1715. The high-chimneyed, Tudor-style residences, capped by an elongated clock tower and enfolding a green on which stands a small pump house, replaced the originals in 1840.

The nave and chancel (1888-90) of **All Saints' Church** were grafted onto the ancient Perpendicular tower of the former building, and now look out on an undistinguished pedestrianised shopping centre. A Gothic clock dates from 1817. There are Catholic and Nonconformist churches, most notably the plain brick **Old Meeting United Reformed Church** of 1726.

To the north, **Griff House** was the home of **George Eliot** (Mary Ann Evans, 1819-80) from 1820 to 1841. Though an early 19th-century building, it has a 17th-century rear wing of Elizabethan appearance. In her novel *The Mill on the Floss*, nearby **Griff Hollows**, a nature reserve traversed by the Centenary Way, is referred to as Red Deeps.

BENTLEY [North Warwickshire]

SP2895: 2 miles (3km) SW of Atherstone

This tiny hamlet on the Atherstone to Coleshill road gives its name to a small parish. It consists of an inn, a burial ground and a few scattered cottages and farms. The **Horse and Jockey**'s sign shows the present Sir William Dugdale (see SHUSTOKE) riding in the 1952 Grand National. It faces St John's Cemetery (formerly the graveyard of the parish church), from which a bridleway leads into the extensive Bentley Park Wood. The brick-built church of 1837 was demolished in the late 20th century.

To the north-west is the site of the ancient manor house. A mile to the south, the sandstone east wall of **Holy Trinity chapel**, recorded as a ruin in 1589, lingers in a field near Chapel Farm.

BIDFORD-ON-AVON [Stratford-on-Avon]

SP1051: 3½ miles (6km) S of Alcester

A village of small town proportions, it stands on the River Avon and near the Worcestershire border. In the second half of the 20th century its size quadrupled, but it retains many old features and is bypassed by the Stratford to Evesham road. There is a teashop and five inns, including the unusually named Anglo Saxon and the Frog and Bullrush.

The Roman Ryknild (or Icknield) Street crossed the Avon at what became known in Saxon times as Byda's Ford. A Saxon burial ground, discovered in 1922, lies beneath the Saxonfields development and the public car park.

The river is spanned by a stone **bridge**, with cutwaters and eight varied arches, that Shakespeare knew. Having been repaired in 1449 and 1545, it suffered near demolition by Charles I's retreating army in 1644. Serious damage again occurred when a combine harvester became stuck there in 1994.

Bidford's most impressive building is **The Old Falcon**, which dates from the 16th century and is built in local oolite and lias. It is now divided into dwellings, but former uses have included workhouse, antiques shop, restaurant and inn. In the last capacity it achieved notoriety as the scene of a fabled drinking contest between the local 'Sippers' and a team from Stratford that included young Will Shakespeare. The story goes that the Stratford lads, having lost, spent the night sleeping off the effects under a crab-apple tree. Another version has it that the Bard binged there with Ben Jonson on the night before his death.

Somehow these apocrypha have become linked with a scurrilous verse about local villages that has been attributed to Shakespeare, though it cannot be traced back earlier than *The Gentleman's Magazine* in 1794:

'Piping Pebworth, Dancing Marston,
Haunted Hillborough, Hungry Grafton,
Dodging Exhall, Papist Wixford,
Beggarly Broom and Drunken Bidford.'

All but the first village are in Warwickshire.

Greensward scattered with decayed gravestones slopes down to the river from **St Laurence's Church**. Though its first incumbent was Rogenus Capellanno in 1260 and the slim tower is 13th century, the rest was restored about 1650 and again, comprehensively, in 1835-36. The broad, light nave has circular pillars and rounded arches, and the chancel was Victorianised in 1886-89. It contains a Florentine-style roundel (1655) of Dorothy, Lady Skipworth, niece of Lady Clarke (see SALFORD PRIORS).

Woodchurch Clarke's monument of 1647 is a reminder that the Clarkes traced their ancestry from the Woodchurches of Kent. The church owns magnificent plate (possibly Spanish) given by Alice, Duchess Dudley, in 1664, and a 14th-century brass mace.

The stone-built Victorian **Vicarage** has timbered gables and an exterior chimney. **Lloyds Bank** occupies a striking stone building with twin timber-framed gables. **No. 1 High Street** displays an old Warwickshire Constabulary badge in a blocked upper window, while **No. 10** is of ancient cruck construction. **Crown House** is evidently a former inn. Icknield Street, named from the Roman road, has the black and white **Old Ford Cottage** and **The Old Fire Station**.

BILLESLEY [Stratford-on-Avon]

SP1456: 4 miles (6km) W of Stratford-upon-Avon

People were settled on the site before Saxon times and Domesday Book recorded a substantial population, yet by 1428 there were only four inhabitants. A combination of bad harvests, the Black Death and evictions of peasants in favour of sheep had depopulated the medieval village of Billesley Trussell. It never recovered, and today the small parish of Billesley centres on a redundant church and a manor house that has become a hotel.

Earl Baldwin held it before the Conquest. Later the Trussells were there for 400 years – the last of them, Thomas, was hanged in 1588 for robbery and felony on the highway. They built the original manor house where three sides of a moat remain in a field, together with lumpy evidence of the abandoned village and a rectangular, 17th-century, stone **dovecote**.

Sir Robert Lee, a Lord Mayor of London, ambitiously built the present house, **Billesley Manor Country House Hotel**, in stone between about 1610 and 1620. It was extended in the 19th and 20th centuries and is of impressive size. The approach, flanked by stone barns, is from the east and through old wooden gates supported on tall pillars capped by urns, but the multi-gabled main front is turned south, towards a yew garden.

Veiled by trees, **All Saints' Church** of 1692 was declared redundant in 1976 and is in the care of the Redundant Churches Fund, though it remains consecrated. In 1998 it was under renovation. Shakespeare's widowed granddaughter, Elizabeth Nash, married John Barnard in its 12th-century predecessor. Old masonry was used in the rebuilding and the medieval porch became the new vestry. Other features include an ogee-shaped bell turret and a rounded apse. A large family pew has a fireplace, before which a Victorian rector, who came by carriage from Alveston, was served meals between services.

BILTON [Rugby]

SP4873: 1 mile (2km) SW of Rugby

Rugby reached out and devoured Bilton in the 20th century, though it remains a village and has a green on which is the stump of an ancient **cross**. The settlement's history is long: the Saxons called it Beolantun (Beola's town) and a perplexed Domesday scribe wrote both Beltone and Bentone.

The spired, red-sandstone, hillside **church of St Mark**, from the mid-14th century, is Decorated, but was much restored in 1873, when the Perpendicular-style north aisle was added. The Easter sepulchre is large and ogee-headed and the octagonal font may be as old as the building.

The **Church House** has become the village hall, and **Long Barn**, a timber-framed house of about 1600, is presumably another adaptation. Brick-built **Bilton Hall**, with mullioned and transomed windows, has the date 1623, though there are 18th- and 19th-century additions and alterations. Strikingly, the facade of the porch extends for the full height of the three-storeyed house.

The author and statesman **Joseph Addison** (1672-1719), who married the Dowager Countess of Warwick, bought the hall and the manor of Bilton for £8000 in his later years. Their daughter Charlotte, at her own request, was buried secretly at midnight in an unknown grave in the churchyard.

BINTON [Stratford-on-Avon]

SP1454: 4 miles (6km) W of Stratford-upon-Avon

Well-situated on a hill giving views across the Avon valley to the distant Cotswolds, the village is notable for its link with Scott of the Antarctic. **Captain Robert Falcon Scott RN** married Kathleen Bruce, sister of two successive rectors of Binton, where the couple are said to have spent their last weekend together in 1910.

The rectory is now **The Grange**, a secluded 18th-century house beside a 16th-century timber-framed barn. Across the road, a carved **fountain** of 1868 flows copiously.

Scott's brother-in-law, Lloyd Harvey Bruce, who served until his death in 1924, was the last rector in a line that began in 1286. Today Binton shares a vicar with Temple Grafton, Exhall and Wixford. **St Peter's Church** commemorates Scott's tragic journey of 1910-12 with a stained-glass west window of 1915 by C.E. Kempe & Co Ltd, depicting scenes from the expedition, and a small display of photographs and manuscripts.

Though there was a medieval church, the foundation stone of the present building was laid by the Marchioness of Hertford in 1875. The Marquis – whose family, the Seymours, have been lords of the manor since 1670 – contributed £2000 towards the £3500 cost.

Surviving from the original church are the 15th-century font, with its carved cover of 1640, a stone coffin lid of about 1300 in a north wall recess and a long, dug-out, iron-bound oak chest of great age. A north window, also by Kempe & Co, depicting Sir John Greville and his wife, incorporates a 15th-century fragment of the Greville Arms from the old church. Sir John, who served in five parliaments and died in 1480, is buried at Weston-on-Avon. Also older than the present building are the mounting steps of about 1800 by the gate and the base of an ancient cross, near the porch, which has a sundial fitted.

Binton's other place of worship, the grey stone **Ebenezer Chapel** of 1886, is now a house, and the small, stone-built Gothic school of 1872 has also undergone a change of use to **village hall. White House** (more precisely black and white) has an impressive exterior stone chimney.

Binton was recorded in 710 as Bunintone and is unusual in having four entries in Domesday Book, where the spellings are Benitone and Benintone. The meaning is 'the town of the sons of Bynna'. To the south, the River Avon marks the parish boundary at Binton Bridges, where travellers crossed into Gloucestershire until the county boundary changed in 1931.

BIRDINGBURY [Rugby]

SP4368: 4 miles (6km) N of Southam

Birdingbury is a small village, mainly of 20th-century development, descending from a war memorial at a minor crossroads to a loop of the River Leam. Its origins, however, are ancient – Earl Leofric and Lady Godiva in 1043 granted land there to their new Coventry Priory. Later owners included the Throckmorton family.

St Leonard's Church is a strange hybrid consisting of a Georgian west end, with a pediment and four Doric pillars supporting a large cupola, and a high-roofed Victorian Gothic nave rising behind it. The dates are 1775 and 1876. The Victorian interior (subject to 20th-century refurbishing) consists of a long nave containing box pews and a chancel of the same width and height terminating in a ribbed apse. A Royal coat of arms has been identified as Hanoverian 1816-37.

The vicar behind the 18th-century rebuilding – Henry Homer, who had 17 children and was equally prolific as a writer on many social matters – lies in a churchyard table-tomb. The £1600 cost of the Victorian reconstruction was met by the Reverend Richard Hickman and his wife in thanks for their son's recovery from a dangerous illness. An early 20th-century south chancel window commemorates them.

Dating from 1764 (for Henry Homer), **The Old Rectory** is white-stuccoed. **Birdingbury Hall**, once of the Biddulphs, was stone built in the early 17th century as the manor house by one of the Shuckburgh family (see SHUCKBURGH) and rebuilt in the Jacobean style after a severe fire in 1859. **The Birbury**, the village club, was the school until it closed in the 1930s.

BISHOP'S ITCHINGTON [Stratford-on-Avon]

SP3857: 3 miles (5km) SW of Southam

This is a sizeable village, but mostly modern. There are two inns, almost neighbours, the Malt Shovel and the Butcher's Arms. Sadly, the 17th-century Manor House was damaged by fire and demolished about 1970.

The village's name stems from the nearby River Itchen and a link with the bishops of Lichfield, former local landowners. Earlier it was Itchington Superior, or Upper Itchington. Itchington Inferior lay to the south-east, near Old Town Farm, and was depopulated in 1547 by Thomas Fisher, secretary to the Duke of Somerset, Lord Protector of England. Fisher wanted to rename the village Fisher's Itchington, but has had to be content with a Fisher Road.

Nearby Itchington Holt, one of the Feldon's few large woods, is a noted wildlife haven.

Many village houses were built by Greaves, Bull and Lakin for their employees at the cement works (closed in 1969), as were the white-painted brick **Greaves Club** of 1887 and the deep, square-stoned **Memorial Hall**.

The blue lias **St Michael's Church** of 1872, in Decorated style, replaced a chapel of ease and has a reredos in marble and tile. Its gateway to the churchyard is now bricked up. The former **Vicarage** is a stone-fronted Georgian house to which a tiled verandah was later added.

The Old School and the neighbouring **School House** are Victorian Gothic. They are built of brick and in private use, like the tall **Independent Chapel** of 1836, where modern windows supplement old lancets.

BISHOP'S TACHBROOK [Warwick]

SP3161: 2½ miles (4km) S of Royal Leamington Spa

The genesis of the large and mainly modern village was in Saxon times, when the manor belonged to the bishops of Lichfield. Domesday Book records the name as Taschebroc (Taechel's brook). The Tach Brook divided Mercia from the kingdom of the Hwicce, and was the boundary between the dioceses of Worcester and Lichfield. Above it rises Windmill Hill, on which is set an ancient **mill mound**.

An inn, The Leopard, stands on the

Leamington to Wellesbourne road. Off it, **St Chad's Church** has Norman work in the north doorway and blocked north chancel windows. There are also Norman columns, a Norman font and a blocked Norman window at the east end of the south aisle. The corresponding north aisle window of 1864 is by William Morris and Philip Webb. It commemorates John Garner, a relative of the architect Thomas Garner (see WASPERTON).

Monuments of the 17th and early 18th centuries represent the Wagstaffes of Tachbrook Mallory. A later one to Robert Landor boasts a Latin inscription by his brother **Walter Savage Landor** (1775-1864), the poet and essayist, who lived locally as a boy and also has an inscription. The east window is to the memory of the widow of the novelist and historian Charles Kingsley (1819-75). She lived at The Grove, Tachbrook Mallory, the former home of the Wagstaffes.

Chapel Hill Farm includes the remains of Tachbrook Mallory's stone church; the hamlet was depopulated by enclosures in 1505. To the west, **Grey's Mallory** (formerly Greystoke) is a handsome Jacobean-style mansion. Mostly brick-built and pebbledash rendered, it was designed as an Edwardian country house in 1904.

BISHOPTON [Stratford-on-Avon]

SP1856: 1 mile (2km) NW of Stratford-upon-Avon

The hamlet, in reality a suburb of Stratford, was the setting in 1837 for a grandiose scheme to build a spa that would rival Leamington, but it failed miserably. Of the Royal Victoria Spa, the large **Victoria Spa Lodge**, a Tudor-like brick building with tall chimneys, and two buildings behind it survive. They are **The Pump House**, gabled and bargeboarded, and **Bruce Lodge**, named after a post-First World War resident, **Captain Bruce Bairnsfather**, who drew the famous Old Bill cartoons of life in the trenches.

Though St Peter's Church of 1836 was demolished about 1970, its graveyard survives off a private drive beyond the railway. Its neighbour is the 19th-century, square, red-brick **Bishopton House**. Modern houses line the road south of the Stratford-upon-Avon Canal and a large industrial estate is threatened.

BLACKWELL [Stratford-on-Avon]

SP2443: 2 miles (3km) N of Shipston-on-Stour

This hamlet of Saxon origin – just off the ancient Fosse Way and on the modern Centenary Way – is part of the large Tredington parish. Ilmington Road rises from **The Old Grange** (of stone construction) to **Blackwell Grange**, where an impressive brick barn has tall wooden doors, a high, thatched roof and a stone gable at one end. Between them, **The Old Post Office** retains tin-plated advertisements for Woodbines and Brooke Bond Tea and old farmhouses add variety to the cluster of buildings.

BOURTON-ON-DUNSMORE [Rugby]

SP4370: 5 miles (8km) SW of Rugby

The small village dating from Saxon times lies well away from main roads and forms a joint parish with the even smaller Draycote. Lewin, a Saxon, held it when the Normans came, and the Shuckburghs were there from 1563 to 1906. At the north end, the mainly prefabricated village hall incorporates a small, octagonal brick building known as the **Round House**. It previously served as a laundry for the hall and may originally have been a tollhouse.

Pretty, Gothic **Glencoe Cottage** is brick-built and bargeboarded from 1869 and was a Baptist church. Opposite, the village school, which began as a Free School in 1836, closed in 1974 and is now **School House**.

Cottages, some thatched, lead to the gates of **Bourton Hall**, stone-built in 1791 on the site of a manor house. It included a Catholic chapel, whose bell summoned estate employees to work. When the last private owner left in 1947, it was used by Jesuits before serving as a boys' preparatory school and later falling into ruin. Ingersoll Engineers bought it and restored it as offices in 1979. It remains in commercial use.

Set in a large green churchyard, **St Peter's** is mainly an 1840s rebuilding of a 13th-century church, though the chancel masonry is medieval and the great octagonal carved font possibly early 14th century. The two-decker pulpit for parson and clerk is dated 1607, the communion rail is of the same period and a south aisle window has rich stained glass of about 1890 by Kempe. The effigy of an unknown woman has rested on its stone pillow for 700 years. The bells were last rung in 1942 to celebrate victory at El Alamein. Later, a chiming apparatus was installed.

BRAILES [Stratford-on-Avon]

SP3139: 3½ miles (6km) E of Shipston-on-Stour

The village lies below Brailes Hill, Warwickshire's second highest eminence at 760ft (232m), and straggles the Shipston to Banbury road. It is divided into two parts, Upper Brailes and Lower Brailes, of which the second is the older.

There was a village here before the Conquest, and **Castle Hill** at Upper Brailes is an earthwork erected, it is surmised, by Roger de Newburgh, Earl of Warwick, in Edward I's time (1272-1307). By the reign of Edward VI (1547-53) it was recorded that 'the parisshe ys of greate compasse, and hathe almost 2000 houselying people'. Thus it was probably the third largest town in the county, after Coventry and Warwick. Brailes had a Monday market from 1248, a three-day St George's Fair and several charities established between 1555 and 1910, all but one of which are united as The Brailes Charity. The exception is the Free School Foundation of about 1630, which provides £20 per annum for church repairs and derives from a charity set up in 1433 by Warwick the Kingmaker.

At Lower Brailes, the stone-built **George Hotel** is 17th century, though the original inn is said to have been established for the refreshment of masons working on the church about 1350. The brick and gabled **Brailes Institute** of 1886 has been taken over by the Brailes Mechanical and Crafts Society, established in 1977.

From it, Friars Lane leads to the **Catholic Chapel of St Peter and St Paul**, opened to the public by the Bishop family in 1726 in the upper part of an ancient barn and attached to the early 17th-century **Manor House**. **Dr William Bishop** (1554-1624), the first Vicar Apostolic appointed in England by the Pope after the Reformation, was born there.

Above the road rises the magnificent **St George's Church**, known as the Cathedral of the Feldon. Mainly 14th-century Decorated, it has a 120ft tower and is both long and broad, with two aisles. A restoration took place in 1879. The font of about 1350 is in the pattern-book style, with each of the eight sides having a different design. Its counter-balanced lid was added in 1879. A tomb-chest and effigy, rescued from the churchyard in 1933 and possibly of Robert Bandy (vicar 1433-55), is worn as smooth as a Henry Moore figure. Near it stand an old four-wheeled bier and a Bath chair.

The church's neighbour, **The Old Parsonage** is brick-built Georgian. **Hillside House** of 1844 has 'Glazier' and 'House Decorator' in old lettering above a cart-entrance. The brick Victorian school with stone window frames has a bell turret and is now called **School House**.

At Upper Brailes are a **Primitive Meth-**

St George's church, Brailes

odist Chapel of 1863 (red-brick, Italianate) and The Gate Inn.

BRANDON [Rugby]

SP4076: 5 miles (8km) E of Coventry

Brandon is on the Coventry to Rugby road and is virtually a single entity with Wolston. It is part of a joint parish with Bretford. The Fosse Way ran within a mile and the Centenary Way passes through. The Bull's Head stands near the ten-arched **railway bridge** of 1837, and Brandon Stadium, used for speedway racing, is along the Coventry road.

The main road bisects the village green, overlooked by the thatched **Tiddlybank Cottage** and a row of restored polychromatic brick **estate cottages** of 1866. Downhill, **Goodrest Cottage** is also thatched and **Ivy House Farm** of 1640 is half-timbered, with dormers in a tiled roof.

In Main Street, near thatched cottages and former farmhouses, **Brandon Club** and the disused **school**, of 1885 and 1888 respectively, have black and white gables. **The Brandon Hall**, originally the Regency home of the Salisburys, is now a hotel. Grassy mounds by the young River Avon mark the site of the 13th-century **Brandon Castle** of the de Verdons.

BRETFORD [Rugby]

SP4277: 5 miles (8km) W of Rugby

A joint parish with Brandon, the tiny village lies where the Fosse Way crosses the upper River Avon, though the road was diverted in the early Middle Ages from its Roman line, east of the present buildings, to cross where the bridge now stands. Bretford was then a planned new town, much larger and more important than now. John de Verdon, Lord of the Manor, established a market in 1227 to provide revenue for the Exchequer.

Kenilworth Priory had a chapel here from about 1150, dedicated to St Edmund. Later, Theobald de Clinton built a gallows, apparently a useful facility. Now the only facility is the dormer-windowed Queen's Head, an unamused young Victoria pictured on its sign.

The brick walls of a tiny, roofless **Congregational Chapel** stand at the road-junction. Next door, **Ivy Cottage Farm** of 1662 is partly timber-framed and was formerly the Bull's Head Inn. Facing them is **Old Oaks**, neat and also timber-framed, near a row of dormered cottages.

The first record of a bridge was in 1279. The present **medieval bridge** (stone-built, with five arches) is said to have suffered damage in the Civil War.

BRINKLOW [Rugby]

SP4379: 5 miles (8km) NW of Rugby

Brinklow was one of 400 market towns established between the Norman Conquest (1066) and the Black Death (1349) to create revenues for the Exchequer. Long before that, the Romans came. They were forced to divert their Fosse Way round the great hill known as **The Tump**, and James Brindley had to make a similar diversion when planning the Oxford Canal.

The impressive site of a Norman motte and bailey castle, constructed by the Mowbrays in King Stephen's time, occupies The Tump. A thousand years earlier, the Fosse Way surveyors probably found an ancient burial mound or a hill fort on the summit.

The canal, opened in 1790, brought prosperity. Trades included basket weaving, candle making, silk manufacturing and boat building. Later, Binley Colliery workers turned Brinklow into a mining village.

Aptly named Broad Street climbs to the church. It is lined with shops and houses, some of them former inns where Brindley's navvies slaked their thirsts. There are no real gems, but the whole is pleasing. The street widens attractively at The Crescent, a small green bordered by Regency houses. Brinklow has four inns – the Raven and the White Lion in Broad Street, the Dun Cow and the Bull's Head on Coventry Road. Half Moon House is a former inn and the Old Plough (1766) suggests the same function.

The Gregory family have been lords of the manor since the mid-16th century, and the Johnsons began their local business dynasty as wheelwrights, builders and undertakers before the Armada sailed.

Behind its later front, the **United Reformed Church** (formerly Congregational) is Georgian, as is **Dunsmore House**. The **Church of England School** of 1826 has Gothic extensions and a turret.

The Late Perpendicular **church of St John Baptist** rises nearly 12ft from west to east, a feature accentuated by an 1860s restoration. A timber-framed 16th-century porch leads into the oldest part of the building, the 13th-century north aisle. In the chancel, a lancet window depicting the baptism of Christ by St John is in memory of Richard Rouse Bloxam (rector 1793-1840). Two of his sons, Matthew Holbeache Bloxam and John Rouse Bloxam, were influential in the Oxford Movement in the early Victorian Church of England.

The appropriateness of the chancel's Minton tiles is a matter of taste. Five of the six bells date from 1705, but Thomas Bolton, who died in 1779 and is buried south of the church, never heard them. A deaf and dumb woodcutter, he lies with the tools of his trade carved on his gravestone, as does another artisan nearby – John Blakemore, maltster and brickmaker, who died in 1820.

BROOM [Stratford-on-Avon]

SP0853: 2½ miles (4km) S of Alcester

This village on the little River Arrow was the 'Beggarly Broom' of the rhyme (see BIDFORD-ON-AVON), because its inhabitants were traditionally basket-makers, knife-grinders or pedlars. Its once great landmark, the tall tower of the 19th-century mill, disappeared in the late 1990s – marking the end of a local industry dating back to medieval times.

Though part of Bidford parish, Broom had, until it closed in 1992, **St Matthew's Church** in Mill Lane. The small, stone building of 1878, with lancet windows, is now a house. Its neighbours include black and white houses and cottages, including the buttressed **Yew Tree House** and **The Grange**, which is partly stone-built.

High Street has a former inn, **The Holly Bush** (black and white, thatched), and the brick and half-timbered **Broom Tavern**, originally a farmhouse. Its sign depicts Shakespeare and friends under a crab-apple tree, sleeping off the effects of a fabled drinking contest (see BIDFORD-ON-AVON).

The Old Post Office is a house, and **The Old Beams** of 1536 and **Baker's Cottage**

have overhanging thatch and half-timbering. In Bidford Road are **The Malthouse**, capped by a turret and weathervane, and the gabled **Broom Hall Inn** – both black and white. The hall, built by Sir Thomas Throckmorton in 1577, served for some years as a youth hostel.

The mainly 18th-century **Broom Court** retains a Jacobean portal with Tuscan columns from the original house of 1618, built by Sir Simon Clarke (see SALFORD PRIORS). The Heart of England Way passes through the village.

BROWNSOVER [Rugby]

SP5077: 1½ miles (2km) N of Rugby

The Oxford Canal separates the village from Rugby. Its modern development lies east of Leicester Road; west of it stand the church and the hall, the latter in parkland, through which the River Swift flows south to join the Avon.

St Michael's Church is mainly a creation of Sir George Gilbert Scott in 1877, though from its 13th-century predecessor he spared the west doorway, the chancel arch and several windows. The organ is German from about 1700.

Scott also built **Brownsover Hall**, a curious red-brick Gothic work with a high porch-tower and spired turret. The building is now a hotel. An earlier hall may have been the birthplace of **Lawrence Sheriff**, the London grocer whose bequest led to the foundation of Rugby School after his death in 1567.

In 1939, **Sir Frank Whittle**, the inventor of the jet engine, worked on his designs at the hall.

BUBBENHALL [Warwick]

SP3672: 4½ miles (7km) NE of Kenilworth

The compact village, originally Bubbas Hill, stands among level fields and above the River Avon. There are two inns – The Malt Shovel, passed by the Centenary Way, and the Three Horseshoes. Near the former, a black and white **cottage** faces the red brickwork and half-timbering of **The Old Forge**. **The Manor House**, small and

St Giles's Church, Bubbenhall

red-bricked, has unpainted timbering and gables.

The pleasant, chestnut tree-bordered Church Road leads to the 19th-century gabled **Church House**, with its pedimented door, and the 13th-century **St Giles's Church**. The central part of the unusual triple chancel arch is Early English, but the sides Victorian. The south windows of the nave and chancel have stained glass of 1901 by Kempe. The brick porch was added in 1616.

A stone churchyard seat of 1994 'in thanksgiving for the life of Dorothy Jean Cadden', with elaborately carved angels, is curiously old-fashioned and reminiscent of the Egyptian-influenced Thames Embankment furnishings. **The Old Rectory** (attractive and in pre-Victorian red brick) stands away from the church on the Leamington road, as does a small, brick **school** with a bargeboarded porch.

BUDBROOKE [Warwick]

SP2565: 2 miles (3km) W of Warwick

Budbrooke, Hampton-on-the-Hill (formerly Hampton Curlieu) and Hampton Magna combine to make a large, modern village in Budbrooke parish, but older elements survive. The early settlement was beside Old Budbrooke Road, where uneven ground indicates the site of an abandoned medieval village, nearer to the church than most later housing.

On 18 August 1642 (more than two months before the Battle of Edge Hill, the Civil War's first major encounter) Royalist and Parliamentary forces clashed at Grove Park, Hampton-on-the-Hill, the home of the King's supporter Robert Dormer, 1st Earl of Caernarvon.

Hampton Magna occupies the site of the Royal Warwickshire Regimental Barracks, vacated in 1960 when the soldiers moved to Glen Parva in Leicestershire. The only remaining military building is a water tower on Old Budbrooke Road, though the modern village pub's name is Montgomery of Alamein. Field Marshal Viscount Montgomery was the regiment's commander-in-chief. In 1968 the Royal Warwickshire ceased to exist, when it became part of the Royal Regiment of Fusiliers.

St Michael's Church has a blocked Norman north doorway and an Early English chancel with lancet windows. Other features were added through the centuries, until the north transept was built in 1838. A large wall monument of 1712 commemorates Roulard, Baron Dormer of Wing, in Buckinghamshire. There are handsome Tables of Pious and Charitable Benefactors, and regimental memorials remind us that St Michael's was the garrison church.

Grove Park is a Tudor-style house built in 1834 and noted for its four large 17th-century chimneypieces. Once the home of the Dormer family, earls of Caernarvon, it was long ago abandoned. The architect was C.S. Smith, who designed the Royal Pump Rooms at Leamington Spa. Previous buildings on the site were an Elizabethan house and a hunting lodge of Queen Elizabeth's favourite, Robert Dudley, Earl of Leicester. The Dormers now have a nearby modern, red-brick country house.

The Roman Catholic church at Hampton-on-the-Hill, **St Charles of Borremeo**, was built by the Dormers in 1819 and has a brick presbytery attached. It is unusual in being T-shaped, having transepts but no chancel. The crypt is reserved for Dormer family burials. A statue of St Mary wearing a cross and chain is believed to be unique in England.

In the churchyard, the grave of **Alfred Newdigate** provides a link with the family at Arbury Hall. Born at Astley Castle in 1829, he became Vicar of Kirk Hallam in Derbyshire, was received into the Catholic Church in 1875, and died in 1923.

BULKINGTON [Nuneaton]

SP3986: 2 miles (3km) E of Bedworth

The Bochintone ('town of the beech trees') of Domesday Book, this large village is part of the Borough of Nuneaton and Bedworth, though separated from the towns by the Nuneaton to Rugby railway line, a neck of countryside and the Coventry Canal. To the east, the M69 traffic skims past.

Weaving was the traditional local industry, brought to this part of Warwickshire by Huguenots after Louis XIV revoked the Edict of Nantes in 1685. George Eliot (Mary Ann Evans) based Raveloe in *Silas Marner* on the village as she knew it, long before its modern expansion. There is another link with the novelist at **St James's Church** – a crumbling table-tomb near the porch is of her uncle and aunt, the Johnsons, portrayed as the Pullets in *The Mill on the Floss*. Both died in 1833.

The high tower is 14th century, but the rest of the building was heavily restored in 1865. There are north and south aisles, both arcades dating from before 1300, and a tomb recess of the same period. The box pews are dated 1821. The font stands on an ancient Roman column drum brought back from the Grand Tour by Richard Hayward of Weston Hall, who carved its marble bowl. He was also responsible for the altar slab of the Last Supper and for a monument of 1781 to his parents.

Number 4 Church Street, a timber-framed house with wattle and daub, set on a brick base, dates from about 1600 and was originally thatched. Neighbouring chequered-brick cottages are 18th and 19th century.

The splendid high-gabled **Weston Hall** was built in ashlar stone in Elizabethan times. It is at Weston-in-Arden and was once the manor house of the De La Zouch family but is now a hotel and restaurant. Its late 19th-century stables were restored in 1988 and converted to upmarket dwellings.

A mile north-east of Bulkington stand the large Gamecock Barracks at Bramcote.

BURMINGTON [Stratford-on-Avon]

SP2637: 2 miles (3km) S of Shipston-on-Stour

From the Stratford-upon-Avon to Oxford road, Burmington's street climbs gently towards Brailes Hill. The renovated former school of 1877 – small, stone-built, bargeboarded and gabled – stands opposite a lane in which a curving row of old brick cottages is flanked by more substantial stone ones.

The **church of St Barnabas and St Nicholas** is a thorough restoration and enlargement in 1849 of a building of 1692. There was a chapel here in 1291, attached to the church at Great Wolford. The base of an old cross survives in the churchyard. The church is small and ashlar-faced. Its unusual, slim north-west tower, or tall turret, has a pyramid roof, and the single bell is of 1592. Within, the 12th-century corbels of the chancel arch were retained and there is a gallery reached from the tower.

Picturesquely bordering the churchyard is the stone and half-timberwork of the **Manor House**, including a 16th-century window and a filled-in double arch from the 13th century. Uphill, beside a brick **cottage** of 1730, a small half-timbered **granary** rests on staddle-stones.

At nearby **Mitford Bridge** two streams meet to form the River Stour. The bridge is named after the family of the former local landowner Lord Redesdale of Batsford Park, across the Gloucestershire border, which included the five famous Mitford sisters.

BURTON DASSETT [Stratford-on-Avon]

SP3951: 4 miles (6km) E of Kineton

The tiny hamlet on the lumpy Burton Dassett Hills has never recovered from the illegal clearance of tenant farmers by the Lord of the Manor, Sir Edward Belknap, in the early 16th century to make way for sheep. An absentee landlord (he lived at Weston-under-Wetherley), Sir Edward, who died in 1521 of a 'pestilential air', had too much influence at Court to need to obey the law. The village of Southend was razed, and today only its great church, a later vicarage and a few farms remain.

All Saints', known as the Cathedral on the Hills, is a great barn of a battlemented medieval church, unspoiled by a restoration in 1890. It occupies sloping ground, the stepped floor rising over ten feet from the base of the tower to the chancel. Both north and south doorways are Norman, the latter with a studded door, and the nave and aisles are high, broad and rough-walled in Hornton stone. Quaint carvings of beasts and men enliven the piers of the north arcade.

Above the chancel arch are ancient wall paintings of three different periods – a Passion series of about 1300, a Virgin, St John and angels of a century later, and a post-Reformation Royal arms. It is uncertain which of them attracted the gunshots that pepper the wall. Memorials include a stone coffin lid under a wall-arch in the north transept, possibly of the church's 13th-century benefactor Sir John de Sudeley, and 16th- and 17th-century tomb-chests. The tower's six bells are all of 1686 and have never been recast.

A 1974 plaque commemorates **John Kimble**, 'whose charitable trust has benefited the inhabitants of Knightcote and Northend since 1474.' John, a beggar-boy, was turned away from the prosperous little market town of Southend, but was treated with kindness at Northend and Knightcote. When he grew up to become a successful farmer at Mollington in Oxfordshire, he remembered what had been done for him and founded a charity that is still benefiting local children.

All Saints' is believed to be the only church to retain its copy of the Puritan *Directory for the Publique Worshippe of God*, which replaced the *Book of Common Prayer* between 1647 and 1662, though it is no longer on display. Outside the gate stands a decaying, Grecian-style **Holy Well** of 1840. Downhill, the former **Vicarage**, built in 1696, displays bargeboards added in 1847.

Warwickshire County Council purchased the 40 hectares (100 acres) of the **Burton Dassett Country Park** in 1971. The uneven ground is the result of iron-ore quarrying from the 1860s to the 1920s. Now the bare, grassy hills, rising to 630ft (192m), are grazed by sheep and provide magnificent views in all directions.

When Sir Edward Belknap drove out the villagers, he built the stone **Beacon** on the hills. Nearby stood a wooden post windmill, until a storm blew it down and killed the miller in 1655. It was rebuilt, but another storm in 1946 destroyed it.

In 1908 a Saxon burial place was discovered by quarrymen on Pleasant Hill, near Northend. It yielded 35 skeletons, some pottery and a sword. Injuries suggested that the men were killed in battle during the 6th or 7th centuries.

BURTON HASTINGS [Rugby]

SP4189: 3 miles (5km) S of Nuneaton

The ancient Watling Street, which marks the Leicestershire border, and the modern M69 pass near the village, as do the 18th-century Ashby-de-la-Zouch Canal and the infant River Anker. It appears in Domesday Book as Bortone. The suffix Hastings (the family name of the earls of Pembroke, who held the manor from the 13th century until 1529) was added in the early 14th century.

The stone-built **parish church of St Botolph**, Burton Hastings with Stretton Baskerville, has a battlemented nave, a large chancel and a plain, ashlared Perpendicular tower. Its chancel and part of the tower are probably 14th century, but the nave was built early in the 16th. Several ancient wrought-iron hooks, which once held the Lenten veil, can be seen on the chancel arch. The date of the carved sandstone font has been variously placed between about 1300 and 1500.

A tablet of 1819 records Isaac Wells's bequest, the annual interest on which (now about £1) still provides bread for distribution at the church door on Christmas Day. His table tomb in the churchyard shows that he died aged 58. The church has two wooden dug-out chests, originally for the storage of registers of births, marriages and deaths, as decreed by Thomas Cromwell in 1538.

A Georgian house stands opposite the church gate, and **The Old School** of 1873 – brick-built and buttressed, with small lancets – is now a cottage. Out beyond the canal, a **mill mound** rises from a field and **Burton Mill**, though not active, still has a waterwheel.

Though **Stretton Baskerville** is part of the ecclesiastical parish, it keeps a separate civil identity. The site of the deserted village lies among level fields east of the canal. Its clearance can be dated to December 1494, five years after Thomas Twyford sold the land and sixteen dwellings to Henry Smith, who drove out the eighty villagers and turned the cultivated land over to grazing. According to a report in 1517, they 'went away sorrowfully to idleness' and the church fell into ruin. It was not until 1633 that the diocese realised that there was still an incumbent living in London and drawing £13 6s 8d (£13.33) per annum for doing nothing.

BUTLERS MARSTON [Stratford-on-Avon]

SP3250: 4 miles (7km) SE of Wellesbourne

The village of grey-lias houses stands above the River Dene, near the Fosse Way and on a former salt road from Droitwich to London. Just outside it rise two ancient features - a **Mill Mound** and a prehistoric **Round Hill** or tumulus. The parish was enclosed and the Kineton road built in 1771. Originally the village lay to the east, beyond the church, but was evacuated after the Black Death in 1349.

One of the local tall-shafted war memorials stands on a small green, near which is a Gothic former school of 1871, now a gabled house with a bell turret. Uphill, a row of ochre-coloured stone cottages has stepped red roofs and tall chimneys.

The brownstone Perpendicular tower of the **church of St Peter and St Paul** is impressively approached by a footpath from the road. Beyond it, the grey stone nave is low-walled but high-roofed. Though mainly Victorian, it has a Norman round-piered arcade and a 17th-century aisle. The octagonal font is also of the Perpendicular period, and the chancel arch Gothic Revival.

In the churchyard, an unusual six-sided, thick, stone pillar commemorates members of the Parker family who died between 1928 and 1987. A neighbouring house, **Monksbridge** is the former vicarage, with stonework of various periods and some half-timbering.

CALDECOTE [North Warwickshire]

SP3594: 2 miles (3km) N of Nuneaton

A small village, it lies just off Watling Street and beside the River Anker. From a row of attractive cottages (the pedimented central pair rising to three storeys), a tree-lined avenue leads to the parish church and **Caldecote Hall**, which has long been occupied as flats. The tall Jacobean-style hall of 1880, in red brick with stone quoins, replaced an earlier house attacked by Prince Rupert during the Civil War. The Royalists came looking for its Parliamentarian owner, Colonel William Purefoy, on 24 August 1642. He was absent, but his wife, son-in-law George Abbot, and servants held out for some hours until Rupert set fire to outbuildings and attacked under cover of darkness. Colonel Purefoy was later one of the signatories of Charles I's death warrant.

When the house was replaced, the door into which Royalist bullets had thudded was moved to the **church of St Theobald and St Chad**. There the bullet holes can be inspected, as can the long scroll hinges, which are, perhaps, from the 13th century. St Theobald is a rare dedication – there are said to be only two others in England.

The nave, chancel and tall, steepled bell-cote are 13th century, but a heavy restoration took place in 1857. Among 16th- and 17th-century Purefoy memorials is one to the previously mentioned George Abbot, who died in 1649 and whose father, also George, was Archbishop of Canterbury (1611-33).

There is something a little gloomy, a little sinister, about the setting of the hall and church, but it is on the far side of the village that we find the Ghost Walk, as the public footpath to Weddington became known after the murder there of Polly Button in 1832. She was killed by her married lover, Joe Danks of Caldecote, who was tried and hanged at Warwick.

CHADSHUNT [Stratford-on-Avon]

SP3453: 1½ miles (2km) N of Kineton

This is a tiny estate hamlet on the Kineton to Gaydon road. At the Battle of Edge Hill, fought two miles away in 1642, the Royalist commander, Prince Rupert, made a furious cavalry charge that only terminated on the Chadshunt-Kineton boundary, at a point known as Rupert's Headland.

When **All Saints' Church**, veiled by trees, was replaced in 1771, a long Norman nave was retained and a tall Georgian chancel and chapel added, the latter with a raised family pew for the Lord of the Manor's party. The Norman font has intersecting arches, the east window is Venetian and there is 16th-century Italian glass in the north transept. The building, which was extended in 1876, is now redundant and in the care of The Churches' Conservation Trust.

Beside the path is the substantial base of an ancient churchyard cross, and on the outside north wall of the chancel are two early 19th-century tablets to the Whateleys. Facing the large north porch is a gate to their former home, **Chadshunt House**, which was rebuilt in the 19th century.

CHARLECOTE [Stratford-on-Avon]

SP2656: 1 mile (2km) NW of Wellesbourne

The tiny village stands where the River Dene meets the Avon in the park of its great house. Domesday Book has Cerlecote, meaning 'churls' cottages'. Since the Avon marks Warwickshire's great divide, Charlecote is at the edge of the Feldon, but Hampton Lucy, its neighbour across the river, lies in Arden. They are linked by a single-span **bridge** cast in 1829 by Horseley Iron Works. Until diverted in 1755, the Stratford road ran through the park.

There are a few half-timbered cottages, and the Charlecote Pheasant, which began as a farmhouse and became an inn, is now a country hotel. Nearby, the picturesque **Charlecote Mill**, a restored, early 19th-century, red-brick watermill, produces stone-ground flour.

The Tudor-style **Vicarage** of 1836 faces the splendid High Gothic **St Leonard's Church**, consecrated in 1853, four years after its 12th-century predecessor was demolished. The grey stone, slim-spired building was 'conceived, planned and wholly paid for' by Mrs Mary Elizabeth Lucy of Charlecote Park, though her ideas were carried out by the architect John Gibson. Mrs Lucy – who died aged 86 in 1890, having outlived her husband George by 45 years – is buried in the Lucy family vault.

There are three monuments from the old

church, each to a Sir Thomas Lucy. The first, an alabaster tomb-chest, was made for Joyce, Lady Lucy, who died in 1595, but enlarged five years later to accommodate her husband – their effigies lie on it. Shakespeare has traditionally been considered to have based Justice Shallow in *Henry IV, Part II* and *Merry Wives of Windsor* on that Sir Thomas.

The second Sir Thomas died in 1605. His effigy also reclines on an alabaster tomb, with fourteen figures of children on its front panel. His widow, Constance (died 1637), kneels on the floor beside him. The third and most impressive tomb is from 1640. Since this Sir Thomas was a scholar, the carving includes books and classical authors' names. He is pictured on horseback, having apparently met his death while hunting. The direct line of the Lucys ended in 1787, but the Reverend John Hammond, who inherited, took the old name.

Charlecote Park, the home of the Lucys since 1257, became a National Trust property in 1946. The 73-hectare (180-acre) deer park, surrounded by a 16th-century oak fence, contains descendants of the fallow deer reputedly poached by Shakespeare, plus a herd of red deer introduced from Scotland in the 1840s and Jacob sheep imported from Portugal in 1756. The grounds, laid out by Capability Brown in the 1760s, can be partly explored on a one-mile walking trail.

The brick house is approached through an impressive Elizabethan gatehouse with polygonal turrets. Most of it, though begun in 1558, is 19th-century Elizabethan Revival. The two-storeyed porch, with Ionic pilasters and Corinthian columns, is probably original.

The richly decorated interior is hung with many Lucy portraits, including a Gainsborough, and there is a library of early 17th-century books. Among items purchased at William Beckford's Fonthill Abbey sale in 1822 is a superb pietra-dura table from the Borghese Palace in Rome, but perhaps the greatest treasure is a rare silver-gilt Tudor wine-cup dated 1524. Other features include a Victorian kitchen and brewhouse, and a collection of 19th-century carriages.

East of the village, visible from the air, is a **cursus** or enclosure, used in Neolithic times for ceremonial purposes.

CHERINGTON [Stratford-on-Avon]

SP2936: 3 miles (5km) SE of Shipston-on-Stour

One of several lovely villages surrounding Brailes Hill, Cherington forms a joint parish with nearby Stourton and is separated from Sutton-under-Brailes by the young River Stour. To the west, **Cherington Mill** has a large, stone, gabled house and a tall, chequered-brick mill building that remained active until about 1948. **The Mill House** (stone-built, dormered and ivy-covered) lies along the Sutton road.

The Cherington Arms is small and stone-built, and a nearby gabled house of 1761 is one of several bearing 18th-century dates. The many modern houses in stone and brick are old enough to have blended in.

A clean-cut, honey-coloured and thatched stone cottage faces the handsome, grey stone **church of St John the Baptist**. This is mainly 13th century, though there have been several restorations, the last in 1917. In the broad, white-walled interior, an effigy recumbent on a tall, carved tomb-chest, set in the arcade, catches the eye. This unusual monument of about 1320 is said to be to a franklin or squire – perhaps William de Lucy, Lord of the Manor, though local tradition favours John de Cherington.

A mural monument in Latin, with carved draperies and a skull, commemorates the Reverend Christopher Smith, who died in 1688, and his wife Constance. The communion table includes parts of a reredos removed from the Roman Catholic chapel at nearby Weston House when the Elizabethan building was demolished in 1780, and several windows incorporate stained glass from the 14th to 18th centuries collected by the Reverend John Warner (rector 1741-64).

Beside the church stands the classical, stone **Rectory**, which, like the gabled Victorian school, has become a private house. Stone cottages lead out to **Cherington House**, where a Georgian wing facing the road and a Gothic porch were added to the 17th-century original.

The gables, mullions and studded door of the 17th-century **Stourton Manor** stand flush with the road, opposite the bright Cotswold stone of the renovated **Stourton Farmhouse** of the same period, its grounds given over to new building. Behind the house, a former **Wesleyan Chapel** of 1809 in chequered brick is now a cottage.

CHESTERTON [Stratford-on-Avon]

SP3558: 5 miles (8km) SE of Royal Leamington Spa

Chesterton is a lonely place, having lost its village, which moved west to tiny Chesterton Green in the Middle Ages to escape plague, and its great house. The Romans passed within a mile or so – along the Fosse Way, where they had a staging post, its site indicated by an earthwork – as does the modern traveller on the M40. The name (in Domesday Book 'Cestretone') is Saxon, meaning 'town of the fort'.

St Giles's Church, overlooking a long pool, is approached via an unfenced lane, past timber-framed houses at Chesterton Green and Old School House. Founded by Richard the Forester and presented to Kenilworth Priory in Richard II's reign (1377-99), it later passed to the Vicars Choral of Lichfield.

The battlemented and fortress-like building, of limestone and Northampton stone, is long and narrow, without aisles and with bare, scraped walls. The church mainly dates from the early 14th century and was restored in 1862. Registers from 1538 onwards are in the county archives. Enter through its oldest feature, the early 13th-century south doorway of carved ballflowers, above which is a sundial. A north door, filled in as a war memorial, was used by the Peyto family for direct access from the hall.

The Peytos were the great family at Chesterton. Busts of Sir Edward (died 1643) and his wife Elizabeth stare rather haughtily down the nave, while those of William (1619) and Elinor face across it but seem to avert their gaze from Humphrey (1585) and Anna, who lie composedly on a tomb-chest, their hands in prayer. Their line ended in 1746 and the great mansion of the 1650s was demolished in 1802. The Verneys succeeded them and are still patrons of the church through Lord Willoughby de Broke, 21st Baron.

In the churchyard stands the brick-built **Peyto Gateway** of 1630 (restored in 1990) that linked the church with the house and is said to have been designed by Inigo Jones. Prominent on a great domed hill and sometimes attributed to the same architect is the unique **Chesterton Windmill** of 1632, though it may have been the work of Sir Edward Peyto himself. Restored by the county council (1965-71), it is built of limestone in the classical style and stands on six semicircular arches. It is in working order and has four sails with an 18-metre (60ft) span. Whether it was built as a windmill or simply as a piece of landscape furniture is uncertain.

Downhill, by the large Mill Pool and watermill, stands **Mill House**. It was built of stone about 1660, with cross-windows and a pedimented doorway on Tuscan columns.

CHILVERS COTON [Nuneaton]

SP3590: 1 mile (2km) SW of Nuneaton

The village is unusual in having a church

rebuilt by German prisoners of war after being bombed by the Luftwaffe. Though now a suburb of Nuneaton, it is separated from the town by the Coventry Canal. Domesday Book recorded the settlement as Celverdestoche and a century later it was Chelvercote. The Saxon name meant 'Ceolweard's cottage'.

At **All Saints' Church**, the ancient Perpendicular tower and the chancel of about 1890 survived the air raid in 1941. The rest, with square piers and Gothic windows, was rebuilt and decorated (1946-51) by the POWs. **Henry Beighton, FRS** (1687-1743), who lies buried in the churchyard, was a cartographer and engineer who improved conditions for the local miners. **Mary Ann Evans** (the novelist George Eliot, 1819-80) was baptised at All Saints' and her parents are buried there in a table-tomb.

About 1800, Sir Roger Newdigate of Arbury Hall (see STOCKINGFORD) rebuilt the **Free School** founded by his mother in 1745. It is now a heritage centre.

CHURCH LAWFORD [Rugby]

SP4576: 3 miles (5km) W of Rugby

The small village lies south of the River Avon, which divides it from King's Newnham and is crossed by a bridge of old sandstone. Most of the interest lies along or just off School Street, where the Old Smithy (an inn known until the late 1990s as the White Lion) stands near a green overlooked by the Georgian **Hall**.

The red-brick, single-storey **Church Hall and Reading Room** of 1912 survives, though the neighbouring modern school has closed. Nearby, a high brick wall largely hides **The Old Rectory** of Victorian times. Just down Green Lane from the inn lies a lovely, brick-built, black and white, thatched **cottage**.

St Peter's Church (rebuilt in 1872, but retaining earlier features) stands among fields, its tower overtopped by a turret. It has clean-cut Victorian traceried windows in the rock-faced walls. A simple, filled-in south doorway survives from about 1210 and the north arcade is 14th century. There is a Kempe window of 1884 in the chancel, which has panelling of 1618. The pulpit is Jacobean.

Next door, the large Tudor **Manor House** has twin half-timbered gables, a two-storeyed porch and extensive pargetting.

CHURCHOVER [Rugby]

SP5180: 4 miles (6km) N of Rugby

The village lies in a triangle formed by the Roman Watling Street, now the A5(T), the modern M6 and the dismantled Rugby to Leicester railway line. Nearby, the little River Swift flows down to meet the Avon at Rugby, and beyond it is the site of the deserted medieval village of **Cestersover**. Ashlar-faced **Coton House** of 1787 (a management training collage) is attributed to the architect Samuel Wyatt. It was a manor house site from Saxon times, and former lords include the monks of Coombe Abbey (see COOMBE FIELDS), who built a monastic grange. Nearby stands a large **round barrow**.

About 1900 Arthur James was tenant of Coton House. His wife became godmother to Queen Elizabeth the Queen Mother, who donated the oak chancel screen at **Holy Trinity Church** in her memory.

The church has a 15th-century Perpendicular tower supporting a spire rebuilt in 1885, both rather squat, and an Early English doorway. The rest is mostly of 1896-97, though the south arcade of about 1300 was retained, as was the flower-pot-shaped Norman font and its octagonal, spired cover of 1673.

There are monuments to Robert Price and family (about 1595) and to Charles Dixwell of Coton House (1641). His grandson **John Dixwell** (1607-89) was a judge at the trial of Charles I and a signatory of his death warrant. After the Restoration in 1660, he fled to America and became a founding father of Newhaven, Connecticut.

Near the church stands a later **Manor House** – a plain, rendered early Victorian building. Its neighbour, **The White House** is a mixture of late 16th-century half-timbering and brick.

Below, tucked out of sight near the small green, is the village inn, the Hay Wagon. The village hall of 1895 is of red brick, with a single bargeboarded gable. Classical **Churchover House** is set back from the road. The brick-built Georgian-style **school** of 1841 closed in 1973 and has become a community centre.

CLAVERDON [Stratford-on-Avon]

SP1964: 3 miles (5km) E of Henley-in-Arden

A sizeable but compact village, where old and new agreeably coexist, it was the Clavendone ('clover down') of Domesday Book. Since Bovi held it before the Conquest, lords of the manor have included the earls of Warwick, one of the ubiquitous Throckmortons, the Spencers (ancestors of the late Princess of Wales) and the Archers of Umberslade.

Today Claverdon has a village shop and two inns – the Red Lion, with close-set 16th-century studding, and the Crown, once a butcher's shop but an inn since the 17th century. There is also a station on the Stratford-Leamington line. There was a Saxon church here and a medieval one that was pulled down in 1830, except for the 15th-century Perpendicular tower, which also survived a rebuilding in 1877-78.

The present **church of St Michael and All Angels** has a tall 14th-century chancel arch and contains the columned monument of Thomas Spencer 'of Claveydon', who died in 1630. That of his steward Christopher Flecknoe – a pointed arch against an outside wall – has seen much heavy weather.

Later memorials include plaques to the Galtons, most notably **Sir Francis Galton, FRS** (1822-1911). A cousin of Charles Darwin, he undertook a wide range of scientific research, especially concerning the effects of heredity, and was knighted for his discovery of the uniqueness of fingerprints.

The nave is broad and high, with wide bays, and the east window of about 1890 is by Kempe. A list of vicars begins with W. Comin in 1208. The neighbouring **Vicarage** is mid-19th-century and of red brick. Quaint neighbours include the old **forge**, entered through a giant wooden horseshoe added to the 17th-century building by Darwin Galton of Claverdon Leys, and **Bonnet Cottage**, with its thatch, plastered walls and exterior chimney.

Curious square dormer windows, without heads, peer through the corner-shop's thatch. At the nearby Italianate **National School** of 1848, the windows are narrow

The Stone Building, Claverdon

and blue-brick with rounded arches. **Claverdon Hall**, part timber-framed, stands off Lye Green Road and is thought to be 17th century or earlier.

Along Manor Lane are **The Malthouse** (lovely, unpainted half-timbering on a stone base) and the small, black and white **Manor House**. Between them, **The Stone Building** is one of the county's most puzzling properties. Three-storeyed but narrow, with high brick chimneys, it has been likened to a north country tower house. In fact, it was probably an angle-tower of a great mansion built by the Thomas Spencer whose monument stands in the church.

CLIFFORD CHAMBERS [Stratford-on-Avon]

SP1952: 2 miles (3km) S of Stratford-upon-Avon

The village stands on the River Stour, near its junction with the Avon, and below outlying hills of the Cotswold plateau. It was part of Gloucestershire until 1931 and the parish church is still in the Gloucester diocese.

Clifford ('ford by the cliff') dates from Saxon times. 'Chambers' was added to the name after the Conquest, when the advowson passed to the abbot of Gloucester and was administered by his Chamberer, or Chamberlain. Later holders of the advowson and lords of the manor were the Rainsfords (or Raynesfords), who lost it after supporting the Royalist cause in the Civil War, the Dightons until 1807 and the Annesleys (three of whom were rectors) up to the late 19th century.

The village consists mainly of a single street, happily a no-through road, which starts with the New Inn and terminates at a small green by the wrought-iron gates of the **Manor House**. Before the Reformation the site of the manor was occupied by a community of monks, some of whose skeletons have been unearthed in the garden of the present mansion. The moated manor, frequently visited by the poet Michael Drayton (see HARTSHILL), was replaced about 1700 by the present handsome, brick-built house, which has pre-Reformation features. After the First World War it was substantially rebuilt to plans by Sir Edwin Lutyens, who also designed **estate cottages**.

Its neighbour is **The Old Mill**, where a wooden mill wheel can be glimpsed.

The splendid, but rather worn-looking, former **rectory** is a large, gabled, 16th-century house with vertical half-timbering. When the Annesleys were rectors in the 19th century, it was divided into two cottages. The fact that a John Shakespeare lived there in 1564 raises questions. Was he William's father, and was the poet born in the house? A likely reason for the family moving out of Stratford would have been an outbreak of plague.

The uncommon dedication of **St Helen's Church** is to the Roman Emperor Constantine's mother. The Saxon building was replaced in Norman times, but there is original work in the slim Perpendicular tower and the foundations. A necessary but drastic restoration took place in 1886. A Victorian porch shelters an ancient door in a large Norman doorway with scalloped capitals. In its rounded arch is an old scratch (or mass) dial.

Rectors are listed from Robert de Wise in 1274. The unusual, plain, seven-sided font is probably Saxon. On the chancel wall are brasses of 1583. A large tablet to Sir Henry Rainsford (died 1622) and his wife, kneeling, has three small figures of children, one swaddled and still-born. A scroll memorial to the Nash family includes Susanna, who died in 1879 aged 100 years and 11 months. Under the tower is a bier presented by John Shakespeare in 1608.

St Helen's owns one of the oldest examples of church plate in England, stamped with one of the oldest Royal hallmarks. This dates the silver chalice and paten to

1494-95. A metal alms dish is of German 16th-century work.

By the Stour on the main road, **Clifford Mill**, a corn mill in 1550, became the post-Second World War workshop of the Hungarian-born fabric manufacturer **Tibor Reich**. It is now in multiple occupancy, including apartments. Its neighbour, **Clifford Forge House** – Georgian, flat-roofed and stuccoed – was probably the mill manager's residence.

CLIFTON-UPON-DUNSMORE [Rugby]

SP5376: 2 miles (3km) NE of Rugby

The most easterly village in the county, it lies where Warwickshire, Leicestershire and Northamptonshire meet and just off Watling Street, which marks the county boundary. The River Avon and the Oxford Canal pass nearby.

St Mary's Church stands at the village centre. Its predecessor at the time of the Domesday survey was probably built by the monks of Coventry and was the mother church to the then smaller settlement of Rugby. The present building is mainly 13th century, though the low sandstone tower was completed 300 years later and has an ancient carving of a muzzled bear's head peering from a window. The bear was the crest of a local family, the Barfords.

A priest's doorway in the chancel survives from the previous church, and a great marble tablet of 1721 commemorates Sir Orlando Bridgeman. There are Townsend table-tombs in the churchyard. During an 1894 restoration, a human heart was found in a lead casket.

The plain, red-brick **Townsend Memorial Hall** of 1885 has white bargeboarding on a large gable. The **Bull Inn**, a former farmhouse, is of dark 18th-century red brick. Behind a brick wall rises **Clifton Manor** of about 1710. It was enlarged in the Queen Anne Revival style in 1895 and has panelling made from the church's former Georgian box pews.

On the outskirts, **Clifton Old Hall** is long, low and brick-built, with a tiled roof and half-timbering. The **Wesleyan Chapel** of 1862 has become a house with modern windows, except for two old circular ones high at the back. The **village school** is still in use and has the date 1850 in its brickwork.

COLESHILL [North Warwickshire]

SP2089: 10 miles (16km) NW of Coventry

This old market town, dating from Saxon times (though a Roman temple was discovered at nearby Grimstock Hill in the 1970s) has narrowly escaped being absorbed into Birmingham. It occupies a ridge between the rivers Cole and Blythe, which converge to the north and become the Tame. In coaching days, when Coleshill was on the London to Holyhead route and had over twenty inns, such ancillary trades as blacksmiths, saddlers and wheelwrights flourished. Many fine buildings remain, most of the interest lying along, or just off, High Street and Coventry Road.

The Digbys have been lords of the manor since Henry VII appointed Simon in 1496. In 1605 the chivalrous and, perhaps, naive young Sir Everard took part in the Gunpowder Plot and was hung, drawn and quartered. Earlier lords were the Clintons and the de Montforts.

Another traitor, during the Second World War, was cinema owner John Wynn – caught transmitting information to Germany.

Lord Plumb, former president of the National Farmers' Union and European Commissioner, has nearby **Southfields Farm**, where the rear wing includes timber-framing of about 1600.

There is a bizarre tale of an elephant that choked on a mangold outside the Bell Inn on the Birmingham road and is buried under the Sons of Rest bowling green.

An unusual survival in Church Hill is the combined **pillory, whipping-post and stocks**, restored in 1998. Uphill are Georgian buildings, including **Old Bank House**.

They face the magnificent **church of St Peter and St Paul**, its 170ft (52m) steeple visible for miles around. Near the stone porch is the base of an old cross. A church existed before the Norman Conquest, but the present building dates from 300 years later and was heavily Victorianised in 1859. A major feature is the drum-shaped and intricately carved Norman font of the mid-12th century. A chancel brass (1586) of John Fenton is an oddity – his right hand has five fingers and a thumb. There are two other 16th-century brasses and an array of tombs, mostly Digbys, in the chancel, plus two knightly Clintons recumbent in the nave.

The early 18th-century **Swan Hotel** is a survivor of coaching days. The essayist Joseph Addison stayed several times and in 1711 described a horse race on Coleshill Heath.

Between the inn and the River Cole – crossed by a six-arched, broadened **packhorse bridge** of 16th-century sandstone and later brick - is the hipped roofed **Laburnum House** of about 1700. By the river stands the 18th-century **St Paul's House**, and number 37 (brick with timber-framing from 1402) is the town's oldest house. Number 131, the early 18th-century, blue-brick **Queen Anne House**, with a carved pediment and frieze, is said to be haunted by the figure of a woman on the stairs.

Coleshill Library (No. 141) has a Roman Doric porch, and **Coleshill Hotel** encompasses several old buildings, including a half-timbered black and white cottage.

Father Hudson's Homes occupy a long line of brick buildings constructed between 1884 and 1906. Beyond is the Byzantine-style Roman Catholic **church of the Sacred Heart and St Teresa** (1938-42), which has a rood, or cross, by Pugin. It was built in memory of **Father George Vincent Hudson** (1873-1936), who devoted his life to helping destitute Midland children, and is believed to be the only church completed in England during the Second World War.

The neo-Elizabethan **town hall** is of 1926, and the **Colehaven Trust Almshouses** are an astonishing 1930s line of single-storeyed, high-chimneyed buildings in quaint Tudor-style.

A mile west, the Gothic **Coleshill Hall** of 1873 was the home of the Digbys and is now part of a hospital.

COMBROKE [Stratford-on-Avon]

SP3051: 3 miles (5km) SE of Wellesbourne

The hamlet nestles in a secluded valley below the Fosse Way. Originally part of Kineton, it became a separate parish in 1853. Its name has had several spellings during a thousand-year history, but despite the widespread use of Combrook for maps and guides, Combroke is locally preferred and appears on road signs.

The church, the square-windowed former school and the Elizabethan-style estate cottages are all stone-built and probably contemporaries from the mid-19th century. The school and church were designed by John Gibson (see COMPTON VERNEY).

A thatched house opposite the church is older, as are former rows of cottages converted to single houses. An old Free School, still in existence with 67 pupils in 1867, is believed to have been held in the former vicarage, now **Combroke House**.

The grey stone **church of St Mary and St Margaret** was built in 1866 by the Dowager Lady Margaret Willoughby de Broke of Compton Verney. Its immediate predecessor may have been Tudor, but the first church on the site was dedicated in Henry I's time (1100-35).

Bellcote, SS Mary and Margaret, Combroke

An awkward west end is capped by an over-large bellcote in contrasting brownstone, from which angels seem to strain at a leash. Beneath it are a rose window and an ornate ogee-shaped doorway. The interior is broad, with two aisles, and in the style of about 1300, though the small chancel of 1831 is refreshingly plain. The Norman font has survived the rebuildings, and the base of an old preaching cross remains in the churchyard. There are no memorials.

COMPTON VERNEY [Stratford-on-Avon]

SP3152: 2½ miles (4km) SE of Wellesbourne

Not a village, because the villagers were ordered out in the early 16th century to create parkland, but an elongated parish, with a chapel adjoining the great house of **Compton Verney**. To the north-west it is bounded by the Fosse Way.

The mansion was stone-built in 1714 for George Verney, 12th Lord Willoughby de Broke and Dean of Windsor, on land owned by the family since the 15th century, when the original manor house was built. Though its architect is unknown, the style has been likened to both Vanbrugh and Hawksmoor. Alterations were made in 1760 and 1855, the first (the not entirely successful south and east fronts) designed by Robert Adam and the latter by John Gibson (see COMBROKE).

In 1998 Peter Moores of the Littlewoods Pools and Stores family, who set up a charitable trust to rescue the building from semi-dereliction in 1964, opened the house as an art museum. It displays British portraits from the 16th to 19th centuries and the British Folk Art Collection.

Capability Brown laid out the 40-acre park, creating the two long Compton Pools on either side of the Wellesbourne to Kineton road from five small ones along Com Brook. Adam designed the **bridge** (reputedly built of stones from the demolished manor house at Little Kineton) that crosses the north pool.

A classical 18th-century **Coach House** by James Gibbs, with pediment and bellcote, has been converted to apartments. The **chapel** of 1772, which replaced the medieval village church that had become a private Verney chapel, is again the work of Capability Brown. It houses 16th-century Verney brasses and later family memorials, and in 1852 was consecrated as the parish church.

COOMBE FIELDS [Rugby]

SP4079: 4½ miles (7km) E of Coventry

The parish of Coombe Fields is large but has no village. **Peter Hall** is now a farmhouse. Through an arch can be glimpsed a building that was once the parish church and later a chapel for the monks of **Coombe Abbey**.

The Cistercian abbey was founded about 1150, and by 1300 was the county's largest and wealthiest monastery. The present house, incorporating parts of the abbey, was built by Lord Harington in 1581 and was linked with the Gunpowder Plot of 1605: James I's daughter Elizabeth, whom the plotters planned to set up as a child queen, lived there with the Haringtons.

The Craven family bought the abbey in 1622 and stayed 300 years. Since 1966, the 150-hectare (372-acre) grounds have been a country park run by Coventry City Council and containing Warwickshire's largest heronry. The house became a hotel in the mid-1990s.

To the north-east, on the Centenary Way route, is the hummocky site of an abandoned medieval village, **Upper Smite**. Its occupants were evicted by the Coombe Abbey monks in the mid- 12th century to make way for sheep.

COPSTON MAGNA [Rugby]

SP4588: 6 miles (10km) SE of Nuneaton

A hamlet near the crossing of two Roman roads, Watling Street and the Fosse Way, the first of which marks the Leicestershire border.

A Victorian postbox is set in a cottage wall by the small village green, from which **St John's Church** is approached up a long, sloping graveyard. The church was built in 1849 by sisters of the 7th Earl of Denbigh at Newnham Paddox, who opposed his conversion to Catholicism. The style is early 14th century, with an open bellcote and mostly clear windows.

In a garden at High Cross, near the site of **Venonae**, a Roman settlement beyond the county boundary, is the base of a monument erected by the 4th Earl of Denbigh to commemorate Britain's gains in the War of the Spanish Succession (1702-13). Lightning in 1791 destroyed its four Doric columns and a globe, but an inscription refers to Venonae and the Roman roads.

CORLEY [North Warwickshire]

SP3085: 3½ miles (6km) W of Bedworth

Corley is best known as the name of a service station on the M6. Half-a-mile south, however, a village has stood since Saxon times. Earlier still, an Iron Age fort was constructed on neighbouring **Burrow Hill**, where the 3-hectare (7-acre) site remains impressive.

The Normans built a **church** (of uncertain dedication) in the 12th century, with thick rounded piers supporting its north arcade. A chancel was added about 1300 and neo-Norman windows date from an 1893 restoration. The oldest of the five bells in the wooden belfry is said to have been cast about 1350.

Timber-framed and cross-gabled **Corley Hall** (from the early 16th century) has Early Renaissance panelling. It was perhaps the Hall Farm of George Eliot's *Adam Bede*, the piers of its gateway having illustrated the novel's first edition. To the west at Corley Moor stands a derelict **tower windmill**.

COUGHTON [Stratford-on-Avon]

SP0860: 2 miles (3km) N of Alcester

The small village lies on the Studley to Alcester road (the Roman Ryknild Street), where stands the railed base of an ancient **cross** that once marked the boundary of the Royal Forest of Feckenham. To the east flows the River Arrow. The Romans called their settlement Wike and Domesday Book has Coctune. There are several ancient cottages and some Georgian and Victorian houses.

Just over the Sambourne parish boundary is the Throckmorton Arms, licensed in 1780 and named from the family that has lived since 1409 at **Coughton Court**. They transferred the freehold to the National Trust in 1946, but still manage the property. Its present custodian is Mrs Clare McLaren-Thockmorton. The family has spread to the USA, where in Texas there is Throckmorton City and Throckmorton County. The 'stately castle-like Gate-house of freestone' (Dugdale) and flanking late 18th-century Gothic wings are striking from the main road.

The Thockmorton's Catholicism has made for an eventful family history. In 1583 Francis Throckmorton was executed for his part in the Throckmorton Plot to replace Elizabeth I by Mary, Queen of Scots, and in 1605 the wives of the Gunpowder Plot conspirators gathered at Coughton to await the outcome. They included the sister of Sir Thomas Throckmorton, head of the family, who was married to the leader of the plot, Robert Catesby (see LAPWORTH). Another conspirator, Sir Everard Digby (see COLESHILL), was tenant of the house at the time.

During the Civil War, Parliamentarians captured and occupied the Court, looting and damaging it, and in 1688, at the time of the Bloodless Revolution, a Protestant mob raided and virtually destroyed the chapel that once connected the early 16th-century half-timbered gabled wings at the rear.

On a summer's day in 1811, the 5th baronet, Sir John, won a thousand-guinea wager when the 'Throckmorton coat' was manufactured between sunrise and sunset, from the shearing of the sheep to the finished garment. It is on display in the house, together with the chemise in which Mary, Queen of Scots was executed.

London's famous Throgmorton Street was named after the Protestant Sir Nicholas Throckmorton (1515-70), courtier and diplomat in Elizabeth I's reign and father-in-law of Sir Walter Raleigh.

Two churches stand in the grounds. **The parish church of St Peter**, built between the mid-15th and late 16th centuries in Perpendicular style, is of considerable interest. Its oldest item is the 13th-century font, set on an upside-down font 500 years older. The workings of the clock, which chimes but has no face, can be seen on the ground floor of the tower. It dates from about 1690 and was restored in 1978.

In the centre of the nave is the cenotaph of Sir Robert Throckmorton, who died in the Holy Land in 1518. The body of his namesake, the 4th baronet, was put into it in 1791. Beside it is a touching and intriguing memorial of 1681 to two 25-year-olds – the Reverend Henry Teong and Mrs Elizabeth Dewes.

In the chancel, superb brasses top the tomb of Sir George Thockmorton and his wife Katheryn (aunt of Henry VIII's Catherine Parr). The couple had 19 children and 112 grandchildren.

Other tombs include Sir John (died 1580), 'master of ye requests unto Queene Marie', and Sir Charles (died 1850). When the latter was interred, the remains of Dame Elizabeth Throckmorton (died 1547), the last abbess of Denye in Cambridgeshire, were discovered, together with those of three nuns. A plate on the end of the tomb commemorates them.

In the nave, a stone plaque and wooden breadbasket record William Dewes's foundation in 1717 of a charity providing bread for poor widows who attended divine service. The east window illustrates the Doom, or Last Judgement, as provided for by the Sir Robert who died in 1518. Above are the arms of the Spineys, into whose family John de Throckmorton married in 1409.

The base of the ancient churchyard cross, near the 18th-century porch with its ogee-shaped arch, supports a 17th-century column with a Tuscan sundial.

The grey stone Catholic **church of SS Peter, Paul and Elizabeth** was built in the 1850s with a pepper-pot tower, and has a large gabled presbytery attached.

CUBBINGTON [Warwick]

SP3468: 2½ miles (4km) NE of Leamington Spa

Though almost a suburb of Leamington Spa, Cubbington has been a parish since 1331. Early versions of the name were Cubitone (Domesday Book) and Cobynton ('the town of the descendants of Coba'). Set in rolling countryside, Cubbington retains a village atmosphere, its High Street dropping past white-painted houses with bow windows to a classical grouping of church, inn and manor house.

West of it runs Welsh Road (here called Windmill Hill), along which Cambrian drovers for centuries herded their cattle to London's Smithfield Market, and the A445 Leicester Lane is the ancient Leycestrewey from Warwick, dating from the 14th century.

The inventor of the clover-head gathering machine, Joseph Russell, farmed nearby from 1780 to 1820. In 1938, L.B. Thwaites established the Thwaites dumper manufacturers in the village. The company is now based at Leamington.

St Mary's Church rises from a vast graveyard above the road. Building began after Geoffrey de Clinton granted the chapelry to Kenilworth Priory in 1122, and features were added piecemeal over the next 300 years. Major alterations were carried out in 1885.

The Easter sepulchre in the north wall is a stone recess, rather than the usual cupboard. A wooden cartouche recalls Captain Abraham Murcott, drowned off the Scilly isles in 1703, though the craftsman, in error, carved the year as 1702. The Murcott family tomb is in the churchyard. The vicar from 1792 to 1820 was the Reverend James Austen, brother of the novelist Jane Austen. The Austens were related to Lord Leigh of Stoneleigh Abbey, the church's patron at that time.

A small Georgian inn, the **King's Head**, looks out on the church. Tucked behind it is a Perpendicular-style Victorian **school**. Nearby stands **The Old Manor House**, a mixture of periods in brick, stone and half-timbering, with mullioned windows. **Ledbrooke Hall**, a tall, gaunt former chapel of 1844, now in commercial use, rises from High Street.

CURDWORTH [North Warwickshire]

SP1792: 3 miles (5km) NW of Coleshill

The sizeable village is now a dormitory for Birmingham. In 1086, however, Credeworde was recorded in Domesday Book as much the larger of the two. The historian Dugdale was the first to use the present spelling, and it was he who marched a party of Royalist troops to the village in August 1642, en route from Kenilworth Castle to join Charles I at Nottingham. Attacked by Parliamentarians from Coventry and Birmingham, they fought them off in a hollow of the present recreation ground south of the church.

Church Lane, now a cul-de-sac, was then the road to Birmingham. It was superseded in the 18th century by Kingsbury Road, probably as a turnpike. Another historical link exists through Dr Henry Sacheverall. Found guilty in a show-trial at Westminster Hall in 1710 of preaching against the government, he was married at Curdworth in 1716.

When the Birmingham and Fazeley Canal was opened north of the village in 1790, the land was still farmed under the medieval strip system. Today vast prairies predominate. Curdworth has two inns, the Beehive in the village centre and the White Horse on Kingsbury Road.

The **church of St Nicholas and St Peter-ad-Vincula** (St Peter in Chains) celebrated its 800th anniversary in 1965, the year 1165 having seen the advowson, or presentation, of a priest to the parish. Since Curdworth was a Saxon settlement, a church of that period probably occupied the hilltop site. Today the tower of about 1460 is Perpendicular, the nave and chancel Norman, and the chancel arch has dog-tooth carving. Warwick the Kingmaker is credited with building the tower.

Inside, deeply splayed windows contain ancient wall paintings and inscriptions, and there is said to be a Civil War bullet hole in one of the nave windows. The Norman font was buried under the floor at that time and not found until 1895, when a restoration corrected the errors of a 1799 rebuilding.

Lord Norton of Hams Hall paid for it; his friend Gladstone came to view the work.

A headless figure on the south side of the nave, believed to be the Archangel Gabriel, was removed in 1926 from Water Orton's ancient bridge. A 10ft-long oak chest was carved from a tree trunk in the early 13th century, and in the nave floor is set a memorial to Cornelius and Anne Ford, maternal grandparents of Dr Samuel Johnson.

A silver bell, the oldest of the church's peal of three, was given in the 15th century by a traveller who, lost in the Forest of Arden, was guided by the tinkling of the small bell then in use.

In Farthing Lane, the 17th-century **Curdworth Hall Farm** rests on a medieval sandstone base and may at one time have been an inn for travellers along the Kingsbury road. Three **cottages** at the corner of the lane were formerly a coaching inn, the Royal Oak, though originally built as a timber-framed Tudor farmhouse. The middle one preserves an inglenook fireplace with an oak-leaf motif from its coaching days.

In the main street, **Red Lion Cottages** indicate another former inn. A timber-framed **tithe barn** stands opposite. Nearby **Dunton Hall**, a gaunt, late 17th-century farmhouse, was the home of the above-mentioned Cornelius and Anne Ford.

DARLINGSCOTE [Stratford-on-Avon]

SP2342: 2 miles (3km) NW of Shipston-on-Stour

One of a string of small Saxon villages just off the Fosse Way, it forms part of the large Tredington parish (but has its own chapel of ease) and is included in a variant of the Centenary Way. The horse-drawn Central Junction Railway (1826-69) from Stratford to Moreton-in-Marsh trundled nearby, as did its successor the Great Western. The line closed in 1961.

St George's Church was stone-built in 1873 along the Ilmington road, with a high red roof and open bellcote. The plain interior has heavily carved bosses and a stern-looking medieval-style face. A brick vestry has been added.

Set on the wall of **Darlingscote House** (Cotswold stone, ashlared) are a well-preserved sundial of 1621 and, from the time when each fire insurer had its own brigade, a Sun Assurance fire-mark.

DORDON [North Warwickshire]

SP2600: 1 mile (2km) S of Polesworth

A former mining and brick-making village north of Watling Street, from which terraced cottages lead uphill to the bellcoted **St Leonard's Church** of 1867-68. Brick-built by G.E. Street, in late 13th-century style, it was extended in 1901 and renovated in 1998.

Flanking the churchyard, a red-brick Gothic **Sunday School** with blue-brick lancets has a foundation stone laid by the Marchioness of Hastings in 1884. Nearby, the **United Methodist Free Church** of 1882, with blue-brick arches and a modern porch, is boarded-up.

Down by Watling Street, the **Congregational Church** of 1908 had a **Sunday School** seamlessly added in 1937, its gable and doorway almost a mirror image of the church.

A mile east, **Dordon Hall Farm** began as a timber-framed moated house. A stone front, stepped gables and a vast doorway were added about 1715, leaving the picturesque timber-work at the rear. Old brick farm buildings stand opposite, one with four great archways.

DORSINGTON [Stratford-on-Avon]

SP1349: 2½ miles (4km) SE of Bidford-on-Avon

Part of Welford-on-Avon parish, the tiny village on the Worcestershire border is approached by quiet lanes. Along a narrow avenue of yews, the small **St Peter's Church** (1758) of chequered brick, with a

Cotswold-stone roof, stands on a low base of blue lias that may have belonged to an earlier building. It has perhaps the plainest tower in Warwickshire, a short, narrow chancel and Victorian Gothic windows, but a Perpendicular font rests on a base from the mid-17th century and the pulpit is Jacobean.

Nearby, **New House Farm** is Georgian, and large, thatched cottages stand back from the road. **Moat House Farm**, which has an old mill wheel, was formerly a retreat of the bishops of Gloucester.

Of outlying **Dorsington Manor**, only gables and chimneys can be glimpsed from the lane. Beside it stretches a long, thatched, domestic building. Felix Dennis, a defendant in the 1971 *Oz* magazine trial and now a successful publisher, lives at the house.

DRAYCOTE [Rugby]

SP4470: 5 miles (8km) SW of Rugby

The hamlet has several cottages and old farmhouses, plus a Baptist Chapel of 1811 (rebuilt in 1869) that closed before the Second World War and became a house. Near Draycote Water reservoir (see THURLASTON), the half- timbered and thatched **Glebe Farm** dates from the 16th and 17th centuries. Features include a minstrel gallery reached by a spiral staircase.

DUNCHURCH [Rugby]

SP4871: 2½ miles (4km) S of Rugby

Though it is a village of small-town size, almost fusing with Rugby, Dunchurch's features of interest are all near the crossroads, where the statue of **Lord John Douglas Montagu Scott** (1809-60), a son of the Duke of Buccleuch, was erected by his 'tenantry'. Since the 1970s, a tradition has developed of clandestinely dressing it up on New Year's Eve in the garb of a cartoon or TV character. Lord John's wife, **Alicia Ann Spottiswoode**, was the composer of 'Annie Laurie' and, by attribution, of 'The Bonny, Bonny Banks of Loch Lomond'.

In coaching days Dunchurch was the crossways of the London to Holyhead and the Oxford to Leicester routes – the mileages appear on the restored **market cross** of 1813. On a green, beyond a thatched bus shelter, stand the two-seater **stocks**.

There are many old buildings, some thatched, and several inns, though not the 27 once listed. They include the 18th-century, stuccoed **Dun Cow** which retains a coach entrance. Changing times were indicated by a plaque recording that the railway engineers George and Robert Stephenson dined there in 1837 on completion of the Kilsby Tunnel in Northamptonshire. Despite the legend of the slaying of the great Dun Cow by Guy of Warwick on Dunsmore Heath, the beast on the inn sign looks perfectly innocuous. Across the road, **Dunchurch and Thurlaston Working Men's Club** was rebuilt in Georgian style in 1951, after having been bombed in 1940.

The Square, beyond the crossroads, is overlooked by the former Lion Inn, now **Guy Fawkes House**, with picturesque vertical half-timbering and an overhanging upper-floor. Some forty Catholic gentry were dining there on 6 November 1605 when Robert Catesby (see LAPWORTH), who had galloped 80 miles in seven hours, arrived with news that the Gunpowder Plot had been discovered, whereupon – spurning his plea to rise – they fled.

Nearby, **The School House** (red-brick, with stone pilasters and a hipped roof) dates from 1707 and was designed by Francis Smith of Warwick.

The monks of Pipewell Abbey in Northamptonshire began **St Peter's Church** of red sandstone. The nave piers stand on 12th-century bases, but much of the building is Perpendicular, including the great tower, which has an unusual large window and an arch to the nave nearly 30ft

(9m) high. There is an east window by Kempe, picturing the Crucifixion, and a triptych to Thomas Newcombe, printer to three kings – Charles II, James II and William III. In 1693 Newcombe founded the simple **almshouses** in The Square, which were rebuilt in 1818.

Adjoining the churchyard, **The Old Vicarage** is chequered-brick Georgian. Its neighbour in Vicarage Lane, **White Lodge**, retains a fine 18th-century wrought-iron gate between ball-topped pillars. **Dunchurch Hall**, of about 1840, was a hunting lodge for the Duke of Buccleuch and served as a boys' preparatory school until 1993. In 1999 the Ionic-porticoed house was converted to retirement flats and the stables refurbished as homes.

Outside the village, **Bilton Grange** (1841-46) was designed by A.W.N. Pugin, but has been called his least successful venture for his most difficult client (Captain J.H. Washington-Hibbert). It has been a school since late Victorian times. Features include a porte-cochere tower and a long gallery of about 100ft (30m). The many later additions include a chapel of 1889.

A mile north-east, Lord John Scott's **Cawston House** was rebuilt (1907) in Georgian style (but roughcast).

EASENHALL [Rugby]

SP4679: 3½ miles (5km) NW of Rugby

The hamlet lies at a lane junction between the Oxford Canal and the M6. It was an estate village of Newbold Revel (see STRETTON-UNDER-FOSSE) and may have been named from its position east of the hall. Though part of the ecclesiastical parish of Harborough Magna, Easenhall is a separate civil parish.

A small, brick-built former **Congregational Chapel** of 1873 looks up a green to an old brick **barn** with a vast gateway, through which the red-brick **Manor Farm** can be glimpsed. A tall cedar tree, said to have stood since the 18th century, sets off the picture. The nearby **Golden Lion** dates from 1640 and includes wattle and daub work. Beyond it rise three sets of solid Victorian semis, red-brick and gabled.

EATHORPE [Warwick]

SP3969: 5 miles (8km) NE of Leamington Spa

Since Eathorpe is a civil parish in the Leam valley, but not an ecclesiastical one, there is no church. Its cottages, including a pair with overhanging thatch, are scattered along lanes west of the Fosse Way, together with the Plough Inn and a village store. For over 200 years before 1858, the Eathorpe Estate belonged to the Vyner family (see WAPPENBURY).

The 18th-century red-brick **Eathorpe Hall** was the home of **Samuel Shepheard** (1816-66), who made his fortune in Egypt. About 1850 he established Cairo's world-famous Shepheard's Hotel, to which the military traffic of the Crimean War and the Indian Mutiny brought prosperity. Born near Daventry, Northamptonshire, and brought up at the Crown Inn, Leamington, Shepheard retired to Eathorpe in 1860 and is buried at Wappenbury. His initials and the date 1862 appear on several Eathorpe cottages, and a stone set in the nearby bridge over the River Leam indicates that he built it in the same year.

ETTINGTON [Stratford-on-Avon]

SP2649: 5 miles (8km) SE of Stratford-upon-Avon

There were originally two settlements, Upper and Lower Eatington. Today's village occupies the site of the former, but the other used to be the main one, where the parish church, a mill and the manor house of the Shirleys clustered by the River Stour. The Fosse Way passed nearby.

The present village developed where the Warwick to Moreton-in-Marsh and Stratford to Banbury roads crossed. Both were turnpikes. The Warwick-Moreton road now bypasses the village, which has two inns: the White Horse and the Chequers. There has been an inn on the Chequers site since the mid-18th century. The premises were once the village court-house and served as a toll (or checking) house on the Banbury road – hence the name.

Dr William Croft (1677-1727), composer of several famous hymns and organist at Westminster Abbey, was born at Ettington.

The Stanleys – perhaps the only land-owning family in England with an unbroken connection through the male line from Saxon times – adapted their house of 1641 to the splendid chateau of **Ettington Park** in 1858-62. A major example of Victorian Gothic, its use of the spiky Early English style was then a novelty for a private mansion. The building (now a luxury hotel) is noted for the sculptures representing events in the family's history. Behind it is a 17th-century loggia from the Digby's house at Coleshill Park (see COLESHILL).

The ruined 12th-century **Holy Trinity Church** (or St Nicholas's) stands nearby, across a lawn. It became disused as the result of an Enclosure Act of 1798, but the north transept was preserved as the Shirley mortuary chapel. Earlier monuments include Ralph Shirley (died 1327) and his wife, both defaced.

It replacement, the **church of St Thomas a Becket**, was jerry-built in 1798 and reputed to be the ugliest in the county. It had to be replaced a century later. The grey stone pyramid-capped tower, part of the private St Thomas a Becket House, stands near the bypass island. The present large, stone-built **church of Holy Trinity and St Thomas of Canterbury** (1902-03), at the old village crossroads, incorporates classical monuments and its predecessor's pulpit.

Down the old Moreton road, a small, stone **Friends' Meeting House** of the 1680s is one of the oldest in the Midlands.

The pyramid-capped tower of the former church of St Thomas a Becket, Ettington

In the village, a red-brick former **school** of 1871 has an impressive Italianate clock tower.

A mile north, the stone-fronted and E-shaped **Thornton Manor House** is mid-16th century.

EXHALL [Nuneaton]

SP3485: 1½ miles (3km) SW of Bedworth

This small former mining village has become a suburb of Bedworth. To the west flows the little River Sowe and the M6 separates it from **St Giles's Church**, which shares its dedication with Warwickshire's other Exhall (see below).

The Early English chancel of the Perpendicular-towered church was built about 1300. A window in the north aisle has a date (1609) and the aisle contains monuments of the Hales of Newland Hall. The south aisle was added in an 1842 restoration. Outside, below the tower, stands a 15th-century font found in a local garden and returned to the church in 1981.

Near the motorway junction, 18th-century **Hall Farm** (or Exhall Hall) is surrounded by an ancient moat. A mile west, **Newland Hall Farm** (as the former Hales' home is now known) is also moated and has traces of medieval fishponds. On its front are four small heads of about 1300, said to have been label-stops or corbels.

EXHALL [Stratford-on-Avon]

SP1055: 2 miles (3km) SE of Alcester

Heralded on the approach from Wixford by the gabled Victorian **Exhall Court** in pale red brick, the village straggles along a lane below a steep hill, at the edge of a flat-bottomed valley. It is the 'Dodging Exhall' of the rhyme (see BIDFORD-ON-AVON), perhaps because of its former inaccessibility.

At **St Giles's Church** (see also the other Exhall above), we encounter first its tall west end – restored in 1863, though the Church Building Society did not approve and refused a grant. A large stone bellcote caps it and a central buttress hides an old doorway seen from the inside. Conversely, a rather rough and ready 12th-century double-arched north doorway, still framing a wooden studded door, is only visible from outside.

Though heavily restored, the long, narrow building is Norman. When the church was redecorated in 1959 its pitchboard panelling was so badly rotted that it had to be removed. In the chancel floor lie small brass figures of John Walsingham (died 1566), wearing Elizabethan armour, and his wife Eleanor. The rector from 1698 to 1723, Dr William Thomas, is described as 'the continuator' of Dugdale, whose *The Antiquities of Warwickshire* he edited in 1730.

Beside the church, the old brickwork and 17th-century timber-framing of **Glebe Farm** can be seen through the gateway of a barn. **Glebe Cottage** stands opposite, with dormer windows and half-timbering.

A row of tall black and white cottages (probably late 16th century) placed end-on to the lane has an exterior chimney on a stone base. The names of the red-brick **Post Office Cottage** and the bow-windowed **Old Mill Cottage** recall earlier uses.

FARNBOROUGH [Stratford-on-Avon]

SP4349: 6 miles (10km) E of Kineton

The village lies just off the Coventry to Banbury road and south-east of the Burton Dassett Hills. Its early name of Fernberge meant 'the little hill of ferns'. The Raleighs, possibly a branch of the Devon family whose most famous member was Sir Walter, were lords of the manor from 1322. They sold the estate in 1684 to the Holbeches (of Dutch origin), who are still at **Farnborough Hall**, though as administrators for the National Trust since 1960.

The original manor house was rebuilt in two harmonious phases in the 1690s and the 1750s and is of mid-18th-century appearance. Its glories are the Palladian entrance hall and the dining room, which looks much as it did in its Georgian heyday. They show Italian influences picked up during William Holbech's Grand Tour in the mid-18th century.

Landscape features include a green Terrace Walk, passing an Ionic Temple and Oval Pavilion, and an obelisk of 1751. Sanderson Miller (see RADWAY) was architectural adviser and landscape designer. The Farnborough Wake is held at the hall on the first Saturday in July.

Both stone and brick were used for the old houses of the village, some of which are thatched. In School Lane, the **Butcher's Arms**, once a simple beer house, is a stone inn with mullioned windows, and the **village pump** survives in an alcove.

The **Reading Room and School** has become a private house. Archdeacon Holbech endowed the Victorian stone building and was responsible for Sir George Gilbert Scott's addition of the north aisle and steeple to the medieval **St Botolph's Church** in 1875.

A tall porch encloses a Norman doorway, with a zigzag arch and tympanum, and the door has strange curving metal bands. Within are memorials to the Raleighs and the Holbeches, and the head of an effigy of about 1200. Mrs Wagstaffe's brass inscription of 1667 has a pretty leaf and scroll surround and a long, adulatory verse, and Jeremiah Hall's cartouche (1711) unusually depicts an open book. On the outside south wall of the chancel is the faintly lettered 17th-century tablet of George Brooke. Nearby, veiled by trees, stands the white stucco former **vicarage** of Regency times.

FENNY COMPTON [Stratford-on-Avon]

SP4152: 5 miles (8km) E of Kineton

The compact village below the bald Burton Dassett Hills lies near the Banbury to Leamington railway line (the old GWR) and the sinuous Oxford Canal. It has had its own water company since 1866, fed by a spring on the nearby hills, and retains a fire station. The village inn, the Merrie Lion (stone-built, but partly brick), has a jester with a lion's head on its sign and an old sundial on a wall.

Henry Bate Dudley was born in Fenny Compton in 1745. He became prominent in literary circles and founded *The Morning Post* (incorporated into *The Daily Telegraph* in the 1930s), among other newspapers, but failed to impress Dr Johnson: 'Sir, I will not allow this man to have merit.'

Visitors arriving from Avon Dassett find, on a small green, a signpost displaying the county emblem of the Bear and Ragged Staff. It was erected in response to a national appeal by George V for signs illustrating local traditions.

The **church of St Peter and St Clare** is said to be one of only two in England with that dedication. It was originally St Peter's; the Blessed St Clare of Montefalco was added by the Augustinian Canons of Kenilworth in Henry I's reign. The first rector, in 1250, was Clyner de Valence, Prior of Kenilworth, a half-brother of Henry III and later Bishop of Winchester. His church was rebuilt about 1320 in Hornton stone. A squat spire (shortened after a lightning strike about the year 1800) caps the tower. Outside, placed against its disused west doorway, is a font (probably 17th century) that until 1840 supported the font used inside the church.

The building consists of a nave with two aisles, the south one added in 1862, and a chancel with a tie-beam roof. A Gothic porch of 1673 shelters the Decorated north doorway. Holes in its wooden door are said to have been made by shots fired during the Battle of Edge Hill in 1642.

A stained-glass window commemorates locally born **Thomas Payne** (1761-1834), who 'eminent as an engineer, designed and constructed the great embankment across the estuary of Traethmawr by which large tracts of land were recovered from the sea and the towns of Tremadoc and Portmadoc were originated.' A small stone head is set high on the chancel wall, where Eliz. Croke's large memorial tells us that she was 'pure and unspotted from the world' when she died aged '22 yere' in 1719. Richard Willis's memorial dates from 1597. In the tower is a detailed plan of Fenny Compton in 1779 and a map showing land ownership in that year.

The Old Rectory stands concealed by trees, but **Red House**, when rebuilt in 1707 (its date on a large sundial), was then the rectory. Brick with a hipped roof, its entrance hall incorporates Jacobean plasterwork and an overmantel of the same period, or a little earlier. The brick-built **Old School** has become a picture-framing specialist's premises, but the nearby larger, stone-built school remains in use. Squeezed between houses in High Street is a passageway to a small **Methodist church**.

Bridge Street has several fine buildings. They include the high-roofed and mullioned **Contone House, The Post House** (18th century, ashlared), thatched cottages and the L-shaped **Woad House**, which has a Decorated window and a small, worn head set near the door.

Where the Oxford Canal, at a height of 400ft (120m), passes under the Banbury to Coventry road stand Fenny Compton Wharf and the George and Dragon Inn. At another crossing to the south is The Tunnel – this has long been a misnomer because Fenny Compton Tunnel was converted to a canal cutting in 1888.

FILLONGLEY [North Warwickshire]

SP2887: 6 miles (10km) NW of Coventry

A compact village in a hollow at the centre of a large parish in the former Forest of Arden, from which later houses have spread along Coventry Road. The monks of Coventry Abbey owned the original settlement, Old Fillongley, when the Normans came, but it was abandoned by the mid-16th century. Surviving traces were obliterated by the M6 in 1972.

There are two pubs: the Butcher's Arms and the classical **Manor House**, with its two porticos, which had fallen into deep neglect before it became an inn. The Working Men's Club in Ousterne Lane, established in 1890, was formerly the Cock Inn.

In the 19th century there was a Mormon Chapel in Broad Lane, near Fillongley Hall. The sect emigrated to Salt Lake City and the building is now **Chapel House**.

The Durham Ox Inn stood nearby, until the Hon. Arden Adderley closed it, complaining that it was 'rowdy' and frequented by miners from Arley, who raced whippets and whistled after his daughters. Adderley was heir to Lord Norton of Hams Hall (see LEA MARSTON), succeeding him in 1944, when almost ninety.

An annual six-day fair used to begin on the Eve of St John the Baptist. Of various church charities, one for supplying bread for the poor no longer operates, but a Christmas charity providing money for aged and poor people exists, as does an educational charity.

The tall church of pale red sandstone is dedicated to **St Mary and All Saints**. Its Early English tower has a Perpendicular top, and the large nave is a rebuilding of about 1300. A restoration took place in 1887.

In the churchyard, the base of a medieval market cross supports a later shaft. Items for sale at a weekly Monday market used to be placed on its steps. A fee went to the lord of the manor. The table-tomb of Isaac Pearson and family, beside the path, has a literary link – the prosperous farmer, who died aged 48 in 1826, was an uncle of Mary Ann Evans (the novelist George Eliot).

Until its mysterious disappearance in 1940, a plague stone stood in the churchyard. It commemorated the death 'In tempore Plage' of William Smith of Birchley Hall in 1623 and of 26 unnamed persons in 1666.

Along Church Lane is the brick-built **Methodist Chapel** of 1892, now a private house. A spire originally capped its tower. The older part of the **school** dates from 1877. Uphill, a **Sunday School** of 1840 was built on land given by Lord Leigh of Stoneleigh Abbey.

Ancient **castle sites** lie north-east and south-west of the village. The former was probably a wooden fortification of the de Fillongley family. Robert de Hastings built the other in William the Conqueror's time; Oliver Cromwell is said to have destroyed it.

Fillongley Lodge is a late Regency house of stuccoed brick, with a Doric portico. It stands in parkland and was owned from 1975 to 1998 by Ronald Potter, grandson of Richard Bevan, who became coachman there in 1898. The Grecian **Fillongley Hall** was built about 1840 for the Reverend George Bowyer Adderley. At Chapel Green, just beyond the M6, stands **Old Fillongley Hall**.

Also south of the M6, at a lane junction on the county boundary, is the thick trunk of the **Wesley Tree**, beneath which John Wesley and other divines preached. A queer tale of its origin tells that it grew from a stake that took root after being driven through the bodies of a couple hanged for poultry stealing.

FLECKNOE [Rugby]

SP5163: 6 miles (10km) E of Southam

The village on Bush Hill overlooks the plain spreading beyond the Grand Union Canal towards Rugby. A mile to the east is the Northamptonshire boundary. The settlement was Flachenho in Domesday Book, probably meaning 'Flecca's hill'. There is a small, red-brick inn, the Old Olive Bush, and nearby are the **stocks**, restored in 1987.

St Mark's Church, with blue-patterned brick over the window arches, dates from 1891. Downhill, and similar in design, is the former **school**, now the village hall. The **Wesleyan Chapel** (converted to a house) is older, bearing the date 1837.

The handsome, twin-gabled **Manor House**, approached through a gateway with ball-capped pillars, is of Georgian red brick with stone quoins. With its steep roof (suggesting former thatch) broken by two levels of dormers, **The Old Oak House** looks rather Norman Shaw-ish. On the outskirts, a derelict brick building of three stepped floors is a survival of a Second World War camp.

FRANKTON [Rugby]

SP4270: 7 miles (11km) NE of Leamington Spa

This village of mingled old and modern houses lies away from main roads. Earl Leofric and Coventry Priory were early lords of the manor, a role held by the Biddulphs from 1680 until after the Second World War.

The gabled, red-brick **Manor House** rises behind the church, its lawn sweeping down to a ha-ha. It was built in 1662, but the William and Mary-style Hornton stone porch was not added until 1926. A Georgian staircase reputedly came from The Priory at Warwick.

St Nicholas's Church has grey stone walls and a stout 13th-century tower, capped by a Perpendicular belfry, in which a small, pointed-arched doorway stands well above the present ground level. Most of the rest was by Sir George Gilbert Scott in 1872.

The rather narrow nave is flanked by a south aisle, in which stands a weathered pinnacle, probably 17th century, removed from the tower in 1976, when new ones were erected. A plaque commemorates twins, Jane and Lucy Biddulph, who died at advanced ages in 1896 and 1904. The village war memorials are unusual in taking the form of wooden boards set on the nave wall.

John de Clungenford was the first rector in 1304, and there are links with two notable headmasters of Rugby School. The first, Henry Holyoake (see HARBOROUGH MAGNA), was rector from 1712. The other is **William Temple** (1821-1902), Archbishop of Canterbury, whose signature appears in the Register of Burials.

The Old Rectory – small, Georgian and entered by a white Doric porch – stands uphill, opposite the church. **The Friendly Inn** is of white-painted brick, with some half-timbering.

GAYDON [Stratford-on-Avon]

SP3654: 2½ miles (4km) NE of Kineton

Most of the small village lies off the

Warwick to Banbury road, where the **Gaydon Inn** stands. An old coaching inn, though much altered, it has served travellers for centuries. In 1789, a highwayman, John Smith, carved his name on a beam in an upper room while detained there before being tried and hanged at Warwick.

Gaydon's other inn, the ivy-covered Malt Shovel, is in the village centre. Opposite stand a thatched cottage and the **Village Hall** of 1886, formerly thatched, with rustic wooden side walls.

St Giles's Church, in dark stone, is an 1882 Gothic rebuilding of a chapel. It has a corner broach spire and a south doorway probably retained from its predecessor.

Half a mile away, on an old airfield site, the **Heritage Motor Centre** boasts the world's largest collection of historic British cars.

GRANDBOROUGH [Rugby]

SP4966: 5 miles (8km) S of Rugby

A quiet village, away from main roads and near the infant River Leam. In the early 20th century it was spelt Granborough – little changed from Graensburgh in 1043. There is an inn, the Shoulder of Mutton, and a former hostelry by the church is now the white-walled **Old Royal George Cottage**.

At **St Peter's**, lawns are lined with old headstones. The steepled church rises beyond them, its tower Perpendicular and the rest mostly Decorated. Outside, below the east window, is an old canopy arch. Adjoining the churchyard, **The Old Vicarage** of 1844 was built in Jacobean style.

In the small, plain, red-brick **Primitive Methodist Chapel** (erected 1856, with a 1991 extension) a plaque records how a local preacher, Elijah Cadman, became so worked up during his sermon that he kicked the front panel of the pulpit down the aisle.

The **Benn Memorial Hall** (1897) and **The Old School** (1840), which closed in 1974, are both built of red brick. **The Manor House**, in plain brick, has a large converted stone barn. Attractively set beside the narrow Leam and veiled by trees, **The Mill House** is white-painted.

A mile north, the red-brick and gabled **Woolscott Manor** has a cart entrance, and there is impressive vertical half-timbering at **Harrow Manor** (once the Harrow Inn). Set behind a long roadside green at nearby **Sawbridge** are lovely old half-timbered and thatched cottages, one with a loft conversion under the thatch. **Manor Farm** of 1654 has tall chimneys, rendered walls and the remains of a Gothic Revival wing. Roman urns were found there in 1689.

GREAT ALNE [Stratford-on-Avon]

SP1159: 2 miles (3km) NE of Alcester

A straggling village on the Alcester to Henley-in-Arden road, named from the nearby River Alne. The Alne Hills, rising to a modest 335ft (102m), extend northwards. There is evidence of a settlement as early as 809, and in 1251 the village was referred to as Ruwenalne. A later name, used in the 17th century, was Round Alne.

Though now a private dwelling, **Station House** is a reminder that the Alcester Railway, linking the town with Bearley on the North Warwickshire line, served the village from 1876. It was soon taken over by the Great Western Railway, which ran a quaint locomotive known as the 'Coffee Pot'. The line has long been abandoned, but a GWR notice on the house wall still threatens trespassers with a fine of forty shillings (£2), or one month's imprisonment.

A small bell turret caps the white-walled **St Mary Magdalene's Church**. Though the building has medieval stonework and there is a 13th-century lancet in the chancel, its origin is uncertain. It was enlarged in 1837 and a board lists charity donations from 1606.

The probably unique name of the Georgian **Mother Huff Cap Inn** refers to the froth on a glass of ale. There is a record of the inn as the Huff Cap in 1746.

At Alne End, a small Italianate **National School** of 1840 stands opposite a modern successor. Near the door is the ring to which its founder, the Reverend Richard Seymour, used to tie his horse. The vast **Great Alne Mills** building has been converted to a magnificent private house. Domesday Book records a mill on the Alne.

GREAT WOLFORD [Stratford-on-Avon]

SP2434: 4 miles (6km) S of Shipston-on-Stour

The village lies only two miles from **The Four Shire Stone**, which marked the meeting place of Warwickshire with Gloucestershire, Oxfordshire and Worcestershire until the boundary of the last moved away. Like No Man's Heath in the north of the county, it was once a lawless place, with illegal bear-baiting and cock-fighting taking place where the offenders could easily dodge into another shire to avoid the law.

Until 1924 Great Wolford was an estate village of Lord Redesdale of Batsford Park (father of the five famous Mitford sisters), across the Gloucestershire boundary. An ancient earthwork borders it and the general appearance is Cotswold-like. The village's oldest building is the stone **Fox and Hounds**, which may date from the 13th century.

The hilltop **St Michael's Church**, ashlar-faced and impressively steepled, goes back no further than 1833-35, though it had a 12th-century predecessor and owns plate from the 16th and 17th centuries.

Medieval-style carved heads and brasses support the door and window arches, and a spacious porch houses a two-wheeled bier and the mechanism of a former clock. Inside, the building is broad and aisle-less, with Ingram family monuments in the short chancel.

Nearby, the former **school**, now a house, is tall, bellcoted and gabled. The neighbouring cottage is **The Teacher's House**.

GRENDON [North Warwickshire]

SP2800: 2 miles (3km) SE of Polesworth

This small village near the Leicestershire border lies beside Watling Street, the busy A5(T), where an old turnpike road headed south to Coleshill. On the main road are The Boot, an 18th-century coaching inn, and the Black Swan.

Former miners' cottages line a cul-de-sac near the brick-built **United Free Methodist Church** (extended in 1885), which has round-headed, cast-iron windows and a modern porch.

All Saints' Church, a mile north-east, is separated from the village by a railway line, the Coventry Canal and the River Anker. Long, plain and grey, it is medieval and mainly Decorated, but with a fine Georgian-style tower added in 1845.

Furnishings include a canopied 17th-century pew. Monuments to the Chetwynds of Pooley Hall (see POLESWORTH) extend from 1539 to 1850. There are three probable Staffordshire imports – the Mayor's Pew of 1618, a screen under the tower (both from St Mary's, Stafford) and a mid-15th-century alabaster effigy of a lady (from Ingestre, where the hall was also a seat of the Chetwynds). Curiosities are the fireplace in the Chetwynd chapel and an unusually large Table of Kindred and Affinity. The neighbouring **Rectory** is in the Victorian Tudor style, but includes some 18th-century brickwork.

Sir George Chetwynd, who once tool part in a fist fight with Lord Lonsdale for the favours of Lily Langtry, lived so extravagantly that he had to sell the nearby 19th-century Grendon Hall, which was demolished in 1933. In its grounds, a medieval **bridge**, which until 1825 carried a road over the Anker, stands marooned among fields.

All Saints' church, Grendon

Across a lane, **Croft House** (1781) occupies a mill site recorded in Domesday Book. It was the home of Harry Atherton Brown, a famous amateur steeplechaser and friend of the Duke of Windsor, who often stayed at the house. Brown finished second in the 1921 Grand National.

At Bradley Green on the Coventry Canal, **Rectory Cottages** of 1829 were once the Goat's Head Inn. The initials GC above the date are Sir George Chetwynd's. Next door, a small, brick-built, Gothic **school** of 1871 (single-storeyed, with bargeboarded gables) is happily still in use.

In 1947, the Euston to Liverpool express, carrying over 1000 passengers, was derailed at Grendon. Five people were killed and over 30 injured.

GUY'S CLIFFE [Warwick]

SP2966: 1½ miles (2km) N of Warwick

There is no village of Guy's Cliffe and only a tiny parish, but a sad and magnificent ruin beside the River Avon features in both the legendary and authentic histories of Warwickshire.

Guy's Cliffe House stands on private ground west of the river, its great walls of crumbling grey stone rising cliff-like from the narrow Avon. The house is roofless, its high windows silhouetted against the sky. Lower down, intriguing stone archways face the stream, indicating rock chambers of uncertain purpose. The house was built (1751) in the Palladian style by a Mr Greathead; Gothic additions were made in 1818. The whole has fallen into ruin since the Second World War.

Richard Beauchamp, Earl of Warwick, rebuilt the neighbouring **Chantry Chapel of St Mary Magdalen** in 1422. A Gothic facade was added in the late 18th century. Among the early chantry priests was **John Rous** the antiquary, whose Chronical Roll is in the British Museum.

The chapel, partly cut out of the rock, contains a 14th-century figure of **Guy of Warwick** more than 8ft tall. Guy is said to have been a 10th-century Saxon earl who did battle with a giant, a green dragon and the great beast known as the Dun Cow. Having made a pilgrimage to the Holy Land, he returned to live at Guy's Cliffe in a cave that contains allegedly Saxon carved lettering.

Now owned by the Freemasons, who hold services in the chapel and give occasional guided tours, Guy's Cliffe is still a place of romance. John Leland certainly felt it to be in the 1540s when it stirred him to wax lyrical in the usually plain English prose of his *Itineries*.

Among those later drawn to it were the 19th-century writer and critic John Ruskin and the 18th-century painter David Cox. Elizabeth I must have called during her several visits to Warwick and Kenilworth, and the great actress Sarah Siddons worked as a 17-year-old maid at the house in 1773. Just resting?

Immediately north stands the **Saxon Mill** of 1822, grafted onto a 17th-century timber-framed stone mill house and now a restaurant.

Statue of St Mary, Halford parish church

HALFORD [Stratford-on-Avon]

SP2545: 3 miles (5km) N of Shipston-on-Stour

The village stands where the Fosse Way crosses the River Stour. A bridge of 1962 carries the traffic on the Warwick to Stow road, but below it lies a long and narrow medieval stone **bridge**, with four small, well-spaced arches. First mentioned in 1278, it suffered Civil War damage by both Royalists and Parliamentarians, who skirmished there in 1644.

The Halford Bridge Inn (formerly the Bell) has a grey stone Georgian frontage hiding 16th-century features. It faces the main road, but most of the older part of the lias-stone village lies to the west.

The north doorway tympanum of **St Mary's Church** (consecrated in 1150) is reputedly the best Norman sculpture in Warwickshire. Well-preserved within its porch, it is believed to show the Archangel Gabriel holding a scroll containing the message of the Annunciation. The south doorway is also Norman, as is the chancel arch, and the inside walls are of bare stone, the plaster having been stripped away in 1960. Earlier restorations took place in 1635-40, 1862 and 1883.

The south chapel of about 1270 is dedicated to St Thomas of Canterbury (Becket). It contains a coloured statue of Mary holding the Christ Child, which is thought to be 19th-century Swiss. Five bishops' heads cap the painted wooden font cover, and on a wall are two heavy fire-hooks designed for pulling down burning thatch.

The tower is 13th century and one of its bells is said to be the oldest inscribed bell in the county, dating from the 14th century. A massive, heavily worn gargoyle leans threateningly out from the west wall. Overlooking the churchyard is the 18th-century, grey stone former **rectory**, with hipped roof, dormers and sashed windows.

The nearby 17th-century **Manor House** – rather small and in a cramped setting – is a delight, its black and white upper part resting on a stone base and with a long, thatched barn beside it. **The Malt House** has mullioned windows and dormers in a high roof.

Downhill lie a prefabricated **Christadelphian Meeting Room** and the stone **Mill House**

Beyond modern houses in Idlicote Road stands **Folly Lodge**, which is ivy-covered and brick-built with Gothic touches. Trees veil **The Folly** itself. Both are Regency.

HAMPTON LUCY [Stratford-on-Avon]

SP2557: 2 miles (3km) NW of Wellesbourne

The small village is divided from Charlecote by the Avon, which is crossed by a single-span **bridge** cast in 1829 by Horseley Iron Works. The Warwickshire Feldon Cycle Way passes through, though on the Arden side of the river.

Since the land belonged to the See of Worcester from 781 to 1549, the village became known as Bishops Hampton. The change to Hampton Lucy occurred after 1557, when Sir Thomas Lucy of Charlecote Park became Lord of the Manor.

In the attractive village centre the houses are a mixture of old and new. There is an inn, the Boar's Head, a Gothic, bargeboarded brick **house**, and some black and white, thatched cottages formerly of the Lucy Estate.

The medieval church was demolished in 1826, when the high-towered and pinnacled **church of St Peter ad Vincula** (St Peter in Chains) was consecrated. Uninhibitedly designed by Thomas Rickman and Henry Hutchinson in the Decorated style for the Reverend John Lucy, it is a stone-vaulted, Gothic Revival building of some splendour, in now rather crumbling Gloucestershire sandstone. Hutchinson is buried in the churchyard and has a monument in the vestry.

Also involved were Thomas Willement, heraldic artist to George IV, and Sir George Gilbert Scott. The first was proud enough of his brilliantly coloured east window to use it as the frontispiece to a book of his works. Scott redesigned the chancel in the 1850s, adding an apse and the vast north porch (now the choir vestry).

The choir stalls are in the style of the Lady Chapel at Ely Cathedral, and a north window commemorates the Reverend John Lucy, who died in 1874 after being rector for 59 years. The only ancient features are two squares of inlaid floor tiles, believed to be 14th century, at the west end of the south aisle. In 1934 a leaden seal of Pope Innocent VI from the same period was found in a grave. Gates leading to the red-brick former rectory of about 1700 stand nearby, and behind the church is **Avonside**, the schoolmaster's house of 1710.

Warwickshire Wildlife Trust's **Hampton Wood** is a 13.5-hectare (33-acre) reserve (members only) by the Avon, 2 miles north of the village. The ancient woodland is noted for its spring flora, such as bluebells, primroses, wood anemones and yellow archangel.

HARBOROUGH MAGNA [Rugby]

SP4779: 3 miles (5km) NW of Rugby

The small village, together with adjoining Harborough Parva, lies in a narrow neck of land between the Oxford Canal and the M6, and is a mixture of old and modern houses. It appears in Domesday Book as Herdeberge. After the canal was cut in 1832, the main source of employment became William Ivens's sawmill at nearby Cathiron.

The Victorian west tower of **All Saints' Church** is flanked by the gable ends of the two aisles, an impressive sight when approaching. Set in the tower is an unusual clock face of 1984, picturing at the quarters the four beasts from Chapter 4 of Revelations (the symbols of the four Evangelists). The mechanism of an old clock, replaced by an electric one in 1973, stands in the large porch.

The church is broad, with aisles of about

the same width as the nave. Its first incumbent was Robert de Farendon in 1305 – the period of the nave and chancel, though the south aisle was rebuilt in 1869. The remains of an Easter sepulchre in the north wall were probably removed from the chancel. Unusually, below the roof are two white fans for ventilation.

Henry Holyoake (see FRANKTON), who became rector in 1712, was the first notable headmaster of Rugby School, and **Dr J.B. Lightfoot** (1828-89) began his career as curate at All Saints' and ended it as Bishop of Durham.

The east window, depicting the Ascension, was presented in 1875 by the rector, Andrew Bloxam, a member of a distinguished family of clergymen (see BRINKLOW). Backing onto the churchyard, **The Old Rectory** is in early Victorian red brick, has a pedimented porch and is now a guesthouse.

The **National School** of 1845 – small and brick-built, with stone quoins – is now a nursery and has a modern porch. A white cottage, **The Smithy**, probably dates from the 17th century. The 18th-century **Old Lion,** formerly the Golden Lion, was severely damaged by fire in 1986, but has been restored.

HARBURY [Stratford-on-Avon]

SP3760: 3 miles (5km) SW of Southam

This large village, with many attractive stone buildings, lies east of the Fosse Way and is visited by the Centenary Way.

Nearby, the Leamington to Banbury railway line runs through a cutting claimed to be the world's deepest when dug in 1852 – the village's five inns were, no doubt, put to good use by the Victorian navvies.

In 1927, a 190 million-year-old macroplata, a 15ft-dinosaur, was dug up in a local quarry and sent to the Natural History Museum. Bronze Age cooking pots have been found, and the village's name is said to stem from Hereburgh, a woman tribal chief of about 500BC. Domesday Book has Edburberie. The Romans built a culvert that still carries water, and in medieval times the Knights Templars were landowners, as the area known as Temple End recalls.

At **All Saints' Church** the tower catches the eye because of the early 19th-century brick top built uneasily on a 13th-century stone base. More rebuilding of the medieval church took place in 1872-73, after it had become 'almost ruinous', and a Church Room was added in 1989. Within, the building is very broad, with aisles and bare stone walls – all rather plain except for the canopied stone reredos. The Georgian font on its tapering pillar is unusual.

There are floor brasses of 1563 (incomplete) to Alys Wagstaffe, and of 1685 to Jacob Wright. The Wagstaffes, lords of the manor, were patrons of All Saints' from Henry VIII's time until 1942, when the benefice was transferred to the bishops of Coventry. The vicars, who are listed from

Harbury windmill and Old Mill House

1251, include the poet **Richard Jago**, who served 1745-71.

Gabled and mullioned **Wagstaffe School**, stone-built north of the church in 1611, is now a house. An older stone **house** of 1577, with a bull's head carved above the door, stands opposite the Dog Inn.

Nearby, the **Wight School**, now a chapel, was erected in 1856 by the Reverend William Wight in red-brick Gothic, and a tall, sail-less **tower-mill** of brick stands on a stone base. **Old Mill House** adjoins it.

Grey-lias **Flecknoe House** of 1832 is the former chapel from which Chapel Street is named. Along Park Lane, **The Manor House** is 16th century and H-shaped, with ancient stonework, mullions, and unpainted timber gables.

To the east, **Harbury Spoilbank** is a 7-hectare (17-acre) Warwickshire Wildlife Trust reserve (members only) beside the railway line. It is formed from calcareous lias clay excavated during the line's construction and has two contrasting habitats: gullies containing dense hawthorn scrub and limestone grassland ideal for wildflowers and butterflies.

HARTSHILL [North Warwickshire]

SP3294: 2½ miles (4km) NW of Nuneaton

The large hillside village, which has become virtually a suburb of Nuneaton, slopes down to the Coventry Canal and the River Anker, beyond which stretches the Leicestershire plain.

At Hartshill Green, a stone bus shelter in the shape of a scroll commemorates the locally born poet **Michael Drayton** (1563-1631), though the plaque recording its dedication by Sir John Betjeman in 1972 has disappeared. By the green, the small, gabled and white-walled **Meeting House Cottage** was formerly a Friends' Meeting House. The Stag and Pheasant overlooks the green, and down Grange Road is The Maltshovel. Beyond it, the **Wesley Chapel** of 1836 has a two-storeyed house built onto its back.

Further down, near a great pyramid of quarry waste, is **Grange Farm**, or Hartshill Grange, with large, twin white gables, some half-timbering, a red-tiled roof and a broad, turret-like chimney. Merevale Abbey owned it before the Dissolution, and later it belonged to Elizabeth I's favourite, the Earl of Essex. George Fox (1624-91), the founder of the Society of Friends, stayed there.

The porch at Holy Trinity, Hartshill

At **Holy Trinity Church** (1843-48), the magnificent west front, a mixture of brick and stone, includes a great doorway with six orders of columns and arches, a large wheel window and a brick bellcote. Otherwise it is a typical Commissioners' church, aisle-less and with tall, round-headed windows.

Warwickshire County Council's **Hartshill Hayes Country Park** covers 55 hectares (137 acres) of woodland, mainly replanted in the 18th century. An open hilltop provides superb views, enjoyed by Centenary Way walkers, north to Charnwood Forest and the Peak District heights, and it is said that forty churches can be counted on the great plain below.

A covered reservoir built on the hilltop by Severn Trent in 1977 to serve Nuneaton holds 15 million gallons. A nearby prehistoric **hill fort** is on private land, as is the 18th-century **Oldbury Hall**, but below in the woods the scanty remains of Hugh de Hardreshulle's **motte and bailey castle** of 1125 can be visited.

Nearby, the early 20th-century **Oldbury Grange** was built by William Garside Phillips, owner of Ansley Colliery and great-grandfather of Captain Mark Phillips, first husband of the Princess Royal. His sarcophagus can be seen at St Laurence's, Ansley Common.

HASELEY [Warwick]

SP2368: 4 miles (6km) NW of Warwick

A tiny village, dating back to Saxon times, at the south end of a long, narrow parish that extends to include the hamlet of Haseley Knob and the Honiley Court Hotel and Restaurant (formerly the Boot Inn).

The old manor house, built in 1561 by Clement Throckmorton of the Protestant branch of that notable family, was demolished in the mid-1960s. In 1598, the printing press on which the scurrilous anti-episcopal 'Marprelate Tracts' attacking 'wainscot-faced bishops' had been produced at various locations ten years earlier was discovered there. Its Puritan occupier, Job Throckmorton, was arrested on suspicion of being the writer 'Martin Marprelate', but escaped punishment.

The original settlement was near the **Manor House** (now the Haseley Business Centre), a Tudor-style stone mansion of 1875, built for a mining engineer named Hewlett and noted for its variety of interior tiling.

An unusual chancel window – mullioned, gabled and probably 17th century – gives an almost domestic look to the **church of St Mary the Virgin**. The tower is 15th-century Perpendicular and the south doorway dates from about 1200, though its porch is imitation Norman. Clement Throckmorton lies in a tomb-chest of 1573 and is depicted with his wife and 13 children on palimpsest brasses – second-hand Flemish imports, previously engraved on their other sides.

The Old Coach House, a timber **tithe barn** and **Haseley House Hotel**, formerly the vicarage, stand nearby.

HASELOR [Stratford-on-Avon]

SP1257: 2 miles (3km) E of Alcester

Below Church Hill lie the picturesque cottages and farms forming the hamlets of Upton, Lower Haselor and Walcote in the parish of Haselor – Haselove ('hazel bank') when the Domesday Book surveyors called.

Upton's Crown Inn no longer exists as such, and Paul Pry Cottage at Walcote was formerly the village pub, but the village **stocks**, last used in 1841, survive at Upton, as does the former workhouse, now **Little Manor**. **Manor Farm** at Upton dates from about 1600, though its distinctive timber gable was rebuilt in 1810.

Flaxhide, a long medieval house with unpainted timber-framing at Walcote, reminds us that, in the pre-cotton age, the pale blue flax was a common crop here and its processing a cottage industry. Walcote also has an 18th-century **cider-press** in a garden and a cottage of cruck construction. **Walcote Manor** is a 17th-century house, timber-framed at the gable-ends, but otherwise refaced in late 18th-century brick.

The grey stone Early English **church of St Mary and All Saints**, Haselor, stands strikingly on the hill, probably occupying a pagan site of worship. Reached by a tarmac path linking Upton and Walcote, its isolation may be due to the parishioners moving away after the Black Death in 1349.

Entering via a broad, stone and timber-framed porch, we find a white-painted, light interior and a Norman font of Cotswold oolite. The Mortuary Chapel in the north wall is in memory of the Reverend Cornelius Griffin, who in 1846 found the building a near ruin ('The tower will collapse at no distant date,' he wrote) and presided over its repair at local ratepayers' expense. Later he was imprisoned at Warwick, possibly for debt. A plaque recalls another benefactor – a lady squire, Maude Mary Cheape, who died in 1919.

In a beech wood towards Walcote, the base of a **village cross** destroyed at the Reformation has been resited beside the path. By the River Alne stands **Hoo Mill** – a private house, but with the mill wheel restored to use in 1945. Though the building is 19th century, there was a mill on the site in 1559.

HATTON [Warwick]

SP2367: 3½ miles (5km) NW of Warwick

Hatton (the Saxon 'heath town') is a small village, most of it just off the Warwick to Birmingham road at Hatton Green. The outlying Falcon Inn takes its name from the crest of the Throckmortons, a branch of whom lived nearby at Haseley. For many years it was kept by the post-Second World War cricketer **Tom Dollery** of Warwickshire and England.

The other local inn, the Waterman at Hatton Hill, has an attractive rear outlook over the Grand Union Canal and part of its flight of 21 locks (1779), which descend to the site of a prehistoric lake. Nearby stand British Waterways' **Hatton Workshops**, in classical style.

The grounds of the former Central and King Edward VII hospitals, closed in 1995, have been developed for housing, though the main buildings are preserved. They include the Jacobean-style **County of Warwickshire Lunatic Asylum** of 1852.

The 40-hectare (100-acre) site of **Hatton Country World** houses rural attractions, including rare breeds, a craft centre, a farm park and a nature trail. The landowner, John Arkwright, who opened it in 1982, is a descendant of Sir Richard Arkwright, the inventor in 1769 of a process of spinning yarn through water-powered rollers.

Holy Trinity Church is entered via a magnificent timber lych-gate. Its Perpendicular tower is 15th century, but the rest was built in 1880 for the Hewletts of Haseley Manor. A tower window has early 16th-century German glass from a Tree of Jesse. The churchyard tombstone of a Mrs Maynard is by the sculptor Eric Gill.

Monuments include **Dr Samuel Parr** (1747-1825), rector for 39 years and chaplain to Queen Caroline. He was known as 'Dr Johnson's double', because of physical and intellectual likenesses to the great man. Johnson spoke well of him, though politically they were poles apart: 'Parr is a fair man. I do not know when I have had occasion for such free controversy.' Parr's residence, **The Old Rectory**, veiled by trees, was built between 1749 and 1757 and enlarged by him in 1785.

Nearby, **Post Office Cottage** and **Wheelwright Cottage** proclaim their previous functions, and on the Birmingham road is the red-brick, towered and Gothic **Hatton Village Hall**, formerly a school.

At crossroads south of Hatton Green, a **cottage** is quaintly fronted by a broad, 16th-century stone chimney, flanked by 17th-century timber-framing and gables. This may have been the original Hatton House.

HAWKESBURY [Nuneaton]

SP3684: 1½ miles (2km) S of Bedworth

Though its name dates from Saxon times, the hamlet on the Coventry boundary grew up at the junction of the Coventry and Oxford canals. The Centenary Way, the Sowe Valley Walk and the Coventry Canal Footpath Trail all use the towpaths. **Hawkesbury Junction** (also known, after its first lock-keeper, as Sutton Stop) is of considerable interest (information boards on site).

The Coventry Canal was one of the most prosperous waterways. Its section linking Coventry with the Bedworth coalfields was opened in 1769, though the extension to Fradley Junction, beyond Tamworth, had to wait until 1790. The Oxford Canal (providing a link with the River Thames and thence to London) was authorised in 1769, but it, too, was not completed until 1790. Both canals were designed by James Brindley, but after his death in 1772 Samuel Simcock took over the Oxford project. The 91-mile route wound inordinately and was cut by 14 miles in an 1830s modernisation.

At the junction, where the canals are linked by a lock with a fall of only seven inches, stand a graceful cast-iron **bridge** of 1837 and a former **pump house**. The bridge has a 50ft-span and was from the Britannia Foundry, Derby. The pump's Newcomen-type steam engine of 1725 was brought from Griff Colliery, near Nuneaton, in 1821 and retired to the museum at Dartmouth, Devon (Newcomen's birthplace), in 1963.

The canal-side **Greyhound Inn**, which dates from before 1832, stands near a row of chequered-brick cottages.

HENLEY-IN-ARDEN [Stratford-on-Avon]

SP1566: 8 miles (12km) NW of Stratford-upon-Avon

Its long High Street, a Conservation Area lined with buildings representing the architectural styles of seven centuries, is one of Warwickshire's glories. Yet the town is junior to adjacent Beaudesert, a much smaller settlement whose church serves a separate and older parish.

Recorded history began in the late 11th century, when Thurstan de Montfort raised a motte and bailey castle on The Mount, the great hill above Beaudesert. Along the ridge beyond The Mount runs Edge Lane, an ancient trackway of which there is evidence from 1360. The Heart of England Way, which passes through the town, briefly uses it. The 'beautiful wasteland' of the Norman invaders, Beaudesert was originally Beldesert and was known locally as 'Belser' until well into the 20th century.

After the Empress Matilda granted a charter for a weekly fair and market at the castle in 1140, Henley grew and prospered. The boom ended when the Lord of the Manor, Peter de Montfort, joined his kinsman Simon against Henry III's forces at the Battle of Evesham in 1265. Henry's men won, the de Montforts were slain, and the town and castle were burnt in reprisal.

Henley recovered and became a borough in 1296, though it remained in the parish of Wootton Wawen. A chapel of ease was built in 1367 on the present church's site.

During the Hundred Years' War, Henley sent 160 archers to France for the Battle of Crecy (1346). At Easter 1643, Prince Rupert, heading north from Oxford to attack Birmingham in the Civil War, paused to plunder the town.

From 1893 Henley-in-Arden was synonymous with ice cream, until, sadly, the manufacturer withdrew from the town in 1997.

The ancient Court Leet and Court Baron were revived in 1915. They are held, under the authority of the Lord and Lady of the Manor, in the timber-framed **Guildhall** built by Sir Ralph Boteler in 1448 and restored in 1915. A High Bailiff is elected annually.

The tall **market cross** is also 15th century, but lost its engraved head in the 1890s. Nearby are a small brick **Methodist church** of 1894, the classical **Stone House** and the 16th-century, timber-framed **George House**, once the Old George Inn.

Across the road stand a slim-steepled Baptist church of 1867, rebuilt after a fire in 1936, and the twin-gabled **White Swan**. Though most of the inn dates from about

1600, since 1358 it has been extending the welcome that, according to once-famous lines said to have been written by the poet Shenstone within its walls, life's travellers find to be warmest at an inn. Dr Johnson and James Boswell, returning from their Scottish jaunt in 1776, were among the 18th-century coach passengers who stayed at Henley, but at which inn is unclear. A **milestone** attached to number 185 reads, 'From London CII miles, from Stratford VIII, from Birmingham XIV 1748.'

Henley has many more buildings of interest, and a **Heritage Centre** was opened in 1997 at the expense of Joseph Hardy of Pennsylvania, USA. As Lord of the Manor from 1990 to 1994, he succeeded the 17th- and 18th-century Archers of Umberslade and William Pitt, Prime Minister during the Napoleonic Wars.

Beside the Guildhall and linked to it by an internal door, the Perpendicular **church of St John Baptist** juts out into High Street. Replacing the chapel of ease in 1448, it housed a Chapel of the Guild of St John, a medieval order of charity.

Unusually, the nave and chancel are one, undivided by an arch. Though outwardly little changed since the 15th century, the church long ago lost its original furnishings, possibly when Henry VIII confiscated it in the 1540s. His successor Edward VI was persuaded to hand it back, because (as a report put it): 'The Town of Henley is severed from the Parish Church with a brook which in winter so riseth that none may pass over it without danger of perishing ...' The first vicar was not appointed until 1868, previous incumbents having been perpetual curates.

Down Beaudesert Lane, but across the River Alne and in its own parish, the Norman **St Nicholas's Church** stands below The Mount. The two churches have shared a rector since 1915, though Beaudesert's list goes back to Ric de Budiford in 1327.

Built about 1170, it has a fine timber lych-gate, a Norman south doorway with a zigzag arch, and a magnificent Norman chancel arch. The small east window is probably original, but the tower was added in the 15th century. Its weather vane shows St Nicholas with three children he saved from a frying vat. The building is narrow and without aisles, the north wall having been brought in by almost two metres in the late 16th century, perhaps for safety reasons. The church was restored in 1865.

Outside the east wall is a monument to the Reverend Richard Jago (died 1741), father of the poet of the same name (see HARBURY). John Hannett, author of *The Forest of Arden*, who died in 1893, aged 89, lies in the churchyard. In the troubled mid-17th century, John Doughty became rector in 1636, was ejected by Parliament, reinstated after the Restoration in 1660 and buried in Westminster Abbey in 1672.

HILLMORTON [Rugby]

SP5374: 2 miles (3km) E of Rugby

In the 18th century Hillmorton was a village on the London to Chester coach road and by 1790 the Oxford Canal had been routed round its high ground. In the 19th, the London to Birmingham railway was built, hemming in expansion to the north, and the 20th saw it become a suburb of Rugby. Among the developments there survives an old **mill mound.**

To the east, Watling Street became the A5(T), which marks the Northamptonshire border. With the coming of radio, a forest of masts over 800ft (240m) high sprouted at Rugby Radio Station, and in 1959 the M1 was built just across the county boundary.

The towered **church of St John Baptist** stands near the canal and is separated from Hillmorton by the railway. It is far older than either, having (it is said) been built by Thomas Astley, who died at the Battle of Evesham in 1265. Later parts include the 16th-century clerestory and the east window dated 1640. The box pews were added in 1777; one of them has a trapdoor concealing a large 15th-century brass of an unknown lady.

Three monuments date from the 14th century: a cross-legged knight and a priest, both defaced, and a more than life-sized lady under a canopy. The knight and the lady are thought to be Astleys.

HONILEY [Warwick]

SP2472: 2½ miles (4km) W of Kenilworth

Opposite the Honiley Court Hotel and Restaurant (a massive late 20th-century expansion of the gabled and ivy-covered Boot Inn), a lane heads east to the delightful setting of **St John Baptist Church** of Arden sandstone. It is approached between two widely spaced service wings of the 17th-century Honiley House, the rest of which was demolished in 1820. The house stood beyond, to the north of the church.

The churchyard of yews is entered through gates whose piers display the elephant head motifs of John Sanders, Lord of the Manor and builder of the church in 1723. Legend has it that Sir Christopher Wren, in the year of his death, sketched the design on the tablecloth when dining with Sanders, but the architect is more likely to have been Francis Smith of Warwick.

Ahead rises the fine Baroque west tower capped by an octagonal spire. Within, most features are original 1723: smallish nave and apse, west gallery on marble pilasters, font, oaken box pews and pulpit. The rich blue tints of the 20th-century east window are a delight.

Three 19th-century members of the Willes family (see ROYAL LEAMINGTON SPA) are buried in the churchyard. There is known to have been a church here in 1318, and Dr Thomas's edition of Dugdale says that it was founded by Simon de Montfort, Earl of Leicester.

North of the church is the site of **St John's Well**, once a place of pilgrimage 'for such men as had offended God and lived a lewd life and had gotten maidens or women with child'.

The nearby Jacobean-style **Honiley Hall** was built in 1914. Its owner is the former swimming coach and television commentator Hamilton Bland, who refurbished the house after acquiring it in a rundown state from Warwickshire Education Authority.

It is said that in 1469, during the Wars of the Roses, Warwick the Kingmaker captured Edward IV nearby in the Forest of Arden, though other places (see WOLVEY) make the same claim.

During the Second World War, the RAF had an airfield to the west. It is now a vehicle proving ground.

HONINGTON [Stratford-on-Avon]

SP2642: 1½ miles (2km) N of Shipston-on-Stour

The small, unspoiled village by the River Stour was the Hunitone of Domesday Book, a name thought to refer to the production of honey.

From **Old Tollbar Cottage** on the Stratford to Oxford road, built for the opening of the turnpike in the 1730s, a lane drops and crosses the river. The lane and the 17th-century classical, five-arched **bridge**, with low stone walls and ball-capped finials, were originally parts of the Honington Hall estate.

By a green, the half-timbered and gabled **Magpie Cottage** gazes up the broad village street and the stone-built and mullioned **Shoemaker's Cottage** faces the gates and lodge of **Honington Hall**.

Sir Henry Parker, a London merchant, built the hall, a brick mansion of seven bays and two storeys with dormers in a hipped roof, in 1682. Busts of Roman emperors are set above the ground-floor windows and the doorway has an open pediment with a coat of arms. Outbuildings include mid-17th-century stables and an octagonal dovecote with a sundial. The interior decoration is sumptuous, especially in the Octagonal Saloon, which has a ceiling painting attributed to Bellucci.

The Parkers sold to Joseph Townsend in 1737 and his family stayed until 1932. Among them was **Mary Elizabeth Townsend**, who founded the still existing Girls' Friendly Society in 1875. She died in 1918 and is buried in the churchyard.

All Saints', in a secluded setting, is a surprising church for a small village. Its basis was a traditional medieval building of west tower, nave and chancel. The 13th-century tower remains, but the rest was rebuilt, or adapted, in the 1680s to resemble the London churches of the time. Its pitched roof above a classical parapet seems a touch incongruous.

The nave has Tuscan arches and there is a broad apse, the Royal Arms of the Stuarts set above its arch. Some box pews survive, with children's seats. Monuments include a vivid Sir Henry Parker and his son Hugh, walking and talking with animation. They died, respectively, in 1713 and 1712. A Rococo tablet of 1763 to Joseph Townsend features a putti, or naked boy, variously described as 'macabre', 'grotesque', 'hydrocephaloid' and 'perhaps the most unpleasant cherub in all England'.

HUNNINGHAM [Warwick]

SP3768: 4 miles (6km) NE of Leamington Spa

The small village ('the ham of Hunna's people') lies just off the Fosse Way, where the modest Hunningham Hill descends to the sinuous River Leam and the Saxons Ernwy and Saewulf were farming before the Normans came.

There are several thatched cottages, the name of one of which, **The Old Bakehouse**, reveals its former use. The river **bridge** on the Weston-under-Wetherley road is medieval, though rebuilt in 1651 at a cost of £20. Beside it stands the Red Lion Inn.

St Margaret's Church, approached by a short avenue of yews, was originally a chapel of ease to Wappenbury, because villagers were sometimes cut off from worship when the Leam flooded. As late as 1819, a vicar drowned when trying to cross the ford, but he was said to have been 'much intoxicated'.

Though Domesday Book records a church, Sir Geoffrey de Corbicum (or Corbicion) constructed the present small, red-roofed, sandstone building, possibly about 1200. It was heavily restored in 1868. There is a blocked Norman doorway and, unusually, a window in a buttress. Inside, the white-sandstone font is 14th century, and one of the two bells, which have had to be removed from the weather-boarded turret, rests on the floor. The tenor bell was cast about 1350 and the treble in 1510.

A wall plaque commemorates the curiously named Hanyball Horseye. The modern oak altar has a dragon with a sword in its mouth, the symbol of St Margaret.

HURLEY [North Warwickshire]

SP2495: 5 miles (8km) SE of Tamworth

A former mining village on a plateau in Kingsbury parish, its name means 'a forest clearing' (the forest, of course, was Arden). For 200 years the village inn has been the Holly Bush, which once overlooked the Bull Ring and the stocks. The much less populous Hurley Common has the White Hart (currently closed) and the Anchor, which probably speaks for the miners' thirsts.

The name of The Forge Garage on Knowle Hill indicates the building's former use by a blacksmith. To the south, Dexter Colliery operated from 1927 to 1968. No spoil heaps disfigure the site because a railway took the coal to the Kingsbury mine at Piccadilly.

At the top of Knowle Hill, the wooden **church of the Resurrection** is 1861 Gothic, with cast-iron supports and a fleche. Originally a dame school, but used for services on Sundays, it became a church in 1895 when the impressive school was built behind it in stone. That building is now unused, modern ones having taken over.

Next door, **Atherstone House** (originally Old East House), is 17th-century brick. A Civil War cannon ball, said to have dropped down its chimney, lay in the garden until recent years.

The cemetery, established about 1904 on colliery land in Heanley Lane, has a large **cross** of rough stonework concealed among yews. It came from St Edmund's Chapel, demolished in the 17th century, which stood where the modern school now is. In the lane, **Peach Cottage** is half-timbered black and white.

Along Atherstone Lane, the three-storeyed **Hurley Hall** dates from about 1720. It occupies the site of a medieval moated manor. The earlier building was the home of Waldive (or Wildive) Willington, a prominent Parliamentarian in Cromwell's time, whose family remained until the mid-19th century. A Magistrates' Court used to be held at the hall.

IDLICOTE [Stratford-on-Avon]

SP2844: 3 miles (5km) NE of Shipston-on-Stour

The tiny village is set among quiet lanes below Idlicote Hill – at 435ft (133m) one of the great viewpoints of the Centenary Way. The present population is smaller than when Domesday Book recorded 29 'heads of families' and Robert de Stafford was Lord of the Manor.

Later, Kenilworth Priory held it until the Dissolution, when Henry VIII bestowed it on his Master of the Revels, Thomas Cawarden. His successor, Ludovic Greville, was hanged for killing a servant as part of an unsuccessful con trick involving a will. He sold the manor to William Underhill, who was poisoned by his son Fulk, but not before he had found a buyer for his New Place property at Stratford in 1597 – a successful poet and playwright called William Shakespeare.

In 1780 Mrs Margaret Underhill left £100 to the poor of the parish, which is still providing interest for the Honington, Idlicote and Whatcote Charity.

The plain, stone-built **Idlicote House** is mainly of the early 19th century and dubiously attributed to the architect Sir John Soane. A grange, at which Elizabeth I is said to have stayed, previously occupied the site. There were once signs of a moat, and subterranean passages still exist. During the Second World War, the Women's Land Army was billeted at the house, which served as a boys' preparatory school from 1953 to 1972, before returning to private use.

Its neighbours are a battlemented, octagonal, early 18th-century Gothic **dovecote** for 1002 birds, a stone-built former **rectory** and the **church of St James the Great**, in grey lias, with a shingled bellcote and clock. Rectors are listed from Robt. de Ketene in 1301. Most of the building dates from about that time, but the Norman north doorway is one hundred years older. At the west end is a domestic-looking mullioned window.

The Tuscan-columned Underhill Chapel was added in the 17th century, as was the rare three-decker pulpit, with its sounding board. A pew door hangs on late 16th-century cock's head hinges, and the deep, 18th-century lord of the manor's pew has padded seats. Tablets to the Peach and Peach Keighley families, 19th-century lords of the manor, indicate links with the East India Company. A large, stone coat of arms is that of the Ettington branch of the Underhills. On the north nave wall is a sizeable fragment of a mural.

Near the Idlicote House gates stands an early 18th-century stone **cottage**. On the Halford road, **Badger's Farm** (17th-century, stone-built, with mullioned windows) faces **Badger's Cottage**, a lovely, thatched, stone building.

From the Second World War until 1952, Idlicote Hill was used by the Air Ministry as a bombing range.

ILMINGTON [Stratford-on-Avon]

SP2143: 7½ miles (11km) S of Stratford-upon-Avon

A large village of honey-coloured stone, it stands where the Cotswolds rise from the Feldon plain. The hills, Ilmington Downs, are the county's highest, reaching 850ft (261m) on the Gloucestershire border and topped by police and transmission masts.

In nearby fields, beside a footpath used by the Centenary Way, is Newfoundland Well. The chalybeate spring, discovered in 1684, raised false hopes of developing Ilmington as a spa town in the 19th century.

The village has two inns – the Red Lion, established in 1849, and the Howard Arms, which takes its name from the family formerly at Foxcote House. There is a tradition of morris dancing going back at least 300 years. A local fiddler, Sam Bennett, played many old tunes for the folk song collector Cecil Sharpe. He died in 1951 and a violin is carved on his headstone in the churchyard.

The cruciform Norman **church of St Mary the Virgin** has above its porch the arms of the de Montforts, patrons from 1290 to 1492 – five members of the family served as rectors. Nearby is the tall Gothic tomb of members of the Sansom family who died between 1750 and 1919, and the weathered gravestone of Hutton Corbett, laid to rest in 1706 aged 106 years, 9 months and 11 days. The base of an ancient preaching cross survives in the churchyard, where, beside the path, twelve lime trees represent the apostles.

The tower and chancel arches and the doorway are all impressively Norman, and there are memorials to the Cannings of Foxcote House and to the Palmers of Compton Scorpion. That of Francis Canning (died 1806) and his wife is in the Grecian style and by Sir Richard Westmacott. The Brents of Lark Stoke (see ADMINGTON) are also commemorated.

A tablet mentions Sir Nicholas Overbury, father of the poet **Sir Thomas Overbury** (1581-1613) of Compton Scorpion Manor. Sir Thomas, the victim of an intrigue at the Court of James I, was poisoned at the instigation of Robert Carr, later Lord Rochester.

In the belfry stands a defaced effigy of a priest from about 1400. Visitors should look out for mice – carved ones. There are eleven of them, the trademark of Robert Thomson of Kilburn, Yorkshire, who replaced the woodwork in the 1930s.

The gabled and mullioned **Ilmington Manor**, reached via Middle Street, is a handsome 16th-century Cotswold house, extended about 1920. A nearby **Methodist Chapel** of ashlar-covered brickwork on a stone base was converted to a house in 1998. The large wooden **village hall** of 1933 was restored in 1998. Across the road, a notice on a stone wall indicates the former site of the local **pound**.

Above Upper Green rises **St Philip's Church** (RC) in Victorian Gothic. The building was a school until 1931 and later became a house. Below, a **drinking fountain** dating from 1864 was restored in 1920.

The long **Crab Mill** (the name refers to crab apples) bears the date 1711. Occupiers have included Professor Dorothy Hodgkin, who in 1964 became the only female British scientist to receive the Nobel prize. A rare survival in Back Street is the business of 'M.D. Vincent, Hurdle Maker'.

South of the village stand **Foxcote House** and **Compton Scorpion Manor**. The former, a large, early 18th-century pedimented mansion, has an old Catholic chapel in its garden. Its owners were the Cannings until 1843, when their relatives the Howards succeeded. The current American owner has restored the house and spacious classical stables. Though Compton Scorpion Manor goes back to the early 17th century, its mullion-windowed face was built about 1700 and sashed windows and a parapet added in the 18th century.

The Old Wharfe, a long stone house of about 1800 on the Armscote road, served as an inn on the horse-drawn railway connecting Stratford and Moreton-in-Marsh.

KENILWORTH [Stratford-on-Avon]

SP2872: 4 miles (7km) N of Warwick

Kenilworth is a town of two parts. The old High Street stands to the north, beyond Abbey Fields and the broad Finham Brook; the later development, including the shopping centre, grew up to the south after the opening of the railway in 1844.

A settlement, Chinewrde, was established before the Domesday survey and had become Kenilleworth by 1265. Trades have included tanning, comb making and a brick-works.

In 1264 Simon de Montfort called the first English Parliament at Kenilworth. A field known as **Parliament Piece,** owned by the Open Spaces Society, is claimed as the site. Edward, son of Henry III, defeated Simon de Montfort the Younger at the Battle of Kenilworth in 1265, during the Barons' War. In the following year, de Montfort adherents were besieged in Kenilworth Castle for six months – the longest siege in English history.

Elizabeth I gave the fortress to Robert Dudley, Earl of Leicester, in 1563 and paid three costly visits there. The last, in 1575, inspired Sir Walter Scott's *Kenilworth.* (Scott stayed at the **King's Arms and Castle Hotel** while researching the novel.)

The red-sandstone **Kenilworth Castle** (English Heritage) has been a romantic ruin since the Civil War, when Cromwell blew up the Norman Keep and stripped the roofs. We enter via a causeway used for jousting in the Middle Ages, when it was known as the tiltyard. Two buildings dominate: the massive 12th-century Keep and the Great Hall built by John of Gaunt in the 14th century. Lesser ones include Leicester's Gatehouse and Stables. The visitor will be struck by the thought that graffiti carved on stonework is not just a problem of the modern age.

In a field to the west, two diamond-shaped dry moats indicate the site of **The Pleasance,** where Henry V laid out a summer house and garden in 1414. Lovely old cottages stand on Castle Green, from which Castle Hill climbs to the splendid High Street. On the way, an appealing group of thatched cottages known as **Little Virginia** is said to indicate where the first English potatoes were grown.

Latimer House was the home of **Bishop Latimer,** who, according to tradition, preached his last sermon from its porch before being burnt at the stake as a Protestant martyr in 1555.

St Nicholas's Church has what Pevsner calls 'the most sumptuous Norman doorway in Warwickshire'. It probably came from the nearby abbey ruins. The church is mainly Perpendicular, but an 1864 restoration was severe. Inside are impressive fragments from the abbey and a marble figure of Mrs Caroline Gresley (1817) by Westmacott.

Geoffrey de Clinton founded the **Abbey** in 1122, originally as an Augustinian priory; he may be buried beneath it. After the Dissolution in the 1530s, some of its stone was used to repair the castle. Today little more than an old gatehouse of the 160ft-long (49m) building remains standing.

The broach-spired **St John's Church** of 1851-52 is a striking sight when entering the town from the south, but Pugin's Catholic **St Augustine's** is a modest creation of 1841, though enlarged over the next decade. A simple red-brick **Baptist church** dates from 1829.

The town's most intriguing residence is **The Water Tower,** white-walled and 90ft (27m) high. Originally a windmill and built in the mid-18th century, it was converted to a house in 1974 and won an award from the United Kingdom Council for European Architectural Heritage.

KINETON [Stratford-on-Avon]

SP3351: 4½ miles (7km) SE of Wellesbourne

A large village (the Kington of Domesday Book), Kineton is the first settlement on the River Dene as it flows down from Edge Hill. On the outskirts rises a **motte and bailey earthwork**, with remains of the bailey wall. It is known as King John's Castle, from a belief that he held a Court Leet there. A large, sail-less **windmill** caps a hilltop near the Wellesbourne road.

In 1642, the **Battle of Edge Hill** (see RADWAY) was fought south-east of Kineton on land now owned by the Ministry of Defence and closed to the public. A memorial to those who died in the battle was erected a mile along Banbury Road by Warwickshire County Council in 1949. Another stands on the battlefield.

There are two inns: the white-walled Carpenters Arms and the stone-built, mullioned and dormered **Swan** of 1668, opposite which is a chequered-brick early Georgian **cottage**. Nearby, the tall-shafted war memorial occupies a small green that is encroached upon by 18th-century houses.

The fine brownstone **St Peter's Church** has a rugged, buttressed tower built between the late 13th and the 15th centuries, with Gothic battlements and pinnacles. The ashlared nave and chancel were rebuilt in 1755 by Sanderson Miller of Radway, and again by his descendant Frank Miller, vicar of Kineton from 1873 to 1889.

Enter via the Early English doorway in the tower and go through a curious, vaulted passage attributed to Sanderson Miller. Within, the building consists of nave, broad north aisle, north and south transepts, and large, wide-arched chancel. A smooth-faced 14th-century stone effigy has its feet placed stiffly on a little dog, and a brass plaque of 1730 commemorates John Venour, whose family manor house stands at Wellesbourne. A metal-bound 16th-century churchwardens' chest has three locks.

The Dutch-gabled **school** of 1840, which replaced the market house, has become a doctors' surgery. In the secluded **Market Square**, 17th-century stone houses surround an incongruous, brick and chapel-like former library, now The Studio. A Mop Fair is held there annually in October.

In Southam Street, the **Wesleyan Methodist Church** of 1893 is brick-built, with a stone-framed door and windows. The chequered-brick **Oddfellows Cottages** overlook a green. Nearby, another former Victorian **school** (brick and tall-gabled) has been converted to houses.

Down Manor Lane is the **Manor House** of lias and brownstone, and Bridge Street has handsome stone Georgian houses. It leads out to Little Kineton, where cottages surround a large green on which stands a rare Victorian pillar box. The **Manor House** was built by the Willoughby de Broke family in place of an Elizabethan predecessor pulled down in 1790.

KINGSBURY [North Warwickshire]

SP2196: 4½ miles (8km) S of Tamworth

The Chinesburie ('royal fortified house') of Saxon times, Kingsbury, set above the River Tame, was a long time growing – into a disturbing mixture of the worthwhile and the shoddy.

In the mid-19th century, when the main landowner was the Prime Minister, **Sir Robert Peel** (of Drayton Manor, across the Staffordshire border), it was a self-sufficient hamlet. The Birmingham to Derby railway line was built in 1839 and industry came – chiefly coal mining and gravel extraction. Kingsbury expanded, and the mining villages of Piccadilly and Hurley grew up.

The mines have gone and the railway station closed in 1968, but the village, mainly a post-Second World War development, lives on as a dormitory for Birmingham, Tamworth and Coventry. To the east is a large oil storage depot. There are two inns, the **Royal Oak** and the **White Swan**. The first opened in the 1850s, as an extension of a wheelwright's business. The second may have been an 'ale house' recorded in 1637.

By the Birmingham and Fazeley Canal at Bodymoor Heath stands the **Dog and Doublet**. Probably a wharfinger's house, it was an inn by the 1830s. Near the canal bridge is a small, brick **Wesleyan Chapel** of 1844. Aston Villa FC has its training ground in Bodymoor Heath Lane.

Osbert de Arden built Kingsbury's large **church of St Peter and St Paul**, set strikingly above the river, about 1150. The nave is Norman, the chancel and tower were added in the 13th century, and the Bracebridge Chapel, now the vestry, in the 14th for private use by the family at the hall.

There are three defaced medieval effigies and a Georgian benefactors' board. A window installed in less politically correct times depicts children with a golliwog, perhaps the only example in England.

Stone-built **Kingsbury Hall**, on its bluff above the Tame and dating from the 16th and 17th centuries, probably occupies the site of a hunting lodge of the kings of Mercia. The Bracebridge family lived there for 400 years, before ownership passed to the Willoughbys of Middleton and the Peels of Drayton Bassett. Sections remain of the 14th-century stone curtain wall of the earlier fortified house. The building became a farmhouse in the 18th century. Latterly, a coal haulage business has operated from it, while the house falls into dereliction.

Teachers House in Church Lane is the school house for which Thomas Coton left money in 1686. Classes, endowed by the historian Dugdale, had begun in the Bracebridge Chapel in 1650. Next door is the **Kingsbury Board School** of 1884, now residences.

From the churchyard, Red Lane Steps drop to the broad Tame valley and Red Lane Bridge (rebuilt 1947) spans the river, giving access to **Kingsbury Water Park** via an old raised footway known as The Planks.

The 240-hectare (600-acre) county council-run water park has been developed since 1973 from more than 30 pools caused by gravel extraction. It offers miles of waterside and woodland walks, boating, games and picnic areas, plus a visitor centre, café and shop. The Centenary Way starts there and the Heart of England Way passes through, as, unfortunately, does the M42. Vehicle access is from Bodymoor Heath Lane.

To the south, **Hemlingford Bridge**, originally built by subscription in 1783, crosses the Tame. The names of its seven subscribers were engraved on the parapet, but only those of William Bond of Kingsbury Hall (defaced) and William Harrison of Drakenage remain.

Downstream stands **Kingsbury Mill**. Though Domesday Book recorded a mill, bequeathed in Henry II's time (1154-89) to Polesworth Nunnery, the present building dates from 1747. Apart from grinding corn and barley, it made gun barrels during the Napoleonic Wars. Many subsequent uses have left it much the worse for wear and currently unoccupied.

To the north, **The Malt House Inn** was formerly Cliff House, built and extended between 1775 and 1825. East of it, the gabled **Holt Hall Farm** of about 1580, which housed the Bracebridges when they came down in the world, has a fine staircase of the 1630s.

KING'S NEWNHAM [Rugby]

SP4577: 3½ miles (5km) NW of Rugby

Its few buildings stand beside quiet lanes above the upper River Avon, which is crossed by an old sandstone bridge leading to Church Lawford. Yet before John Dudley, Duke of Northumberland, depopulated the area by enclosing the common lands in the 16th century, it was the much larger Royal Borough of Newnham Regis.

North of the lane to Bretford and near the Fosse Way, aerial photography has revealed ditches up to 60 metres (200ft) in diameter from Neolithic or Bronze Age times.

The hamlet's most striking feature is the Norman **church tower** rising from a farmyard, the rest of the building having been demolished in the 18th century. It stood open to the elements until the Duke of Bucceulch, Lord of the Hundreds of Knightlow, added a pyramid roof in 1900. A vault containing coffins, including one of a beheaded man, was found under the rickyard in the mid-19th century.

The Georgian, brick-built **Newnham Hall** is adjacent, and beside it stands a restored, mullioned-windowed and much older stone barn. The three pools, or stows, across the lane were fishponds for Kenilworth Abbey.

To the east, **Manor Farm** (formerly the manor house) is also Georgian, with dormer windows. In fields by the river are the **'baths'** – the remains of an 1857 restoration of an old spa building. Its chalybeate spring – recommended by Elizabeth I's physician, Walter de Bailey, who wrote 'A Brief Discourse of certain Bathes ... neere ... Newnom Regis' – was visited by Queen Anne. By a footbridge spanning the river are the remains of an old watermill, including a metal mill-wheel.

KINWARTON [Stratford-on-Avon]

SP1058: 1 mile (2km) NE of Alcester

Consisting of little more than a church, its former rectory, a farm and a dovecote, the hamlet lies off the Alcester to Henley-in-Arden road. Though its name is of Saxon origin, Roman coins have been found near the church.

Edward Hobart Seymour, born at Kinwarton Rectory in 1840, had a naval career extending from the Crimean War (1854-56) to the Boxer Rebellion in 1900. When Edward VII founded the Order of Merit in 1902, Admiral Seymour became one of the original privy councillors.

At the gate of **St Mary the Virgin** stands the shaft of an Anglo-Danish village cross, its carving almost worn away. Believed to date from about AD900, it now supports a later head. The church was consecrated in 1316, and the south door is probably original. In 1847 the architect William Butterfield restored the building. There are side windows from the church's early years and a rare example of an ancient oak-framed window, probably from the 16th-century, when the weather-boarded bell turret was also added. The font has been speculatively dated from 1316 and its lid as 16th-century pre-Reformation.

In the first half of the 18th century, when clandestine marriages were all the rage, the Kinwarton rectors took full advantage. Instead of sending couples back to their own parishes, they married them with few questions asked and no witnesses, risking a £100 fine. For a time, during which weddings averaged 27 per annum and once totalled 51, Kinwarton became the Gretna Green of the Midlands. The Hardwick Act of 1753 ended the bonanza.

Beside the church is the handsome former **rectory** of 1788, in red brick with three floors. Neighbouring **Glebe Farm**, as its name indicates, once provided part of the clergyman's benefice. A 17th-century black and white house with half-timbering, it hides behind an ancient timber and brick barn.

The National Trust-owned **Kinwarton Dovecote** stands in a field beyond the church. Circular, with thick stone walls, the 14th-century building has a conical roof and a tiny ogee-arched door. It is almost unique in retaining its potence, or rotary ladder, and has nests for nearly 600 pi-

Kinwarton dovecote

geons. Adjoining the field is the **moat** of the manor house, which had disappeared by 1752.

KNIGHTCOTE [Stratford-on-Avon]

SP3954: 4½ miles (7km) NE of Kineton

A hamlet on the plain north of the Burton Dassett Hills and near the little River Itchen, it has a lovely row of stone-built and thatched **cottages**. **The Old Forge** (black and white) is now the post office. There was formerly an inn, the Royal Oak.

The small chequered-brick **Wesleyan Chapel** of 1837, with round-arched windows, remains in use as the Methodist church, but the school, originally endowed by the Kimble Charity (see NORTHEND), is now **The Old School House** in disappointingly rough-cast Victorian Gothic. Across sheep pastures rise the rear gables of the 17th-century stone **Manor House**.

LADBROKE [Stratford-on-Avon]

SP4158: 2 miles (3km) S of Southam

The name of the small village, bordering some of Warwickshire's loneliest countryside, is little changed from the Lodbroc of Domesday Book – referring to Lot Brook, which feeds the River Itchen. In 1985 – seventy years after the matter was first proposed – the busy Coventry to Banbury road was diverted to bypass the village. Useful information boards are found in the church porch and by **The Bell**, the only survivor of three coaching inns.

Tollgate Cottage, a simple brick building, indicates the former status of the highway, which became a turnpike in 1750. Opposite, three low-walled, stone-built and thatched **cottages** retain a picturesque appearance. A First World War army hut, restored in 1980, serves as the **Village Hall**. The tall, red-brick **High House**, with a porticoed doorway, is late 18th century, and **The Old Well House** still has a water pump. **The Croft** is Elizabethan and timber-framed.

A tree-lined lane leads to the handsome brick **Ladbroke Hall**, which the Palmers built in the 17th century to replace a farmhouse. Once the home of **Lord Rootes**, the car manufacturer, and later a girls' school, it has been converted to flats.

W.S. Schwind, who was so successful at betting on horses that a London bookmaker could not pay him out, occupied the hall in the early 1900s. Schwind set up a partnership to take over the firm and changed its name to Ladbrokes, now a multi-million pound hotel and gaming group.

Beyond the hall cluster the thatched and brick-built **Church Cottage**, the 18th-century **rectory**, with hipped roof and dormers, and **All Saints' Church**. The 14th-century tower and later spire of the latter are 120ft (37m) tall, and the 13th-century chancel, with its double-decker windows, has been described as 'a hagiologist's delight'. The Victorian east window alone portrays 58 saints and there are more in the side-windows.

When Sir George Gilbert Scott restored the church in the 1870s, an effigy (said to be Roger de Paveley, rector 1298-1303) was dug up and placed in the south aisle. Four flat-topped stone heads set in the porch are former roof corbels from nearby Radbourne, where the church was demolished in the 16th century.

In a field to the south-east is evidence of the former manor house's medieval fish ponds.

LAPWORTH [Warwick]

SP1671: 3 miles (5km) N of Henley-in-Arden

In prosperous Middle England, the ancient church and tiny village stand over a mile west of the main settlement of Kingswood, which is almost totally modern, though a small Queen Anne house, **Kingswood Hall**, stands opposite the railway station.

About AD125, the Romans were manufacturing tiles in two kilns, and by 816 a recognisable version of the name, Hlappawurthin, had appeared. It meant 'the enclosure at the edge', though of what is uncertain. Domesday Book has Lapeforde.

At Kingswood, where the Boot and Navigation inns were in use before the turnpike was removed about 1810, the Grand Union and Stratford-upon-Avon Canals almost meet – they are connected by a short link canal, near two large supply pools. Towards Hockley Heath, two unusual drawbridges cross the Stratford Canal.

Tall and quirky, the **church of St Mary the Virgin** is one of the county's finest. Though its style is Perpendicular, there is a Norman north window from an earlier building. A 15th-century west porch juts out so close to the lane that it is, in effect, an archway, with openings north and south to pass through. Two spiral staircases lead to an upper room.

The tower (late 14th-century Decorated) supports a spire possibly added later, and was detached from the nave until linked by

The tall and quirky church of St Mary the Virgin, Lapworth

a vestibule in 1872. An alarm system protects the chancel and the north chapel, which contains a 13th-century wall painting of roses, and a Madonna and Child of 1928 by Eric Gill. The font is early 14th century.

A stone in the chancel floor commemorates the Reverend Owen Bonnell, curate on behalf of absentee rectors for 46 years from 1750. What a contrast that exemplary Welsh cleric makes with Bauldwin Nutting, installed by the Catesbys in 1575, who was described as 'Neither preacher nor good reader, of ruffianly behavor and suspect life'! Near the porch is the worn table-tomb of **Robert Catesby**, who instigated the Gunpowder Plot in 1605 and was killed in the final shoot-out at Holbeche House, near Stourbridge.

The **school** of 1828 stands adjacent. It has bargeboarded gables at each end, where the schoolmaster's and parish clerk's houses were incorporated. The first pupils paid three old pence per week.

The oldest house in the parish is probably the late medieval **Bushwood Common Farm. Bushwood Hall**, rebuilt in 1705, was Robert Catesby's reputed birthplace in 1573.

Harborough Banks at Kingswood is all that is left of an Iron Age fort (later used by the Romans) after much of the 10-hectare (25-acre) site was dug up for gravel in the 18th century.

LEA MARSTON [North Warwickshire]

SP2093: 3 miles (5km) N of Coleshill

A quiet village, reached by lanes and bordered by the Tame – unfortunately one of Britain's dirtiest rivers. Rolling down from Severn Trent's purification lakes, which arrest its flow and allow pollutants to settle, it emerges at Lea Marston slightly less odorous. The village's other industrial neighbour, the vast Hams Hall Power Station, was razed in the mid-1990s and is now a manufacturing and distribution park.

Hams Hall became the Adderley family home when Sir Charles Adderley, an equerry to Charles I, purchased the original building. Charles Bowyer Adderley built a new hall in 1760. When it fell empty after the First World War, a shipping magnate, Oswald Harrison, bought and dismantled the house, rebuilding it at Coates, near Cirencester. The Royal Agricultural College afterwards acquired it.

A later **Charles Bowyer Adderley** (1814-1905), 1st Lord Norton, was a pioneer of colonial independence. As Under-Secretary of State for the Colonies, he drafted the Constitution of New Zealand at Hams Hall. In South Africa, Cape Town's main thoroughfare, Adderley Street, takes its name from him.

Mostly modern, the village centres on a green with a large cedar and some 18th-century farmhouses. It is the first village southbound on the Centenary Way, which starts at nearby Kingsbury Water Park (see KINGSBURY).

The small, wooden **Victory Hall** of 1918 survives on Birmingham Road (once a main route). **The Old Smithy** (17th century) and the former **school**, built in the 1840s, are down School Lane. **Lea Bridge**, spanning the Tame, was reconstructed in 1909. Beside it, **Bridge Cottage** is a charming house in 1840s Tudor-style.

In Church Lane, **Woodhouse Farm** has unusual high brick pilasters. A tall **cross** at the end of the lane is said to commemorate a visit by Gladstone to his friend Lord Norton in 1895. Beside it – at the former Hams Hall gates, but remote from the village – is the **church of St John Baptist**, its nave dating from about 1300, the tower and chancel from 1876-77. A large Adderley tomb, with a cusped cross, stands in the churchyard.

Within, family monuments include the above-mentioned Sir Charles (died 1682), Mrs Lettice Adderley (1784, in Coade stone) and the 1st Lord Norton, to whom there is also a memorial window. Lord Norton's daughters carved its pulpit from an oak. An early 18th-century vicar, Dr Thomas Bray (see OVER WHITACRE), is commemorated by a portrait in brass.

Ladywalk Nature Reserve, established by Powergen, adjoins the churchyard, but is not open to the public.

LEAMINGTON HASTINGS [Rugby]

SP4467: 4 miles (6km) NE of Southam

The small village lies at about the midway point of the River Leam, which upstream is pronounced 'leem' and downstream 'lem'. The second part of the name stems from the Hastang family, medieval lords of the manor. To the north spreads the great Draycote Water reservoir (see THURLASTON).

All Saints' Church, large and stone-built, has a broad Perpendicular

Blackdown Mill, Hill Wootton

tower and a fine, carved north doorway depicting a trailing vine. Within, the south arcade is Early English and the chancel has the date 1677. There are monuments to two Sir Thomas Trevors (1656 and 1698), the first of whom was Baron of the Exchequer to Charles I.

An ogee-gabled west doorway faces a churchyard gate to **The Manor House** (grey stone and red-roofed, with tall chimneys), which was enlarged in Victorian times. Along the lane, an impressive row of stone **almshouses**, with mullioned windows and dormers, were begun by the earlier Sir Thomas Trevor in 1633. Sir Charles Wheeler added the west part in 1696. They were restored to pristine condition in 1980-81.

Hill Farm, in the nearby hamlet of Hill, was, until 1973, one of the last breeding places for the once dominant Warwickshire longhorn cattle.

LEAMINGTON SPA

See ROYAL LEAMINGTON SPA.

LEEK WOOTTON [Warwick]

SP2869: 2 miles (4km) N of Warwick

The Saxon name of this small village in rolling countryside between Warwick and Kenilworth means 'town in the wood', referring, of course, to the Forest of Arden. At a crossroads stands the Anchor Inn. South of it, **All Saints' Church** occupies a pre-Christian site. The present building of 1792, erected by the Leighs of Stoneleigh Abbey, replaced a medieval church and retains a bell cast in the 14th century. Its roof is Victorian hammerbeam and the chancel was added in 1889. Crosses proliferate in the churchyard, some commemorating the Wallers of Woodcote.

The names of the dormer-windowed **Reading Room Cottage** and **The Forge Cottage** (half-timbered) remind us of former uses, as does **The Old School** in Victorian brick. At the bottom of the hill, the low plastered walls and high thatched roof of **The Cottage** are very picturesque.

Outlying **Woodcote**, stone-built in 1861, has 300-year-old cedars in the grounds and is the Warwickshire Constabulary Headquarters. It replaced the Elizabethan house of the Wallers and overlooks The Warwickshire golf course, opened in 1994, beyond which stands the 19th-century **Goodrest Farm**.

On one of her visits to Kenilworth Castle, Queen Elizabeth I is said to have rested at the moated manor house that preceded the farm. The route past it was considered 'the fairest way to Kenilworth', a reference to its relative dryness. Dugdale gives an alternative reason for the farm's name – the manor's use by countesses of Warwick for lying-in during childbirth.

Nearby, beside the Centenary Way, are the grassy dam and hollow of a **fish pool** belonging to the ancient manor.

Wootton Grange Farm, on the Kenilworth road, was the home in the 18th century of the Burbury family. A Thomas Burbury moved to Coventry as a weaver, was transported to Australia for his part in the weavers' riots of 1831 and became a successful sheep farmer.

In a wood on Blacklow Hill, **Gaveston's Cross** of 1832 indicates where Edward II's favourite, **Piers Gaveston**, Earl of Cornwall, was beheaded in 1312. The uncompromising inscription calls him 'the Minion of a hateful King'.

The hill has been identified as a rare Anglo-Saxon pagan sacred grove. In 1971 archaeologists found two burial pits, a sword, and several shallow pits cut into the stone.

At Hill Wootton are **Hill Wootton Farm** (black and white, with an ancient wooden porch), **The Old Farm House** (handsome and stone-built) and **Tower House** (on a hillside, with a pepper pot tower). Down by the River Avon, **Blackdown Mill** has richly carved woodwork and the mill house incorporates Jacobean features from a previous building. A smart Regency **house** with a portico stands opposite.

LIGHTHORNE [Stratford-on-Avon]

SP3355: 3 miles (5km) N of Kineton

The village lies along a valley, the generous gaps left between its old cottages now filled by modern developments. **The Antelope**, an inn of 18th-century stonework capped by a hipped roof with dormers, overlooks the smaller of two greens. Above the other, which slopes down from the road, stands the stone and thatch **Smithy Cottage**. Below it, **The Old Stone House** has mullioned windows and high brick chimneys.

At the east end of the village, **The Old School House** is steep-roofed and in grey stone. At the west end, **St Laurence's Church** was rebuilt in 1876, its light grey stone nave and chancel, with darker quoins and windows, grafted on to a Gothic tower of 1771. Unusual stained glass of the 17th century depicts Saints Laurence and Sebastian.

Enclosed by a stone wall, the former **rectory** is a handsome 17th-century stone house with an 18th-century front. Nearby, the large **Church Hill Farm** – stone-built, pleasantly quaint, with dormers and a tall, brick chimney – probably dates from the 16th century. In front of it is one of several water pumps and wells dotted about the village.

LILLINGTON [Warwick]

SP3267: 1 mile (2km) N of Royal Leamington Spa

The village of Lillington existed before Domesday Book, in which it is recorded as both Lillintone and Illintone, the second spelling being an error. The Saxon meaning was 'Lilla's town'. In 1890 it became part of Leamington and is now a suburb.

Lillington is one of several places claiming to be the centre of England. An ancient oak at the junction of Lillington Avenue and Lillington Road, said to mark the spot, was removed for road widening in 1966, but a young tree was planted nearby.

Lillington Manor survives, a plain-fronted, stone house facing the **church of St Mary Magdalene**. The church, an extensive building with a Perpendicular tower, has some 14th-century work in the chancel, but is mainly Victorian. It owns a chalice and paten from the 1570s and three stained-glass windows by Kempe light the rich interior. The oldest bell dates from 1480.

The modern Catholic **Church of Our Lady** is large and lofty, with a tall, slim, copper spire.

LITTLE COMPTON [Stratford-on-Avon]

SP2630: 6½ miles (10km) S of Shipston-on-Stour

Warwickshire's most southerly village,

though the ecclesiastical parish is in the Diocese of Oxford, it stands on the fringe of the Cotswolds and 50 miles from its northern counterpart, No Man's Heath. The village was once known as Compton in Floribus, because of its profusion of flowers.

Ragstone cottages lie scattered along lanes off London Road, between Moreton-in-Marsh and Chipping Norton. They include Old Post Office Row and Brewery Row, and there is an inn, the Red Lion. The Cotswold-stone former brewery was converted in 1998 to **The Old Malthouse**.

The stone-built **Manor House** (now Reed College, an accountancy school) has a link with mainstream history through **William Juxon**, Bishop of London, who attended Charles I at the scaffold in 1649 and afterwards retired to Little Compton Manor, owned by his brother Thomas. When the monarchy was restored in 1660, he emerged, aged 78, to become Archbishop of Canterbury and officiated at Charles II's coronation.

The east wing, bordering the churchyard, is pre-Reformation, and the gabled south front was added in 1620. In the grounds stands a steep-gabled **dovecote**, believed to be Jacobean.

St Denys's Church was originally a chapel belonging to Deerhurst Priory in Gloucestershire, but was extensively rebuilt in 1863-64. Early English windows are set in the chancel south wall and there is an unusual 14th-century saddleback tower.

The building is long, but quite narrow. Windows in the south chapel depict Edward the Confessor, who gave the priory to the Abbey of St Denis near Paris, and scenes from the execution of Charles I. Coincidentally the saint and the king suffered the same fate – beheading.

In the sanctuary window is a fragment of glass rescued from a destroyed church at Villers-Bretonneux, on the Somme, by local glazier Oswald Mace during the First World War. There are Juxon gravestones of the 17th and 18th centuries in the nave floor, and on the wall hangs a framed and illuminated history of the parish. The 13th-century font has long been held together by iron bands.

Outside stands the tomb of the Rt. Hon. Frederick Leverton Harris (of the manor house) by Eric Gill. Unfortunately, the distinguished sculptor botched the date of his death – is it 1926 or 1927? Though the stone-built **Baptist Chapel** survives from the 1870s, it is now a house, cloaked by trees.

Two miles from the village, on the Moreton road, is the **Four Shire Stone**. It originally marked the meeting place of the counties of Warwick, Oxford, Gloucester and Worcester, but the last no longer extends so far south.

LITTLE WOLFORD [Stratford-on-Avon]

SP2635: 3 miles (5km) S of Shipston-on-Stour

The existence of the small village, originally Wolford Parva, on high ground just off the Stratford to Oxford road, was enlivened during the Second World War by the evacuation of London's Old Vic theatre company to one of its farms.

There are brick estate cottages of 1858 dotted about (they have been dubbed 'working-class Gothic'). Stone-built **Broadmoor Lodge**, on the main road, has long outlasted Weston House of the 1830s (pulled down in 1928), for which it was a gatehouse. The architect, William Blore, was chiefly responsible for Buckingham Palace.

The one major building is **Little Wolford Manor**, an L-shaped mansion of early Tudor origin. Lord Camperdown of Weston Park owned it in the early 20th century, but the house fell into disuse, was divided into cottages and became a school, a chapel and a nonconformist meeting place before being restored in the 1930s. Its hall has mid-16th-century heraldic stained-glass windows, and there are said to be bloodstains on the solar stairs from a soldier wounded at the Battle of Edge Hill in 1642.

A badly weathered but still flowing **fountain** near the manor gate has a barely identifiable lion's head and a coat of arms; beside it is a **Victorian postbox**.

LONG COMPTON [Stratford-on-Avon]

SP2832: 5 miles (8km) S of Shipston-on-Stour

Spread along the Stratford to Oxford road and spilling down lanes east of it, the grey stone village lies near the county boundary in delightful, hilly south Warwickshire countryside. There are thatched stone cottages, and facilities include the 16th-century **Red Lion Hotel**, a post office store and a 'traditional family butcher'. The early settlement is indicated by uneven ground in a field beside Buryway Lane, south-west of the church.

During the General Strike of 1926 drivers passing through distributed the *Long Compton Wireless News*. Its printer was the Reverend William Manton (vicar 1922-57) of the local King's Stone Printing Press.

The **King's Stone** is a large Late Neolithic or Early Bronze Age standing stone on a hill south of the village. Nearby, but across the Oxfordshire border, are the **Rollright Stone Circle**, or the King's Men, and a smaller group, the **Whispering Knights**. Naturally, a legend explains how an unidentified king and his followers were turned into petrified monoliths.

In 1875, James Hayward murdered Ann Tennent at Long Compton, because he believed she was a witch. His weapon, a pitchfork, suggests an affinity with the Meon Hill witchcraft murder 70 years later (see QUINTON).

The village's most eye-catching feature is the thatched lych-gate of the **church of St Peter and St Paul**. This was originally a cottage built about 1600, from which the ground floor has been removed to make a gateway. It leads to a churchyard of clipped yews, from which rises a 13th-century nave entered by doors installed about 1620 in the 14th-century porch. The tower (81ft and in three stages, with carved heads clenching waterspouts in their mouths) is rather later. Its height was increased in the 15th century and it was restored in 1930.

Parts of the church are Norman and there are scratched Mass dials in the porch and east of it. Also inside the porch lies a worn early 14th-century female effigy. Beside it is a stone to Joseph Friday, who served Edward Sheldon and his family 'above forty years' and died 'October ye 5th, 1746, aged 55'. The wealthy Sheldons lived in the former Elizabethan house at Weston Park.

The chancel is mainly an 1862-63 restoration, but outside it is a charming little lean-to 15th-century chantry. Within, the church is large and high, with clerestory windows and a variety of carved heads on the capitals supporting its roof trusses.

A legend of **St Augustine**, the first archbishop of Canterbury (597-605), quoted by Dugdale, implies that there was a church at Long Compton even then. The Archbishop excommunicated the Lord of the Manor for non-payment of tithes and specified that 'no excommunicated person should be present at Masse', whereupon a dead man rose from his grave in the church and went outside. Ascertaining that the man had been excommunicated for the same reason, Augustine raised his priest, who promptly forgave him. Not surprisingly, the Lord of the Manor repented and paid his dues.

Almost opposite the church, set back beyond a stream, is a stone Gothic house with gables. Near the post office, the base of the **village cross** has been converted to a fountain. Down side roads are the stone-built **Malthouse** of 1703, **Compton House** (the pedimented 18th-century former vicarage, to which a massive Victorian gable was added) and an ashlar-faced **Congrega-**

tional church of classical style but obscure date.

The **Wesleyan Chapel** (also classical) once ran in competition with **The Meeting House** (1670) of the Quakers and the former **Primitive Methodist Chapel** of 1881.

Wisteria-covered **Peregrine House** has upper windows with curious rounded heads.

LONG ITCHINGTON [Stratford-on-Avon]

SP4165: 2 miles (3km) N of Southam

This village on the busy Coventry to Banbury road takes its name from the little River Itchen. To the south is the Grand Union Canal and beyond it stand the tall-chimneyed Rugby Cement works and the pebble-dashed Model Village built to house the workers.

St Wulfstan (or Wulstan) was reputedly born in the village about 1012 and became Bishop of Worcester in 1062. The only Saxon bishop to swear loyalty to William the Conqueror, he began the rebuilding of Worcester Cathedral in 1084 and was canonized in 1203.

Dispirited-looking **Tudor House** of about 1600 displays its studded door, vertical half-timbering and five equal gables to the main road. Elizabeth I stayed there in 1572 and 1575, when it was the home of Lady Anne Holbourne, daughter of Robert Dudley, Earl of Leicester. The Sitwell family, of literary distinction, latterly owned it.

Most of the village lies beyond broad greens to the west, where (opposite the Jolly Fisherman, one of several pubs) Leamington Road branches off beside a lovely pool ringed by Lombardy poplars. In The Square stand the 15th-century **manor house**, with unpainted half-timbering, and **The Old School House** in red brick.

The large Victorian Gothic **school** faces grey stone **Holy Trinity Church**, where the tower still supports the stump of a 14th-century spire that broke off during a thunderstorm in 1762. The 18th-century clock face was refurbished and an electric quartz drive installed in 1989. In the south wall is a blocked-up round-arched doorway, with roll-mouldings, that Pevsner says 'can hardly be later than 1190'.

The church is spacious, consisting of a nave, with a broad south aisle, and a large, light chancel beyond the 14th-century rood screen. There is a squint in the 13th-century aisle and two great tomb recesses. It also contains the Wulfstan Chapel dedicated in 1961. It is the oldest part of the building, though the arcade was rebuilt in the 15th century and the roof in 1860.

A hatchment of Lady Anne Holbourne records that she left £50 per annum payable to 'Mr Sam Row, minister of this church and to his successors for ever', and 18th- and 19th-century charity boards indicate bequests still administered by trustees. Adjoining the churchyard, the red-brick Georgian **Manor Farm** is disused, its doorway bricked up.

The Green Man (which was originally a farmhouse, dating from 1674) suffered bomb damage in 1940. Black and white **Devon House** is a splendid creation of about 1600, with twin gables and herringbone strutting. A small, stone-built **Congregational church** has a stuccoed Gothic gable, a brick chimney and a tiny bellcote.

LONG LAWFORD [Rugby]

SP4776: 2 miles (3km) W of Rugby

The village lies within a broad loop of the River Avon and is bisected by the Coventry to Rugby railway line, north of which the compact older part contains the buildings of interest. There are three inns, all in Main Street – The Country Inn and, side by side, the Caldecott Arms and the Lawford Arms. The Caldecotts were the family at nearby Holbrook Grange.

The Old House, long, low and roughcast, has the date 1657, and the red-brick Victorian **school**, with gables and lancets, is now houses. A small Italianate **Methodist Chapel**, in red brick with cream pilasters, has been closed and replaced by a modern building to the east.

Closed too, because of its unsafe state, is the **parish church of St John**, built in 1839 as a chapel of ease to Newbold-on-Avon. The tall, creamy-brick building, set in a large, neat churchyard, is noted for its undisturbed original furnishings, including the pulpit and a two-decker desk. The nave is short and the chancel unusually shallow. Services are now held in the neighbouring **Church Hall** of 1939, where the initials of Sunday School children and other contributors to its building costs appear on bricks.

Holford Grange is a mansion built by the Caldecotts to replace Little Lawford Hall, which stood north of the Avon and was demolished about 1790. The hall had been purchased from the Broughtons, the last of whom, Sir Theodosius, was poisoned there in 1780 by his brother-in-law, Captain John Donnellan. The present **Little Lawford Hall** is a stone-built house adapted about 1800 from the stables of 1604.

LONG MARSTON [Stratford-on-Avon]

SP1548: 5 miles (8km) SW of Stratford-upon-Avon

Spread along a lane near the Worcestershire border, with the Masons' Arms to the north, the village was part of Gloucestershire before a boundary change in 1931. An earlier name was Marston Sicca, or Dry Marston, and it was the 'dancing Marston' of an old jingle, said to refer to an ancient tradition of morris dancing.

There is recorded evidence of the village in 1043, when Earl Leofric granted it to the monks of Coventry – they sold it early in the 13th century to Winchcombe Abbey. Elizabeth I's favourite, Robert, Earl of Leicester, was Lord of the Manor from 1566 to 1577.

Charles II, when escaping to the south coast after defeat at the Battle of Worcester in 1651, stayed at the Manor House, now **King's Lodge**. In his disguise as servant to Jane Lane, he was ordered to wind the meat-jack and was beaten by the cook for his incompetence at that simple task. The jack is still there.

Long Marston Airfield, constructed in 1940, has been used for many purposes since the Second World War, including gliding, microlight flying and various forms of racing, but is best known as the site of the annual Phoenix Festival.

The Heart of England Way passes through the village, south of which stands the vast Royal Engineers' Resources HQ, due to close in 2000.

Surprisingly, the hoary, timber-framed porch and bell turret that implement the beauty of the otherwise grey-lias **church of St James the Great** are merely late Victorian. The Decorated-style church was built in the mid-14th century. In the east window, installed a century later, are traces of medieval glass. The pulpit is Jacobean and a bier survives from later in the 17th century, but all are outranked by the Norman font set on a later pillar. In the churchyard, which is entered by a wooden porch rebuilt by the Royal Engineers in 1996, stand a number of heavily weathered table-tombs.

Nearby, a former Tudor-style **school**, small and also in lias, is now a cottage. Among houses lying back from the lane, the timber-framed **Orchard Cottages** has a gabled stone wing containing a 14th-century two-light window.

Just off Wyre Lane is **The Goodwins**, a mullioned and dormered stone house of about 1700, and at the end of the lane stands **Hopkins**, a former farmhouse thought to date from before 1350. The original single-storey house, with its central open space, was upgraded in the 16th and 17th centuries. An inglenook fireplace has the date 1626.

LOXLEY [Stratford-on-Avon]

SP2552: 4 miles (6km) E of Stratford-upon-Avon

This hillside village facing north to the distant Avon valley has been associated with Robin Hood, who was known as Robin of Loxley (or Locksley), but nothing is certain. Most of the houses stand with the white-painted Fox Inn, uphill from the war memorial, on its sloping green, but the real interest lies below.

There the picture-book **Loxley Farm** is thatched and half-timbered, and **St Nicholas's Church** presents itself as 'one of the oldest in England, with Saxon and Norman features', its noticeboard adding that 'thirty generations have worshipped here since circa 760AD'. In that year King Offa of Mercia gave the ground to the Cathedral Church of Worcester.

The Saxon work is the herringbone masonry in the chancel, though some authorities put it as late as Georgian times, when most of the church was rebuilt (c1735-40). The tower, however, is 13th century and within it are the old stocks. The nave is simple and white-plastered, and carved tablets of about 1700 occupy the outside wall of the south chancel. Some of those who died at Edge Hill are said to be buried in the churchyard.

Large, brick **Loxley Hall** is Georgian in origin but Gothic in appearance, having been rebuilt in 1850 and added to about 1868. An eye-catching doorway is set in a tall gable with stone quoins.

The Underhill Trust, established with £100 in 1780 by Mrs Margaret Underhill for the 'benefit and succour of the needy of the Parish', still provides Christmas treats for the elderly.

LUDDINGTON [Stratford-on-Avon]

SP1652: 3 miles (5km) SW of Stratford-upon-Avon

Luddington (the Saxon 'Luda's town') is spread along a lane and looks across the broad valley of the River Avon towards the distant Cotswolds. There are black and white cottages dotted about, but most of the elongated village is modern. It is one of the great might-have-beens of history because claims have been made that Shakespeare was married there. Unfortunately, no registers exist to shed light on the matter.

The chapel of ease of the poet's time burned down in the late 18th century, and the present slim-spired **All Saints' Church** was built (1871-72) of lias and in the style of 1300. The stonework of the steeple and buttresses includes odd-looking yellow-brick infillings, and the font from the original chapel is set on the base of an old churchyard cross.

Fronted by a great cedar, **Luddington Manor** has dormers and large ground-floor bays. Beside it, the village green is bordered by **The Thatched Cottage** (black and white) and **The Old House** (white-painted, with dormers in a red-tiled roof).

The Experimental Horticulture Centre occupies land to the west.

MANCETTER [North Warwickshire]

SP3296: 1 mile (2km) SE of Atherstone

The village merged long ago into Atherstone, but retains a picture-book centre where church, manor house and almshouses face a small green. It stands just off Watling Street, which marks the county boundary with Leicestershire, and between the River Anker and the Coventry Canal. Nearby is **Manduessedum**, a 1st-century Roman station enclosing 2.5 hectares (6 acres). The Romans reputedly defeated Queen Boudicca in the Anker valley.

There are two pubs. The Blue Boar displays the date 1940 and The Plough, though not outwardly ancient, is said to include 14th-century work. **St Peter's Church** was founded in 930, but the present sandstone building is a development of an early 13th-century church to which Guy de Mancestre (died 1365) added the tower.

The large Victorian east window includes early 14th-century figures from the Merevale Tree of Jesse, and other windows have glass of the same period. A tasteful, modern, red-brick church hall has been added.

Within are memorial boards to the Mancetter Martyrs, Robert Glover and Joyce Lewis, who were burnt at the stake for their Protestant beliefs in the 1550s, when Bloody Mary ruled. A bewigged bust of 1690 commemorates Edward Hutton, and there are several monuments to the Bracebridges of Atherstone Hall. The family lived in the county from the 12th century until Charles Holte Bracebridge died in 1872. According to his inscription, he claimed descent from Egbert, the first king of England, Alfred the Great, the Plantagenets and Robert the Bruce.

Attached to the large brick porch are a sundial and a damaged strapwork plaque of 1663 to John Blise. The churchyard table-tomb of Richard Warwick, 'Merchant Taylor and sometime citizen of London', who died in 1633, records that he donated £15 per annum forever to buy 'Gray Coates, Hatts for ... poor housekeepers'. The small stone of a mysterious H.I.M. has a quaint verse on mortality.

There are two rows of **almshouses**. James Gramer, a London goldsmith, endowed the one bordering the churchyard in 1728. The other, with a Gothic veranda, was built in 1822.

The timber-framed **Mancetter Manor**, now a hotel and restaurant, was built about 1330 and its south wing added about 1580. The martyr Robert Glover lived there as Lord of the Manor with his brothers John and William, who, it is said, escaped arrest but died of starvation. It has secret panels for hiding those who were on the wrong side of the religious divide. Corner gazebos were added in the 18th century, as was a long, brick coach house now used for accommodation.

In Quarry Lane, the white-walled 18th-century **Manor House Farm** has become a smart residence, its half-timbered and red-brick barn rendered convincingly domestic as a separate house. **The Old Vicarage** is early 19th century and stuccoed, and three large Arts and Crafts **cottages** of 1908 border The Green. The small, brick **National School** of 1875, which replaced a dame school, is disused.

MAPPLEBOROUGH GREEN [Stratford-on-Avon]

SP0867: 4½ miles (7km) W of Henley-in-Arden

Spread along the county boundary, hard against the large Worcestershire town of Redditch, the village lies in Studley parish. There are two inns: The Dog and The Boat.

The grey stone **church of the Holy Ascension** was built for the Jaffrays of Skilts in 1888. It is a large, towered building, from which medieval-style heads gaze serenely out from below the window arches. A tall, abstract steel sculpture, depicting the Ascension of Christ and the Descent of the Holy Spirit, is being installed in the churchyard as a Millennium project.

Below Gorcott Hill lies **Gorcott Hall**, some features of which are believed to date from the 14th century. It has a two-storeyed brick porch of about 1540, gables and timber-framing, and until the mid-19th century was the home of the Chambers family.

On an eastern hilltop stands **Upper Skilts**, the substantial survival of a brick-built house of about 1560 in quadrangular form, which was partly demolished in the 18th century. It was built for William Sheldon (see BARCHESTON) on the site of a grange of Studley Priory. Sheldon died at Skilts in 1570. A later occupier was Sir John Smith, who recaptured the royal standard at Edge Hill in 1642.

The Jaffrays left soon after the Second

World War, and the shabby, white-walled, timber-gabled house, standing opposite brick barns used for farming, is now a school belonging to the City of Birmingham. At **Lower Skilts**, old stone arches and mullioned windows have been incorporated into brick barns. To the south, **Moat House Farm**, a 17th-century timber-framed house, occupies the site of the medieval manor.

MARLCLIFF [Stratford-on-Avon]

SP0950: 1 mile (2km) S of Bidford-on-Avon

The hamlet, near the Roman Ryknild Street, slopes down towards the River Avon and terminates in 17th-century stone cottages. A small, black and white, thatched **cottage** is strikingly picturesque and the red-brick Bogwoppit Cottage is curiously named.

MARTON [Rugby]

SP4068: 4½ miles (7km) N of Southam

This village on the Coventry to Banbury road stands where the River Itchen flows into the Leam and is only a mile off the Fosse Way. The Leam is crossed by **Marton Bridge**, built in 1414 by John Middleton, a wealthy London merchant born at Marton – who excused villagers from paying tolls. The bridge was widened in 1928.

Nearby **The Elms Farm** is half-timbered and red-roofed, and the long Black Horse Inn is painted yellow. The narrow Itchen is spanned by a stone bridge built by Samuel Shepheard (see EATHORPE).

The parish church has the possibly unique dedication of **St Esprit**, having been a chapel of ease to the French nuns at Nuneaton Priory. Vicars are listed from 1296. A new nave and chancel were grafted onto the lower part of the 13th-century sandstone tower and the ancient south doorway in 1871. The once-battlemented upper tower is believed to be 17th century and its three bells date from the 1620s.

In the nave (which, with two aisles, is broader than it is long), the south arcade was rebuilt with original stones and Victorian metal-painted texts are prominent. The organ, installed in 1875, occupies the area intended for a vestry and there is a grand piano.

Adjoining a thatched house, The Bower, at the end of High Street, is a small, red-brick former Victorian **chapel**, with triple lancets. **The Manor House**, its walls rendered and with large twin, gables flanking a smaller gable, dates in part from the 16th century. **The Old Brew House** has thatch and unpainted half-timbering.

The village hall is modern, as is the **Museum of Country Bygones** building, which displays old craftsmen's tools, farm implements and household utensils. The 1964 Derby winner, Santa Claus, belonged to a local doctor, Frank Smorfitt, and was bred at Marton.

MAXSTOKE [North Warwickshire]

SP2386: 2½ miles (4km) SE of Coleshill

The Machitone of Domesday Book had by 1170 become Makestoke, the recognisable ancestor of today's small crossroads village that gives its name to a large parish.

Maxstoke Castle (occasional opening days) stands beyond a golf course (formerly the deer park) where a prisoner-of-war camp was located during the Second World War. William de Clinton, Earl of Huntingdon, built it about 1345. Sir Thomas Dilke acquired it in 1589 and the Fetherston-Dilkes still live there. It is said that Richard III stayed overnight before the Battle of Bosworth Field in 1485, and his successor Henry VII afterwards.

The large, red-sandstone building has polygonal towers and a lofty gatehouse within a broad, deep moat. Additions were made to the north side about 1820. Interior

Maxstoke Castle

features include the Great Hall, the Banqueting Hall and the Chapel. It houses Sir Everard Digby's table, round which the Gunpowder plotters gathered, and a small, carved chair in which Henry VII is said to have been crowned on Bosworth Battlefield. The richly carved 'whispering doorway' was brought from Kenilworth Castle before the battling kings met at Bosworth.

William de Clinton also founded **Maxstoke Priory** for Augustinian Canons in 1336. Today its ruins stand on private land at Priory Farm, entered via the massive Outer Gatehouse, which is divided into separate ways for carriages and pedestrians. Within can be glimpsed the farmhouse – tall and half-timbered, with stone and brick features – that has grown from the Inner Gateway. The great stone fang of the monks' ruined church tower rises beyond.

A long, stone wall beside the lane leads to **St Michael and All Angels' Church**, on the site of a chantry built in 1333 by (again) William de Clinton. Rather high and quite short, the sandstone building has nave and chancel in one – they underwent a remodelling in Georgian times. The blocked north doorway includes an ancient pointed arch, but the Perpendicular west doorway was added later, its arch supported by weathered heads. The wooden bell turret is Victorian.

Also Victorian is the **Old Rectory**. It lies west of the Priory and is hidden from the road, though a medieval fishpond can be seen.

MEREVALE [North Warwickshire]

SP2997: 1 mile (2km) W of Atherstone

The parish covers splendidly hilly, timbered country, but there is no village. Gothic **Merevale Hall**, gabled and turreted, strikingly caps a wooded hill. It was completed in 1840 – replacing a house of about 1700, whose masonry contributed to it – and has Jacobean features. The architects (for the Dugdales) were the experienced Edward Blore and the young Henry Clutton. The owner, Sir William Dugdale, lives at Blyth Hall (see SHUSTOKE).

The grounds have been partly reclaimed from opencast mining. The **church of Our Lady** stands just within them and is approached through a vast and determinedly medieval-style gatehouse – also by Clutton. The lengthy sandstone church, which originally served the nearby abbey, is rather curiously shaped, its small, 13th-century nave having had a much longer and wider chancel added about 1500. There are large, filled-in arches and a brick bellcote.

Recumbent effigies of the Ferrers family, who came with the Conqueror, include a headless Crusader, which Pevsner calls 'a very early case of crossed legs'. He is possibly William, Earl Ferrers, who died in 1245. Depicted in alabaster of about 1440 are William de Ferrers of Chartley and his wife Elizabeth Belknap. Brasses of 1412 commemorate Robert, Lord Ferrers of Chartley and his wife Margaret.

The early 14th-century glass in the rare Tree of Jesse east window was not designed for its frame and may have come from the abbey. Schnetzler made the organ in 1777. A great treasure owned by the church is a silver-gilt Italian chalice of about 1375 with semi-precious stones.

In the churchyard, the table-tomb of Frank Herbert Pogmore records that he died 'in the 28th year of his age' from injuries received in the Baxterley Colliery disaster of 1882 (see BAXTERLEY).

Nearby Abbey Farm was partly built from the stones of **Merevale Abbey**, the remains of which, including the north and south walls of the refectory, look up at the hall across the monks' lovely old fishpool. Robert, Earl Ferrers, founded the Cistercian house in 1148.

MIDDLETON [North Warwickshire]

SP1798: 4 miles (6km) N of Sutton Coldfield

Probably the Saxon 'tun', or 'farm', midway between Sutton Coldfield and Tamworth, the small village lies south of Gallows Brook, which marks the Staffordshire boundary.

There are 18th- and 19th-century cottages along Church Lane, and an inn, the Green Man (originally a farmhouse), faces the three-storeyed **school** of 1886, which partly conceals an early medieval manor house site. The 18th-century **School House** stands opposite the church.

St John Baptist, built by the Normans on a Saxon site and surrounded by a 17th-century sandstone wall, was altered about 1300, when the north aisle was added. It retains a Norman south doorway, with a zigzag arch, inside an 18th-century brick porch. The Perpendicular tower, added 200 years later, which once supported a wooden spire, houses a 14th-century bell-frame. Restorations took place in the 18th century and in 1876. The base of a 13th-century cross stands in the churchyard.

The chancel, linked to the north aisle by a long squint, contains large, well-preserved floor brasses of Sir Richard Bingham, Justice of the King's Bench (died 1476), and his wife. There are monuments of the Willoughbys of Middleton Hall – Thomas, Earl of Londonderry (1638), dressed for war, and the naturalist Francis (an immense tablet of 1675, for which a window was blocked up). A small brass plate of 1507 commemorates Dorothy Fitzherbert.

The oak chancel screen is 15th century, and fragments of wall paintings revealed by the removal of peeling Victorian plasterwork in 1994 are a century older. Busts of half-brothers Benjamin and Samuel White, who died in the 1680s, recall their father. He left money for the poor, which accumulated to allow the Samuel White Cottages to be built in 1966. The village schoolchildren still receive Whitsuntide loaves at a special church service.

Villagers also benefit from the Lady Middleton Charity and the Middleton United Foundation, the first providing a Bible for every school-leaver and the second giving financial help to students.

Middleton Hall, to the east, was the oldest inhabited house in the county until its tenants, the Averills, were forced to leave the decaying premises in 1966. Middleton Hall Trust, set up in 1980, has the 16-hectare (40-acre) site on a 75-year lease at a peppercorn rent from ARC Ltd, which excavates nearby. A long-term restoration project is well under way.

The building's architectural features, which include a Great Hall, range from about 1285 to 1824. A display of modern embroideries depicts the history of Sutton Coldfield. The hall and grounds are open in season and a nature trail explores an SSSI. Behind a 16th-century timber-framed building is a craft centre and café.

The hall's early owners were the Marmions of Tamworth Castle, but the Willoughbys were installed by 1543, when John Leland rode by on one of his 'itineries'. When Francis Willoughby entertained Elizabeth I, her retinue nearly ate him out of house and home, but he was knighted, as was his successor Percival in 1603, when James VI of Scotland called *en route* to taking up the English throne as James I.

A later **Francis Willoughby** (he of the church's vast monument) was a celebrated 17th-century naturalist and founder member of the Royal Society. With **John Ray** the botanist, who lived at the hall after Willoughby's early death, he put the study of nature on a scientific basis. In his honour, his son was created 1st Baron Middleton while an infant.

The nine-days' queen Lady Jane Grey and the novelist Jane Austen visited the hall in the 16th and 18th centuries respectively. In 1868, when the moat was filled in, skeletons of an armoured soldier and his horse were found. They are thought to have been from the Royalist force at Edge Hill in 1642. The moat has been restored by the trust.

MILCOTE [Stratford-on-Avon]

SP1952: 2 miles (3km) SW of Stratford-upon-Avon]

Milcote has no village, though it dates from Saxon times and appears in Domesday Book, where the scribe wrote it as Melcote ('the mill cottage'). Until medieval times it consisted of two villages – Upper Milcote, or Milcote-on-Stour, and Lower Milcote, or Milcote-on-Avon.

The Grevilles (see WESTON-ON-AVON) had their hall at Upper Milcote, but Colonel Purefoy (see CALDECOTE) burnt it down in 1644. The present Milcote Hall Farm replaced it, though the farm at Burnthouse Barn presumably has a link with the Civil War event.

At Lower Milcote, **Milcote Manor Farm** was originally a castle or moated manor. It has a chimney stack of 1564 and a long, timber-framed barn. For centuries local children have been told tales of the bogyman Wicked Loddy, or Lodvic Greville, who was pressed to death by stones in 1599 for murder.

MONKS KIRBY [Rugby]

SP4683: 7 miles (11km) SE of Bedworth

The village, named from the Benedictine priory founded on the site in 1077, lies just off both the ancient Fosse Way and the modern M6.

The **Priory church of St Edith** is one of the largest and most magnificent in Warwickshire. Its great Decorated tower must have been even more impressive before the octagonal spire was felled by a terrific gale on Christmas Day 1701.

Ethelflaeda, daughter of Alfred the Great, built the first church in the village (then known as Cyricbrig) in 917. After the Conquest, it was replaced by Geoffrey de la Guerche (or Wirce), who dedicated the new building to the Blessed Virgin Mary and St Denis, the patron saint of France. He also endowed the Benedictine priory.

The change of dedication to St Edith (see POLESWORTH) took place after the priory was transferred to the Carthusians in 1399, when hostilities with France rendered St Denis unacceptable. Trinity College, Cambridge, held the advowson from 1546 until the late 20th century.

Well-preserved slate headstones line the paths to the large, stone porch with ribbed roof, which dates from a second rebuilding of the church in 1380, some 30 years after the Black Death caused the priory to fall into ruin.

The interior is wide and high, with two aisles. There are chapels for the Skipwiths, who lived at Newbold Revel (see STRETTON-UNDER-FOSSE) until 1862, and the Feildings, earls of Denbigh, at Newbold

Paddox. Sir William Feilding (died 1547) and his wife Elizabeth recline on an alabaster table-tomb, as do their son Basil and his wife. Basil's children are carved on the side of the tomb, but, curiously, the date of his death (1585) is left blank.

A tablet to Mary, Countess of Denbigh, who died in 1842, reads, 'This little monument was raised by the peasant boys of the villages of Monks Kirby and Pailton in grateful memory of the kind interest taken in their welfare by the good lady.'

Speculation about the mutilated head and shoulders of an effigy built into the north wall has variously dated it from Saxon times, suggested that it represents the founder, Geoffrey de la Guerche, or (Pevsner) placed it in the 14th century. White marble wall monuments commemorate 19th-century Feildings. A humbler resident, said to have a stone in the churchyard, was Elizabeth Mott, who died in 1720 after giving birth to 42 children during a 44-year marriage.

The former Gothic **vicarage** of 1843 has diaper brickwork. A large inn, the Denbigh Arms, stands opposite the church, and down a lane the Bell Inn has old timberwork. At adjoining Brockhurst, **St Joseph's Roman Catholic Church** is of modern red brick and has a spiky turret.

The Feildings lived at nearby **Newnham Paddox** from the 15th century until the house was demolished in 1952, when they moved to Pailton House (see PAILTON). Of their old seat, only the great 18th-century wrought-iron gates remain.

In James I's reign (1603-25), William Feilding became 1st Earl of Denbigh through the influence of his brother-in-law, George Villiers, Duke of Buckingham. The 1st Earl and his son Basil fought on opposite sides in the Civil War – Basil was the Roundhead, though he had earlier helped to broker Charles I's marriage to Henrietta Maria. The novelist **Henry Fielding** (1707-54), who adopted the orthodox spelling of the name, was a nephew of the 4th Earl.

Though the family crest is an innocuous nuthatch carrying a hazel twig, some Feildings used the double-headed Hapsburg eagle, harking back to a tradition that they were descended from the imperial Austrian house. When a genealogist cast doubt on that, the family jokingly dubbed themselves the Perhapsburgs.

MORETON MORRELL [Stratford-on-Avon]

SP3155: 2 miles (3km) E of Wellesbourne

This small village at a junction of quiet lanes west of the Fosse Way was the Mortone of Domesday Book, when the Comte de Meulan was Lord of the Manor. There is a small inn, the Black Horse (formerly the Sea Horse).

The village has links with American history through William Randolph, born there in 1650. He emigrated to Virginia and was a great-grandfather of Thomas Jefferson, third President of the USA. Other descendants were John Marshall, first US Chief Justice, and Robert E. Lee, Commander-in-Chief of the Confederate forces in the American Civil War.

The **church of the Holy Cross** dates from the 13th century. Its flat-topped tower has a curious, unfinished look; the upper stonework having in 1966 replaced a brick capping of 1808, prior to which the upper part was of wood. At the same time the three bells, cast in the early 17th century, were rehung for chiming only. Georgian brick buttresses remain in position.

Enter through a rebuilt wooden porch of 1896, sheltering a 13th-century doorway and a studded oak door. Within, a large alabaster tablet with kneeling effigies commemorates Richard Murden (1604-35) and his wife. Beside it, a tablet of 1623 to Elizabeth, infant daughter of Stephen Hervey, has quaint spelling. By the vestry steps is

Francis Bagshaw's richly engraved 17th-century floor brass.

On a window sill lies a carved Norman tympanum, its arch broken. A long iron-bound chest (probably Elizabethan) retains an ancient padlock, and on the roof trusses are the arms of prominent local families, including the Beauchamps, Earls of Warwick from 1363 to 1488.

Neighbouring **Moreton Manor**'s ball-capped gate pillars are 17th century, as is a wing of the house with mullioned and transomed windows. In a valley, creamy-stoned **Moreton Hall**, now part of an agricultural collage, is an impressive and substantial William and Mary pastiche of 1906. Opposite its gateway, a Queen Anne-style building of the same period houses a real-tennis court.

A tall, black and white, 17th-century **house** behind the village hall (originally a school) is believed to have been the Randolphes' home. Across the road, a long row of Arts and Crafts **cottages** has a gabled centre. Some half-timbering survives, and a former **chapel** with bricked-up windows serves as a garage for the next-door house.

MORTON BAGOT [Stratford-on-Avon]

SP1164: 2½ miles (4km) SW of Henley-in-Arden

A delightful cluster of church and farm buildings on a hillside, with an earthwork above. The original Bagot was Sir William, who sold up in 1296 – roughly when the low, buttressed, grey stone **Holy Trinity Church** was built.

It has happily escaped restoration, though the large wooden bellcote (said to have been originally a pigeon loft) was added about 1600, and contains a rare (but battered) prayer-desk from the Profumo Estate's Catholic chapel at Avon Dassett. The communion rail has panels from an early 16th-century screen, and the east window commemorates three Peshalls (see OLDBERROW) who were incumbents for much of the period between 1788 and 1933.

Red-roofed **Church Farm**, fronted by a long, timber-framed brick barn, is black and white with twin gables and dates from about 1580. The **earthwork** is a ring motte; its hilltop site was that of the ancient moated manor.

The present **Morton Bagot Manor** was expanded in the 1920s from a farmhouse built about 1700, which had also served as the vicarage. The developer was the Birmingham industrialist Sir Oliver (later Lord) Lucas, whom Churchill visited for discussions during the Second World War.

Nearby houses of interest include **Greenhill Farm** (on the Heart of England Way), a timber-framed house of late 15th-century origin with traces of a moat, and **Netherstead**, which is 16th-century and timber-framed, with a 17th-century extension and 18th-century brick refacing.

NAPTON-ON-THE-HILL [Stratford-on-Avon]

SP4661: 3 miles (5km) E of Southam

The village is unique – the only example in the county of a true hill settlement. Napton Hill rises prominently from the Feldon plain near the Northamptonshire boundary and is twin-peaked, its tops occupied by the church and a windmill. The outlook, said to encompass seven counties, includes to the south some of the loneliest countryside in Warwickshire, traversed by Welsh Road (see CUBBINGTON).

To the north, the Leamington to Daventry road skirts the hill. The Oxford Canal half-encircles it and meets the Grand Union Canal at Napton Junction, north of which a small reservoir regulates the water level.

The name Napton-on-the-Hill is tautological, because Napton alone meant 'town on the hill'. Domesday Book has Neptone. In the Middle Ages Napton had a population of about a thousand (similar to that of today) and was one of the largest towns in the county. In 1321 Edward II granted it a weekly market and an annual three-day fair; both are long discontinued.

High in the village, the Crown Inn overlooks a green. On the main road below is Ye Olde King's Head. To the west, the Folly Inn stands by the Oxford Canal.

St Lawrence's Church has a large Norman chancel. Though the tower is 13th century, its parapet and pinnacles were added 400 years later in place of a bellcote. Enter through a deep south porch with stone seats, enclosing an older doorway of about 1200. The broad and rather dark interior has north and south aisles and transepts.

At the base of the chancel arch is an ancient, worn, carved head. On the north chancel wall, the oldest part of the building, John Shuckburgh's brass memorial of 1625, in a marble surround, indicates a link with the family at Shuckburgh Hall (see SHUCKBURGH). A German landmine fin from the Second World War commemorates Harry Griffin, 'who received an award for transporting unexploded mines'.

An unusual feature is the 15th-century vestry door, which has a hatch and grill. Whether it was used as a confessional, as a spy-hole into the nave, or provided ventilation is uncertain.

The stone-built **windmill** (occupied as a house) is a restored tower-mill, with sails, for which records go back to 1543.

A small, speckled-brick **Christadelphian Meeting Room** still functions at Pillory Green, but the **Congregational Chapel** has long been a private house.

NETHER WHITACRE [North Warwickshire]

SP2393: 3 miles (5km) NE of Coleshill

The small scattered Domesday Book village consists of a church, two inns, a former school, a few farms and cottages, and an outlying hall. Set in a secluded churchyard of limes and yews, **St Giles's** has a broad, ashlar-faced, 16th-century sandstone tower, with gargoyles, a carved Saxon stone above the west window and a mason's mark low down. The rest was rebuilt in 1870, though the east window may be original. Its oldest feature is a small, 14th-century stained-glass window of a kneeling angel holding a censer.

In the vestry, formerly the Jennens Chapel, the wall monument to Charles Jennens (see OVER WHITACRE), who died aged 75 in 1773, includes a lengthy eulogy and details of his bequests. Since 'he was never marry'd', who is the weeping woman depicted? Beside the churchyard stands the red-brick **School House** – the school endowed by Charles Jennens about 1775 and closed in the mid-1980s.

At the corner of Dog Lane, **The Old Rectory** of 1872 is brick-built and has small, symbolic crosses on its gables. Though its predecessor along the lane, **Church House Farm**, has two gables, only one is genuinely half-timbered. The other's 'timber-work' is painted on, as is that at the **Dog Inn**, where the older part stands sideways to the road and a gable was added later. For real half-timbering proceed to **Church End Farm**, a long building incorporating a brick barn.

To the north, the small Jacobean gatehouse at the Jennens's **Whitacre Hall** has Civil War bullet holes. The Tudor hall was largely rebuilt in the 17th century and given a shaped Dutch gable and a contrasting straight one. Eastwards, **Botts Green Hall**, its black and white gables and red roof glimpsed among foliage, is late 16th century. Even here, some of the 'timber-work' is painted on.

Beyond Whitacre Heath is Warwickshire Wildlife Trust's **Nether Whitacre Nature Reserve** (members only). A wetland area once used for gravel extraction, it is noted for its birdlife.

NEWBOLD-ON-AVON [Rugby]

SP4877: 1½ miles (3km) NW of Rugby

Deriving from the Saxon Niowebold ('new house'), the hillside village was incorporated into Rugby in 1931. The little River Swift joins the sinuous Avon there and the Oxford Canal passes by via the 230-metre Newbold Tunnel, built when the waterway was straightened in the 1820s. A blocked tunnel near the churchyard shows where the canal originally ran.

St Botolph's Church stands high above the Avon and is mostly Perpendicular. It is entered through a 15th-century north door in a broad, stone porch, which has canopied niches on each side. Part of the early 14th-century tiled floor can be seen by the chancel arch.

The building is well furnished with monuments, especially to the Broughtons of Little Lawford Hall (see LONG LAWFORD). High-heeled Sir William (died 1716) and his wife dominate, standing upright and life-size in black and white marble. Earlier Broughtons date from the 15th, 16th and 17th centuries, but are outranked in age by the tomb-chest (1441) of Geoffrey Allesley and his wife. There are also Leighs of Brownsover Hall. St Botolph's is the only Warwickshire church to have ten bells.

The Old Vicarage of Georgian red brick has a hipped roof and dormers. Off the main road, the Boat Inn and the Barley Mow stand together by the canal, facing **Brindley House**. The plain brick building with Gothic tracery may have been the lodging of the engineer **James Brindley**, who died in 1772 while work on the canal was in progress.

Uphill, **The Manor House** is brick, with some half-timbering. Below are the lovely thatched **Avon Cottage** and **Montagu Cottage**, and a small **Methodist church** of 1879.

Beyond a crossroads stand the Newbold Crown (formerly the Old Crown), a modern red-brick pub, and the **village hall**, in polychromatic brick, which began as a Victorian school.

Newbold Quarry Park, a nature reserve set round a lake, occupies the site of a former Portland Cement quarry pit.

NEWBOLD-ON-STOUR [Stratford-on-Avon]

SP2446: 3½ miles (6km) N of Shipston-on-Stour

The village lies on the Stratford to Oxford road, in the Stour valley, and is part of the large Tredington parish. It has two inns, the Bird in Hand and the 16th-century **White Hart**. The latter was originally a cottage on the Shirley estate (see ETTINGTON) and bears the family arms. It later became a posting house and had a blacksmith's shop at the rear.

There were once several mills along the river. All have gone, or have been converted to other uses, though the last can be identified to the north as **Talton Mill Farm**.

The grey stone Early English-style **St David's Church** was built in 1833 and restored 1884-89. The crumbling spire was removed from its substantial north-west tower in 1948. Across the road stands a sumptuous former rectory, now **The Grange**. The stone-built and gabled Victorian house, displaying an impressive variety of chimneys, is the largest in the village.

The modest, red-brick and Gothic-windowed **Methodist church** was built in 1910 by Primitive Methodists. Newbold's oldest building, **The Bothy**, probably dates from the 17th century. A small former coach house with thick cob walls and a thatched roof, it stands on the spacious village green.

Opposite the church and covered in Virginia creeper, **Newbold House**, in Georgian chequered brick, is now a nursery school. Down Chapel Lane stands a stone

house dated 1714, with mullioned and transomed windows.

A stout pointed milestone at a junction north of the village has the following verse carved on it:

Six miles to Shakespeare's Town whose Fame
Is known throughout the Earth.
To Shipston four, whose lesser Fame
Boasts no such Poet's birth.

NEWBOLD PACEY [Stratford-on-Avon]

SP2957: 1½ miles (3km) NE of Wellesbourne

A hamlet on the Wellesbourne to Leamington road, consisting of little more than church, former vicarage, hall and a few Victorian estate cottages. The name stems from the Norman de Pasci family, lords of the manor from the early 13th to the mid-14th century.

The **church of St George the Martyr** is a stone building of about 1880 in the Early English style and has a saddleback tower. Its east and west ends, with lancets, almost mirror each other.

Two Norman doorways were saved from its burnt-down predecessor. A plain, worn outer one leads into a tall porch, then the nave is entered through the second, which has shafts with carved heads and an arch of four orders.

Within, St George slays the dragon in a Gothic Revival reredos, and memorials include Thomas Castle Southey (vicar 1868-99), nephew of the Poet Laureate Robert Southey (1774-1843). Edward Carew (died 1668) shares his wall monument with his youngest daughter Felicia, who died 'in the 13th day of her age'. Tradition accuses him of bringing the plague from London and causing an evacuation of villagers, who founded nearby Ashorne.

Early 19th-century tablets on the west wall include William Little's of 1834, with its charming Grecian-style charity scene. Unhappily, his wife died in 1817, 'a martyr to the gout'.

The former **vicarage** is a brick Queen Anne house with gables and dormer windows, and the secluded **Newbold Pacey Hall**, on the former manor house site, was the 18th-century stuccoed home of the Little family, Coventry bankers.

NEWTON [Rugby]

SP5378: 2½ miles (4km) NE of Rugby

Part of Newton and Biggin civil parish, Newton lies near Dow Bridge, on Watling Street, where the River Avon flows into the county. A mile north is the site of the Roman settlement of Tripontium, a name referring to the bridges over three streams.

The former Cave's Inn, or Cave's Hole, was the birthplace of **Edward Cave** (1691-1764), founder in 1731 of the *Gentleman's Magazine*, which continued into the 20th century. The small village has plain old cottages along Main Street and later developments off it. Its most attractive building is the thatched **Stag and Pheasant**, with white-painted brick walls.

Newton Chapel of 1905, ('a branch of Rugby United Reformed Church') and the Church of England's **The Good Shepherd** ('in the parish of Clifton-on-Dunsmore and Newton') are both small and of red brick.

Along Pilgrim's Lane stands **Newton House**, Georgian and brick, and at crossroads to the south, a small 18th-century inn has the unusual name of **St Thomas's Cross**.

NEWTON REGIS [North Warwickshire]

SK2707: 5 miles (8km) NE of Tamworth

The village was unassuming Newton-in-the-Thistles when Charles I arrived to pray at the church and fight a Civil War battle at Seckington. Perhaps as a result of the doomed king's visit, the village (which had also been known as King's Newton) resumed the royal title bestowed by Henry II.

The thistles may have been the teasels used for carding flax fibre for linen making.

Flax was a local crop and there were linen looms in what is now the **Queen's Head**. The inn, a red-wigged Elizabeth I depicted on its sign, stands behind a long, thatched, half-timbered and brick **cottage**.

In the early 18th century, Robert Phillips of Newton Hall donated 'Mr Phillip's barley close' in Birmingham as the site of St Philip's Church (now the Cathedral). Since the Phillips family intermarried with the Inges of Thorpe Constantine, across the Staffordshire border, the Thorpe Estate owns much of the village.

There is a striking view along Main Road to **St Mary's Church**, with its 13th-century tower, to which the spire was added later. It was originally a chapel to All Saints' at Seckington. The high, stone porch contains an ogee-shaped doorway, and a squint window in a tower buttress allowed people outside (possibly lepers) to watch the sacrament. Within, the most notable monument is an early 14th-century carved stone coffin-lid.

A curious outcrop of terraced stone, known as **The Rock**, lies beside the road outside the church. Nearby stands the school, built by the Thorpe Estate in the 1840s. In Main Road, a handsome **farmhouse** with dormer windows is inscribed 'RS 1718'. Opposite is an attractive pond formed from a quarry pit.

The **post office store** occupies a timber-framed building with a 17th-century brick front. Off Kings Lane, to the north, stands the early 19th-century **Newton House**.

Newton Gorse, accessible by track, is a lonely 2.5-hectare (6-acre) woodland owned privately but managed by Warwickshire Wildlife Trust. A mixture of broadleaved trees and conifers, it was planted in the mid-1950s and became a nature reserve in 1983.

NO MAN'S HEATH [North Warwickshire]

SP2908: 6 miles (9.5km) NE of Tamworth

The most northern settlement in the county, it lies on the Tamworth to Ashby-de-la-Zouch road, 50 miles (80km) from the most southerly village, Little Compton, and forms part of the parish of Newton Regis. An earlier spelling was Nomans Heath. The heath was for centuries a lawless place, situated where Warwickshire, Leicestershire, Staffordshire and Derbyshire met. Once a popular venue for illegal cockfights and prize-fights, it became the resort of many on the run from authority; if the law appeared, it was easy to slip into another county.

The boundaries, however, were changed long ago, and the boundary stone is said to have been put at the back of the fireplace at the Four Counties Inn. Today only Warwickshire and Leicestershire meet there, though Staffordshire is within a mile. The Leicestershire boundary follows the line of Salt Street, a hedged bridleway. The **Four Counties Inn** sign still depicts it as the junction of four shires and the county badges in stained glass appear in its windows.

Squatters settled on the heath early in the 19th century. The first to build a hut is said to have been Joe Leavesley, a coal-heaving leper from Newton Regis. **St Mary's Church** is brick-built Victorian Gothic of 1863, by which time No Man's Heath had evidently become respectable.

NORTHEND [Stratford-on-Avon]

SP3952: 3½ miles (5km) E of Kineton

The village lies below the north point of the Burton Dassett Hills and is part of Burton Dassett parish, though now much the larger of the two settlements. Its simple undedicated **church** of 1844 is a towerless stone building built in the Early English Revival style as a chapel of ease to All Saints' at Burton Dassett. The chancel has been adapted as a vestry.

The adjacent school (stone with a brick gable end) closed in 1996. Nearby, **Green Farm House** of 1654 is tall and gabled, with mullioned windows and a red-tiled roof. Uphill from a green rise the **Wesleyan Chapel** of 1831 and a grafted-on **Sunday School** of 1900, both in brick. Facing them and stone-built is **The Bakery Cottage**.

To the south, the **Manor House** is 17th century and stone-walled with twin gables. Its stone outbuildings border the road, which leads out to **Chapel Barn**. The dilapidated building with a corrugated-iron roof is the east end of an early 14th-century chapel, to which a two-storeyed priest's house was added in 1642.

Northend has an inn, the Red Lion, and the Centenary Way passes through. Off the Warwick to Banbury road, **Temple Herdewyke** is an old name revived for a modern village housing service families at the Ministry of Defence camp.

NORTON LINDSEY [Warwick]

SP2263: 4 miles (6km) W of Warwick

Appropriately in 'windy Lindsey', the visitor approaching the village along Wolverton Road sees first among features of interest a circular brick **windmill** of 1802-03. It was last worked in 1906. **The Mill House** was added in 1804. Beyond, at a junction, an ornamental metal **signpost** on a stone base commemorates Queen Victoria's Diamond Jubilee in 1897.

In the village, fronted by the black and white **Church Row Cottages**, which began as a Tudor farmhouse and barn, **Holy Trinity Church** presents a striking west end topped by an open bellcote. The perhaps too conspicuous clock celebrates Victoria's Golden Jubilee.

A Saxon church stood here, but only its 11th-century font survives. The church was rebuilt in the early 13th century, and the north aisle, porch and bell turret were added in 1873-74. The building is short, broad and rather dark, its silence broken by the insistent ticking of the clock. The east window in the tiny chancel dates from about 1330.

Among the graves are two whose occupants met tragic deaths. William Blakeman, the miller, was killed in 1892 when he fell whilst setting the sails, six years after James Wakefield, a farm boy, died when trying to stop a bolting horse. On a happier note, Barry Witherington, an Anzac cavalryman wounded at Gallipoli in 1916, survived to sound the Last Post when the War Memorial was unveiled in 1920. Adjoining the churchyard, the brick **Church Room** was built in 1851 and served as a dame school until 1876.

The New Inn stands on the site of a Tudor farmhouse that became a hostelry in 1750, but was rebuilt in 1936. Though not outwardly old-looking, **Big House Farm** dates from the early 14th century and is believed to occupy the site of an 8th-century Saxon holding.

NUNEATON [Nuneaton]

SP3691: 8 miles (13km) N of Coventry

The Saxon Eatun ('the town on the running water') became Nuneaton after a Benedictine nunnery was founded there in the 12th century. Today it is the major part of the Borough of Nuneaton and Bedworth and has engulfed several once separate villages. The River Anker and the Coventry Canal pass through. The textile industry has been the town's main business, though it also profited from the adjoining Warwickshire coalfield.

The district is intimately associated with the novelist **George Eliot**, who was born Mary Ann Evans at South Farm on the Arbury Hall estate (see STOCKINGFORD) in 1819 and died in Cheyne Walk, Chelsea in 1880. Her statue stands in the town centre. From 1820 to 1841 the family home was Griff House (see BEDWORTH). Many local scenes and buildings can be identified under other names in her writings and some of her characters were based on people she knew in the area.

Following Second World War bomb

damage, the architect Frederick Gibberd was appointed in 1947 to create a new town centre around the parish church. Unfortunately, his master plan has been marred by the ring road.

The large, towered **St Nicholas's** has much work of the Perpendicular and Decorated periods, though the chancel is of 1852. John Leeke endowed the Leeke Chapel of about 1350 as a chantry in 1507. Monuments include that of Sir Marmaduke Constable, an alabaster effigy of 1560.

Sir Marmaduke lived at the manor house, which he converted from the ruins of the **Abbey Church of St Mary the Virgin** after the Dissolution. It occupied the site of the nunnery founded about 1160 and had been rebuilt in the 1330s, after the collapse of the original central tower. The nave was partly rebuilt in 1877 and the chancel and north transept in 1906 and 1931.

Near St Nicholas's stand the 17th-century **vicarage**, with tall chimneys and mullioned windows, and the brick-built **Old School** dated 1716. Among its pupils, in an earlier building, was **Robert Burton** (1577-1640), author of *The Anatomy of Melancholy*.

The Catholic church, **Our Lady of the Angels**, was brick-built in 1838 and added to in 1936.

The monumental **Public Library** of 1966, by Gibberd, is late 18th-century neoclassical in style. It houses valuable collections of manuscripts by George Eliot, Robert Burton and the poet Michael Drayton (see HARTSHILL). **Nuneaton Museum and Art Gallery** includes sections on local history and archaeology, and has a George Eliot exhibition.

A late 20th-century addition to the town's architecture is the **Mosque**.

OFFCHURCH [Warwick]

SP3565: 2½ miles (4km) E of Royal Leamington Spa

The small village lies between the Fosse Way and the River Leam. The Grand Union Canal is nearby, and Welsh Road – used for centuries by Cambrian drovers bound for London's Smithfield Market – passes through.

Though not in Domesday Book, Offchurch is mentioned in the *Anglo-Saxon Chronicle*. A Saxon burial ground, discovered south of the church in 1886, yielded weapons and ornaments from about AD650.

The name is probably derived from the powerful **King Offa** of Mercia (757-96), who reputedly had a fortified manor house nearby and built the first church in memory of his murdered son. The site associated with him is **Offchurch Bury**, where a small, stone-faced and battlemented Gothic house, mainly of 1829, stands within a loop of the river. The house and its classical brick stable block can be viewed to advantage across the Leam.

Offchurch Bury belonged to Coventry Priory before the Dissolution of the Monasteries. One of the King's Commissioners, Sir Edmund Knightley, then acquired the estate and it stayed in the family until 1919. The house was built from the reign of Henry VIII onwards, but has been reduced in size in modern times. Since 1923, the Johnsons have lived there and managed the 400-hectare (1000-acre) estate.

The thatched **Stag's Head** on Welsh Road took its name from the Knightley crest. Picturesque cottages stand opposite, and uphill the plain brick school has become the village hall.

St Gregory's Church occupies the hilltop site of Offa's supposed foundation. It is mainly Norman, but incorporates Saxon features, including a serpent carved above an outside south window. The ashlared tower, pockmarked by Cromwellian bullets from the Civil War, is Perpendicular and the south doorway and porch are Early English. Memorials within commemorate the Knightleys.

The church's most intriguing feature is a

broken Saxon stone coffin. Inevitably, the possibility of it being Offa's has been raised. Neighbouring **Offa House**, brick-built and early 18th century, was the vicarage until 1962, when it became a retreat for the Diocese of Coventry.

Offchurch House, dating from Georgian times, served as a convent from 1952 to 1973, and has since been a private dwelling. Offchurch proudly claims the only village croquet club in Warwickshire.

OLDBERROW [Stratford-on-Avon]

SP1265: 2 miles (3km) W of Henley-in-Arden

The tiny hamlet at a junction on the Henley-in-Arden to Redditch road was transferred to the county from Worcestershire in 1896. Not much has happened since, though a visit to a local Women's Land Army hostel by Mrs Elinor Roosevelt, wife of the American president, was recorded during the Second World War. 'Mrs Roosevelt looked almost too regal for the cowshed,' began a news report.

St Mary's Church – small and of grey stone – has a half-timbered bellcote with a mini-spire. There was a chapel here in 1150. The narrow and rather low interior, with nave and chancel in one, is entered through a 14th-century south doorway. A plaque states that the church was rebuilt in 1875, during the incumbency of the Reverend Thomas Peshall. Peshalls (see MORTON BAGOT) were rectors for 150 years.

The chancel has a Norman side window and two from the 13th century. The east window commemorates the Reverend Samuel D'Oyley Peshall, who died in 1859. A 15th-century north doorway is blocked up and not visible from the inside, and five undated charity boards on the nave wall have 18th-century lettering. The churchyard has comparatively few graves, other than the Peshall tombs – nine of them drawn up in a phalanx.

Across the lane, veiled by trees and its stonework ivy-covered, stands the former rectory. Now **Oldberrow House**, it was built, like the church, by Thomas Peshall, and served during the Second World War as the headquarters of the Women's Land Army in Warwickshire. The 16th-century **Oldberrow Court**, with timber-framing and twin gables, is set back from the main road, beyond a walled garden with corner gazebos.

OLD MILVERTON [Warwick]

SP2967: 2 miles (3km) NE of Warwick

The tiny hilltop village lies just beyond the urban spread of Warwick and Leamington. It became Old Milverton in 1890 to distinguish it from the part of Milverton parish then taken into Leamington, and consists of a few estate cottages built by the Heber-Percys of Guy's Cliffe, two farms, a parish room converted to a house, and a church.

The grey stone Victorian Gothic **St James's** stands at the end of a lane. Most of it dates from 1879-80, when a 'restoration' by Lady Charles Bertie Percy turned into a rebuilding. Only the foundations and lower part of the tower survive from its predecessor, a chapel of 1835.

The tall, ashlar-faced tower has a tiled pyramid roof and a weathervane. One of the nave windows commemorates Dr Henry Jephson of Leamington, whose better-known memorial is the town's Jephson Gardens.

Vera Brittain (1893-1970), author of *Testament of Youth* and other books, and her husband Sir George Catlin, are buried in the churchyard. They were the parents of the politician Shirley Williams.

Also in the churchyard, a weathered font has the date 1674. It was removed from the chapel for the rebuilding and served as a bird bath in neighbouring Blackdown before being reclaimed.

At the roadside by Church Farm, a long, half-timbered brick barn has a warning in 18th-century lettering: 'Man Traps and Spring Guns on Theife Premifes'.

OVERSLEY GREEN [Stratford-on-Avon]

SP0956: ½ mile (1km) SE of Alcester

A small village in Alcester parish, it lies just south of the confluence of the rivers Arrow and Alne, and is separated from the town by the downgraded Stratford road. Among its lords of the manor was Henry VIII's executed Lord Chancellor **Thomas Cromwell**.

Old Stratford Road crosses the Arrow via **Oversley Bridge**, first recorded in 1521. Charles Johnson and Robert Wake repaired it in 1659. Eleven years later they were still awaiting payment.

From a hilltop to the south, **Oversley Castle** stares across the Arrow valley, a white-towered, battlemented folly. It was constructed (or developed from an existing building) about 1800 at the suggestion of the Prince of Wales (later the Prince Regent), to set off the view from Ragley Hall (see ARROW). In the 1930s, the grocer **David Greig** revamped it, with a touch of the Odeon style.

OVER WHITACRE [North Warwickshire]

SP2591: 4 miles (6km) NE of Coleshill

There is no village of Over Whitacre – just a parish of scattered houses, its main settlement being the crossroads hamlet of Furnace End. The furnaces (all traces gone) were built in the 18th century by the Jennens family, Birmingham ironmasters.

Charles Jennens, known from his lavish lifestyle as Soliman the Magnificent, became a patron of Handel and was responsible for the Bible-based libretto of *The Messiah*. He is buried at Nether Whitacre. The family also smelted iron at Daw Mill, which lies west of RJB Mining's Daw Mill Colliery – sunk in 1965 and the only deep mine left in Warwickshire.

Furnace End has the 16th-century Bull's Head Inn, a butcher's shop in business since at least 1874 and a post office store. A small 16th-century **bridge** (of stone and brick, and widened in 1924) spans the little River Bourne. **Mill Farm House**, which looks early 19th century, has an older timber framework beneath the brick. The Centenary Way passes through.

The small Baroque **St Leonard's** – known as 'the Squire's Church', from the landowner who built it about 1765 after tearing down its medieval predecessor – stands above Nuneaton Road. Its spire, added in 1850, replaced a dome.

The stone-built front of the neighbouring village hall was originally the tiny **'Bray School'**, established about 1700 by **Dr Thomas Bray** when curate-in-charge. Later he founded the Society for Promoting Christian Knowledge and the Society for the Propogation of the Gospel, and was the Bishop of London's Commissary to the Colony of Maryland.

Along the Nuneaton road lies the handsome, late Georgian **Monwode House Farm**. At Monwode Lea is **Tollgate Cottage**, a red-sandstone Gothic building of about 1800, with a quaint, ogee-shaped gable. A tall chimney, said to be all that remains of a Tudor house, stands lonely in a neighbouring field.

OXHILL [Stratford-on-Avon]

SP3145: 4½ miles (8km) NE of Shipston-on-Stour

The Domesday surveyors found a mill operating here, in the Vale of the Red Horse (see TYSOE). They recorded the settlement as Octeselve; today the local pronunciation is Ocs-shull. The village consists of a single street linking Oxhill House and the church. Midway, a 17th-century inn, **The Peacock**, is single-storeyed and mullioned.

In June 1644 Oxhill billeted the cavalry of Sir William Waller's Parliamentarians before their defeat at Cropredy Bridge, near Banbury. Osborn Atterbury (rector 1746-52) was a son of the Bishop Atterbury, Chaplain to Queen Anne, who supported Bonnie Prince Charlie, was imprisoned in the Tower and fled abroad to end his life in exile.

St Lawrence's Church is a battlemented stone building dating from the mid-12th century. Extensive restorations took place in 1865 and 1876-78, though raising the money was difficult because the changes were rather High Church and the wealthy local farmers were mostly Methodists. Some of the alterations were reversed in 1908, and in a restoration of 1980-81 the decaying pinnacles were removed from the 15th-century tower.

In the large north porch (also 15th century) is a Norman doorway, topped by a smooth-faced carved head with a hand raised to its cheek. A Maiden's Wreath, believed to date from the 16th century, or earlier, hangs in the chancel. There are no wall tablets, but several worn floor slabs. The wording of one, in memory of a Civil War Royalist, Daniel Blackford, is reproduced in a frame on the wall.

The 12th century font, tub-shaped and carved with figures, includes an uneasy Adam and Eve concealing their nakedness with their hands. Outside, set above a well-preserved, triple-arched Norman doorway, is part of a corbel-table carved with seven small heads, one of them grotesque. Near the south wall is the gravestone of Myrtella, a black girl slave who died young in 1705; it was restored in 1969.

The stone-faced former rectory stands to the north. Across the road, a rambling red-brick house is believed to have been a school before the Education Act of 1870.

The large, stone **Methodist church** was built in 1814 and extended in 1839. The small, brick **village hall** was the Board School of 1876, which closed after the Second World War.

Stone-built and gabled, with a small porticoed door, **Oxhill House** has the date 1706 on a lintel and has been rescued from dereliction. **Oxhill Manor**, of similar description and period, stands among fields.

PACKINGTON [North Warwickshire]

SP2184: 3 miles (5km) S of Coleshill

Packington comes in two parts, Little and Great, separated by the River Blythe, but has no village. In 1043 the name was already Pakinton, though the Domesday clerk later mis-spelt it Patitone.

Scattered Little Packington, on a quiet lane, lies near a vast mound that has grown up on what is said to be the largest landfill site in Europe at 160 hectares (400 acres). Its small stone-built **church of St Bartholomew** has been converted to a private house ('Bartholomews'). The period is late 13th century, though the large, timber-framed bell turret is only partly medieval. A small Transitional north doorway has been filled in with stone and there was substantial rebuilding in 1878.

At neighbouring **Church Farm**, tall and of red brick, the outbuildings, including a half-timbered barn, have been adapted to commercial units. Also in red brick and from the 18th century, **The Old Rectory** stands across the lane. Gothic **Park Farm**, strikingly set above the nearby dual carriageway, dates from about 1840.

At Great Packington, in pleasantly undulating country to the east, is the Earl of Aylesford's 1800-hectare (4500-acre) Packington Hall estate. The grounds, laid out by Capability Brown, include a deer park containing 400 rare black-backed fallow deer, fisheries and a golf-course.

Packington Hall ('Strictly Private'), stone-built in 1693, was enlarged and remodelled in 1766. It is noted for its late 18th-century interior decoration by Joseph Bonomi and has been painstakingly restored following severe fire damage in 1979.

In the grounds, **Packington Old Hall** (1680) is much smaller and of brick. It was adapted from a house built soon after the Dissolution of the Monasteries in the mid-16th century. Nearby, an oblong **dovecote** has spaces for over 1000 birds.

On the estate (and also by Bonomi), **St James's Church** is lauded by Pevsner as 'the most important and the most impressive English church of the ending c18'. It is an outwardly plain, square, mainly brick building, with four corner towers capped by lead domes. Particularly striking within are the four strong Greek Doric columns.

The church contains an organ on which Handel played before it was removed from the hall and a monument of 1570 to John Fisher and his wife, who purchased the earlier building from Henry VIII for £626. When the peal of three bells was rung to celebrate victory at Trafalgar in 1805, they came crashing down. Their broken remains were melted and recast as a single bell, which includes a Latin inscription recording the event and a medallion of George III.

PACKWOOD [Warwick]

SP1772: 4½ miles (7km) N of Henley-in-Arden

There has never been a village of Packwood, though Domesday Book records the name as a 'member' of distant Wasperton and a deed of 1190 refers to 'Walter, Chaplain of Packwood'. An ecclesiastical parish was created in 1838, but Packwood remains part of the civil parish of Lapworth.

The Saxon name probably derives from 'Pacca's wood', and it is possible that the tiny settlement by the church began as a religious community founded by the Prior of Coventry in the Forest of Arden. Today it is a joint benefice with Nuthurst cum Hockley Heath.

St Giles's Church has a nave and chancel dating from the 1270s. Nicholas Brome (see BADDESLEY CLINTON), who died in 1517, added its Perpendicular tower. A major restoration took place in 1886.

The eight bells, five of which were cast in 1686, are popular with visiting bell-ringing teams because of their lightness. The tower has an impressive sundial of 1730, and three earlier scratch (or Mass) dials can be seen on a buttress and on the south wall of the nave. Before the tower was built, the low window in the chancel, originally shuttered, was opened for the ringing of a handbell to announce the Eucharist.

We enter by an ancient south door in a late 18th-century porch and find a rare early 14th-century Doom painting above the chancel arch. To the left it shows three kings or noblemen (the Quick) and to the right, less well preserved, are three skeletons (the Dead). The east window of 1913 was designed by Richard Stovington of Birmingham College of Arts, who studied under the Victorian G.F. Watts and was described as 'the last of the Pre-Raphaelites'.

Dating from Norman times are the font (on a modern base) and a dug-out chest. The font was lost for many years, before being found in use as a cattle trough. In the north transept of 1704, the Fetherston Chapel houses the monuments of the Packwood House family. Though its Gothic tracery is Victorian, the window glass includes a 13th-century Crucifixion.

In 1706, a 50-year-old bookseller and his bride of 37 were wed at the church ('Michel Johnsons of Lichfield and Sara Ford married June ye 19th,' says the register). Their son, born three years later, was the famous Dr Samuel Johnson.

Making a perfect setting with the church is a moated manor house, **Packwood Hall**. The gabled brick and timber-framed building was the home of the Wykeham-Martins, lords of the manor, the last of whom, Fiennes, died in a motorcycling accident in 1984.

Sheep graze peacefully in meadows surrounding nearby **Packwood House**. Dating from the 16th century and described by the National Trust as 'a fascinating 20th-century evocation of domestic Tudor architecture', it is surprisingly small; the nearby stables from the 1660s are larger.

Owners included the Burdets of Bramcote (see POLESWORTH) and the

Fetherstons, before Alfred Ash bought the property in 1904. His son, Graham Baron Ash, presented it to the National Trust in 1941, with 40 hectares (100 acres) of land and an endowment of £30,000.

Features include the Ireton Room, where Oliver Cromwell's future son-in-law, Henry (later General) Ireton slept before the Battle of Edge Hill in 1642. Other rooms are named after George V's consort, Queen Mary, who came to tea in 1927, and the Lancastrian Queen Margaret, which contains the bed on which she slept at Owlpen Manor, Gloucestershire, before the Battle of Tewkesbury in 1471.

A portrait on plaster of Charles II dates from the mid-16th century and is said to have been removed from Windsor Castle. The unique Yew Garden, reputed to portray the Sermon on the Mount, was originally believed to be 17th century, but is now known to have been planted about 1850.

PAILTON [Rugby]

SP4781: 7½ miles (12km) SE of Bedworth

Pailton (originally Pailinton) is a sizeable village built in a variety of styles. The neat, red-brick **St Denis's Church** – an unusual design of 1884 – has exterior arches and an apse. Given the dedication, which is linked to the Benedictine priory at nearby Monks Kirby, the style is suitably Norman. It was renovated in 1982.

The Beavers (formerly Pailton Hall) is a large, stuccoed house with elaborate timbering and a black wooden Tuscan porch. It served for many years until 1986 as Lady Mary's Home, a charity endowed by Lady Mary Feilding, twin sister of the earl of Denbigh.

The Bakehouse has a coach entrance and the White Lion's dormer windows are set in a high roof. The polychromatic **village hall** was built in 1860 as a reading room. Further out stands the Fox Inn.

To the west, **Pailton House** became the seat of the earls of Denbigh when Newnham Paddox (see MONKS KIRBY) was demolished in 1952. The nearby **Radio Measuring Station** was established by the RAF in 1940 and taken over by the Ministry of Civil Aviation after the war.

PILLERTON HERSEY [Stratford-on-Avon]

SP3048: 7 miles (11km) SE of Stratford-upon-Avon

The small village east of the Fosse Way was Pillerton Nether until the Herci family acquired it from the earls of Warwick in Norman times. During the Second World War, the Women's Land Army had a hostel there.

A long, upmarket barn conversion faces the towered **church of St Mary the Virgin**. Building began about 1250, producing one of Warwickshire's finest chancels, to which a hammerbeam roof was added in the 17th century. The nave has a carved Perpendicular roof with bosses, but the aisles have been rebuilt – the north one in 1845. The design of the priest's doorway, with its five shafts, is possibly unique.

Nearby, **The Old Vicarage** is Georgian, gabled and in speckled red brick. Secluded **Pillerton House** is stone-built and gabled.

PILLERTON PRIORS [Stratford-on-Avon]

SP2947: 7 miles (11km) SE of Stratford-upon-Avon

This almost entirely modern hamlet stands on the Stratford to Banbury road (a former turnpike), a mile from its crossing with the ancient Fosse Way.

A red-brick Georgian **house** overlooks the main road, south of which is the **graveyard** of the church of St Mary Magdalene, burned down in 1666. It was not rebuilt and the ecclesiastical parish was united with Pillerton Hersey. Reached by a side road, a red-brick **chapel** has been converted to a garage for a neighbouring house.

POLESWORTH [North Warwickshire]

SK2602: 4 miles (6km) SE of Tamworth

A very large village in the Anker valley, on the Staffordshire border, Polesworth has passed through several metamorphoses since an abbey was founded there in 827. The Saxon settlement grew into a medieval village, saw the prosperous Coventry Canal completed in 1790 and underwent a population explosion a century later. Its cause was the opening of Pooley Colliery, which enabled Polesworth to become one of the first villages to enjoy electric lighting.

During the Second World War, opencast mining devastated the landscape and the River Anker was diverted to accommodate it. Today the colliery is an industrial estate, the opencast site a public park, the river flows in its old bed again and most of the population is employed elsewhere.

In the early 19th century, when Polesworth had perhaps the largest mop, or hiring fair, in England, as many as 3000 farm workers walked up to 30 miles to find employment.

The main thoroughfares are Bridge Street and High Street, the former crossing the Anker by the ten-arched **Polesworth Bridge**. At their junction stands **Nethersole School**, founded by **Sir Francis Nethersole** in 1638 and rebuilt, with turrets and a cupola, in 1818.

Sir Francis devoted many years to the service of James I's daughter Elizabeth, who – having married the Elector of Bohemia – suffered in the Thirty Years' War (1618-48). He went to the Tower for criticising the failure of her father and Charles I to intervene.

In High Street, the 15th-century **Abbey Gatehouse** is stone-built, with a timber-framed upper floor. Adjoining cottages are of ancient cruck construction. From the Gatehouse, a tree-lined avenue leads to the **Abbey church of St Editha,** dating from Norman times.

The saint was Polesworth's first abbess. Her father, King Egbert, is said to have founded the abbey in the 9th century, after being cured of leprosy by St Modwena. Sir Richard Herthill of Pooley Hall built the broad 14th-century tower and its parapet was added 400 years later.

The nave and north aisle, divided by massive round piers of the 1120s, are almost equal in breadth – the one may have been for the nuns and the other for the laity. An earlier effigy of an abbess (c1200), claimed to be the oldest in England, tops Sir Richard Herthill's tomb.

Beyond the church stands the **vicarage** of 1868. It incorporates a fireplace and timberwork from the manor house built on the site after Sir Henry Goodere demolished most of the abbey in the 16th century. Surviving stonework of the manor house adjoins the churchyard.

The poet **Michael Drayton** (see HARTSHILL) is said to have been schooled at the manor. His contemporary, the playwright **Ben Jonson,** visited it.

Other buildings of note include the red-brick **Congregational church** of 1828. Near the modern library are a long, timber-framed **tithe barn** and an early 18th-century square **dovecote,** constructed of brick on a stone base.

Along Pooley Lane stands a Pillar of Remembrance to the 32 local miners who 'answered the Nation's call and fell in the Great War, 1914-1919'. Nearby **Pooley Hall** was built by Thomas Cockayne, probably in 1509. It includes some of the oldest brickwork in the county. Later knighted by Henry VIII, Cockayne died by the sword of his neighbour Sir Thomas Burdet of **Bramcote Hall,** a lonely early Georgian house now ivy-covered and falling into ruin.

Above Grendon Road, Hoo Hill is topped by an **obelisk** erected by Sir George Chetwynd of Grendon Hall to mark the site of St Leonard's Chapel, founded in the early 12th century.

PRESTON BAGOT [Stratford-on-Avon]

SP1766: 1½ miles (2km) E of Henley-in-Arden

Its houses lie scattered about the parish in a delightful hilly countryside of small pastures. There is an inn, **The Crabmill**, on Warwick Road. with 17th-century timbering and dormer windows. An early 19th-century **tollbridge** stands in a field.

The Stratford-upon-Avon Canal, opened in 1816, was channelled alongside a broad tributary of the River Alne. It passes the superb gabled **Manor House** built in the 1570s for the Earl of Warwick, with timber-studded walls rising from a stone base. A later owner was Ingram Bagot, whose surname was added to the original village name of Preston, or 'priest's farm'.

Along the towpath stands **Lock Cottage**, one of the canal's characteristic barrel-roofed employees' houses of about 1811, for which bridge-building techniques were used to cut costs. This one has acquired an Italianate extension. Beyond is another typical Stratford Canal feature – a **split-bridge**, which allowed towropes to pass through when the path changed sides of the waterway.

The Norman **All Saints' Church** is unpretentious, with a tall, pointed bellcote. Its hilltop setting provides lovely views of gentle hills. Built in the 12th century, it has small north and south Norman doorways. The chancel was added in 1870. Long ago, when a problem with damp was investigated, two skeletons were found within the walls.

PRESTON-ON-STOUR [Stratford-on-Avon]

SP2049: 3 miles (5km) S of Stratford-upon-Avon

This small village on the slopes of Atherstone Hill, a Cotswold outlier, overlooks the winding River Stour. The lordship of the manor has changed hands many times since it was held by Deerhurst Priory in Gloucestershire, before the Dissolution. The owner who had the most impact on the village was James West, a wealthy antiquary who (his memorial tablet says) 'was many Years Secretary of His Majesty's Treasury' and MP for St Albans.

He bought Alscot Park in 1749 and was soon rebuilding the house and **St Mary's Church**. His plans for the church, however, were never fully carried out, so what we see is a 1752-64 remodelling of the medieval building. It left intact the nave walls and Perpendicular tower.

The nave and chancel are of the same height, their flat-topped walls supporting finials. We enter through the dark base of the tower, passing beneath a gallery to the aisle-less nave. Monuments, mainly to the Wests, cover the chancel walls. James West's is modest, a simple depiction of two overlapping urns done in 1800, though he died, aged 69, in 1772. The tablet of 1624 to Sir Nicholas Kemp and his two wives was, according to Hutton, 'calmly removed' by James West from St Mary's, Islington, and installed here purely to dignify his church.

The church faces a large, sloping green, as does a brick-built Georgian **house** on a stone base, with plain brick pilasters, or lesenes, and the impressive gabled and timber-framed **vicarage**, believed to be late 16th century. Along a side road, **The Old Vicarage** has a rendered classical front and half-timbered brickwork at the rear.

Gabled and high-chimneyed brick **estate cottages** of 1852-55, with Gothic windows and clipped yews, lead down to the black and white **manor house** of 1659. Further on, the former **school**, brick-built in 1848, is divided between a post office and a furniture-maker. It faces another sloping green, above which stands a row of simple, rather Celtic-looking, colour-washed cottages.

In the valley, James West's stone-built **Alscot Park** is a major Early Gothic Revival building of 1750-64. It replaced what Mrs West called 'the comicallist little house you ever saw'. The parkland occupies the site of the deserted medieval village of Alscot.

PRINCETHORPE [Rugby]

SP4070: 6 miles (10km) NE of Leamington Spa

The tiny village where the Coventry to Banbury road crosses the Fosse Way has an inn, the Three Horseshoes, and the small, cottage-like **St Cuthbert's Church**. The latter is brick-built, with stone quoins and stone-mullioned windows.

In the 1950s Roman coins were found nearby at Stoneyford Bridge. Previously, an Anglo-Saxon brooch and an iron spear-head had been discovered. The medieval Coffin Walk to the parish church at Stretton-on-Dunsmore survives as a public footpath.

Princethorpe College Independent Catholic School was built in 1832 as St Mary's Priory, the final settling place of Benedictine nuns from Montargis who had escaped the French Revolution in 1792. Girls were taught there, but when falling numbers forced the nuns to leave in 1966, it became a boys' school until going co-educational in 1995.

The massive tower of rich red brick designed by P.P. Pugin and consecrated in 1901 dominates it. The nave is of matching proportions, as is the impressive ciborium. Masses are attended by the public from many miles around.

The square-turreted Old Church of 1835-37, designed by a mysterious Mr Craven and soon Victorianised by J.A. Hansom, has been divided into two parts – a theatre downstairs and large schoolroom above. Hansom's Guest House of 1840 is in the Georgian style and his Mortuary Chapel neo-Norman.

PRIORS HARDWICK [Stratford-on-Avon]

SP4756: 5 miles (8km) SE of Southam

In a classic village setting, the church and a few old cottages overlook a green with a plain war memorial, below which stands an ancient stone inn. The memorial records that no fewer than eleven local Hayneses fought in the First World War, when the village's population was significantly larger than today's figure of about 180.

The Middle English Herdewyk meant 'the herdsman's dwelling'. 'Priors' was added after Earl Leofric granted the land in 1043 to Coventry Priory, which retained it until the Dissolution 500 years later. By then the village had been depopulated, probably by the monks for sheep grazing. Uneven ground in fields near the church marks the site. The population grew again from the late 16th century.

Though near the Oxford Canal, the village stands remote from main roads. Northamptonshire is within a mile.

St Mary's Church, in Hornton stone, has a slim, castellated tower. The nave is aisle-less and tall, the chancel nearly as large. Most of the building dates from about 1300, but (following an 1869 restoration) the chancel arch is strikingly Victorian. Set in the floor below are 18th-century memorial slabs.

A slab also records that the chancel 'was paved at the proper cost of Sir Robert Spencer, knight, Baron Spencer of Wormleighton' in 1612. Sir Robert was said to be the wealthiest man in England after James I. The late Diana, Princess of Wales's family, the Spencers of Althorp, originated from nearby Wormleighton. Another slab, once part of a mid-15th-century alabaster tomb, has only the incised spurred feet of a knight resting on a Thurber-like dog.

The font is Norman, the piscina and sedilia 13th century. Stone angels and figures of the apostles (with appropriate accoutrements – keys for St Peter, a moneybag for Judas) support the rafters.

Since its Portuguese landlord took over in 1972, **The Butcher's Arms** (reputed to date from 1375) has developed into a prestigious restaurant, its success helping to revive a dying village.

In 1872 the villagers were shaken by the murder of Betsy Handcock, stabbed by her husband Edward, a local butcher. He became the last criminal to be hanged at Warwick.

PRIORS MARSTON [Stratford-on-Avon]

SP4857: 5 miles (8km) SE of Southam

A lovely village, set where the land rises from the level Feldon to the Northamptonshire hills. 'Priors' came from the monks of Coventry, who owned the land before the Dissolution; 'Marston' (Mersctune in Saxon times) meant 'the town in the marsh'. The drovers' route, **Welsh Road** (see CUBBINGTON), and the line of a salt road from Droitwich to Northampton meet at the village.

In 1602 Robert, Lord Spencer acquired the land. Today Earl Spencer of Althorp is still Lord of the Manor and patron of the church. **St Leonard's** is set in a level churchyard containing two great cedar trees and some 500 gravestones.

The tower, with unusual corner pilasters, is 17th century in its lower part, 18th in the upper. The rest, apart from the 13th-century north wall of the nave, was rebuilt in 1863. The porch has stained-glass windows and, set in its floor, a bronze tablet to Elizabeth West (buried 1688) and her husband Richard (1691).

The interior consists of nave, broad north aisle and chancel. The east window and nearby north window of 1875 are in memory of Admiral Sir Henry Prescott, GCB, and his wife, relatives of the Revd I.P. Prescott, vicar at the time of the rebuilding. On a window-sill stands a carved 14th-century cross head recovered from a garden.

Most of the village, which has been a Conservation Area since 1970, is of Hornton stone. **The Old Vicarage** has a south front of about 1660, with mullions and a hood moulding over the door. Its west side was added in 1879. Buildings of interest cluster by a green, where a small grey stone cottage was, until 1920, the Roebuck Inn, once frequented by rowdy drovers. Earl Spencer's agent used the 18th-century **High House**.

At **Westover Farm** of 1663, Blencowe Churchill (died 1764) made longcase clocks. Another craftsman, Edward Gardiner, produced Gimson chairs at **Hillview House** until 1958. At **Keys House** on Keys Lane lived Josiah Key, locksmith to William III and Queen Anne in the late 17th and early 18th centuries.

Set back from the lane is the small, red-brick **Moravian Church** of 1862. It is reached by a long, blue-brick path laid through the village by Mr Ted Masters, so that he could walk there without getting his shoes muddy.

A small, castellated tower is a disguised boiler house and the 17th-century **Falcon House** used to be the Falcon Inn. The present village pub is the **Holly Bush**, an old farmhouse that obtained its licence only in 1947. Also changed in purpose (since 1975) is **Wesley House**, built as a chapel in 1858. **The Priors School**, begun in the 1840s and extended in 1879 and 1960, became independent in 1996. A new and enlarged village hall was constructed in 1999.

QUINTON – LOWER AND UPPER [Stratford-on-Avon]

SP1847: 5 miles (8km) S of Stratford-upon-Avon

The large village at the foot of the Cotswolds was part of Worcestershire until 1931. Since the Second World War it has expanded greatly, but retains an ancient centre at Lower Quinton, with several lovely thatched cottages. The expansion was mainly due to the establishment of the Royal Engineers' Resources HQ, which is due to close in 2000.

Quinton (the Quinentune of Domesday Book) takes its name from the Saxon word *quean*, meaning 'woman' – a reference to the abbesses of Polesworth, who held the land before the Conquest. Afterwards it passed to the Marmion family and to Magdalen College, Oxford, which has now sold most of the land.

Lower Quinton is much the larger of the two parts. It has two inns, the **College Arms** and the **Gay Dog**. The first – double-gabled, partly stone-built and named from its former ownership by Magdelen College – overlooks the village green, where its sign displays the college's coat of arms. The red-brick Gay Dog, in Friday Street, was formerly Magdelen House, a farm dwelling. Beyond it, a gabled 16th-century **house** has vertical timbering.

The large **St Swithin's Church** – heralded across the Feldon plain by a 127ft, 15th-century spire – is of Norman origin. Near the porch stands the base of an old cross, supporting the stump of its reeded shaft.

The church was dedicated to St Swithun (to use the original spelling), Bishop of Winchester, because he was tutor to Ethelwulf, King of Mercia and brother of St Edith, Abbess of Polesworth. The round-arched south arcade dates from about 1100 and the north arcade, added about 1170, has sharply pointed arches with traces of medieval paintwork. At the east ends of the aisles are the Chapel of St Anne and the Lady Chapel.

The chancel is Early English, but suffered in the restoration of 1862, when the Victorian east window was inserted into a previously blank wall. The circular font is late 12th century, with a scalloped underside; the aumbry, double piscina and sedilia were added a century later.

Eye-catchingly set among pews is the effigy of Sir William Clopton, who fought at Agincourt and died in 1419. The table-tomb of his wife, Joanna, was moved in 1739 to St Anne's Chapel. A brass depicts her as a widow who had taken vows as a nun in order to devote the rest of her life to good works.

On a nearby wall is the Lingen Monument, a large, pillared tablet commemorating Sir Thomas Lingen (a descendant of Joanna Clopton), who died in 1742. There is also a bronze tablet to the 'armigerous' Underhills. Captain John Underhill emigrated in 1630 to New Hampshire and founded the American branch of the family.

In 1998 the Royal Engineers donated two stained-glass windows in memory of their 55-year association with the parish.

John Wesley preached twice in the church during the 18th century, once writing that there was 'a thin, dull congregation'.

The black and white **Church Cottage** is 16th century, and two large, impressive, walled houses stand nearby. **The Old Vicarage** (or Cotswold House) is late 17th-century red brick, with a hipped roof. Its neighbour, **The Grange** of 1879, is in the Arts and Crafts style, with a great central gable.

Along the street, the brick-built Victorian Gothic **school** has become a youth club.

Upper Quinton has a few houses scattered round a vast green at the southern end of the county council's 100-mile Centenary Way trail and there is a timber-framed and studded **Manor House**.

On Meon Hill, the north-east corner of the Cotswolds, is a 10-hectare (24-acre) plough-damaged, multivalliate **hill fort**. In the 19th century a large hoard of iron currency bars was dug up.

Meon Hill is better known, however, as the site of the notorious 'witchcraft' murder of St Valentine's Day, 1945. A 74-year-old farmworker, Charles Walton, was found pinned to the ground by his own pitchfork, his throat cut with his own sickle and the sign of the Cross carved on his chest. The famous police detective Fabian of the Yard was put on the case, but (though he had his suspicions) failed to bring anyone to justice. Local people old enough to remember the killing deny that witchcraft had anything to do with it.

RADFORD SEMELE [Warwick]

SP3464: 1½ miles (2km) SE of Royal Leamington Spa

The village stands on the Leamington to Southam road and a mile west of the Fosse Way. Bordering it are the River Leam and the Grand Union Canal, the towpath of which is used by the Centenary Way.

Domesday Book has Redeford, probably meaning 'red ford'; the Semele came from the Simele family, 14th-century lords of the manor. Flints from 30,000 years ago and Roman coins have been found. A mile south at Pounce Hill Farm is the site of a Roman villa.

Since the Second World War, the village has greatly expanded south of the main road, where an old, chequered-brick **school** and red-brick **Baptist church** with a tall clock tower remain in use. Beside the main road is the 17th-century **White Lion**, a black and white, thatched building.

St Nicholas's Church stands away north of the road, its nave, tower and chancel disconcertingly ill-matched. The ashlared tower is Perpendicular, but the rough-walled nave and the chancel date from 1889. A Norman window survives in the nave and the east window is by Kempe. Though the neighbouring vicarage was new in the 1960s, its solid mid-19th-century predecessor, now **The Glebe House**, stands behind it.

The twin-gabled Jacobean **Radford Hall**, its original stonework encased in dark 19th-century brick, overlooks the road and is in multi-occupation. Its outer wall may be older than the house, which contains fine woodcarving dated 1622, attributed to travelling Huguenots.

At the Offchurch turning, **The Manor House** of about 1800, with a plain, brick front, has a massive Arts and Crafts addition, now **Gable House**. A tall, round tower at the rear is often likened to the one on Edge Hill (see RADWAY). Two old thatched **cottages** crouch opposite, one with an unusual chimney dividing round a window.

RADWAY [Stratford-on-Avon]

SP3748: 3 miles (4km) SE of Kineton

The pre-Domesday Book village straggles along minor roads beneath Edge Hill. Its name refers to the 'red road' leading from the hill to Kineton – later called King John's Lane. The monarch possibly travelled along the road when visiting Kineton, where tradition says he held a Court Leet. The Ministry of Defence, whose depot puts the famous battlefield out of bounds, has closed most of the route.

The **Battle of Edge Hill**, the Civil War's first major conflict, was fought between Radway and Kineton on the lovely Sunday afternoon of 23 October 1642. When the Royalist troops under Prince Rupert descended the hill and passed south of Radway to attack the Earl of Essex's Parliamentarians, the landscape was very different from today: Edge Hill had no woods and there was only one hedgerow between it and Kineton.

Some 3000 men were killed in the inconclusive three-hour struggle, before Essex was forced to withdraw. A mile east of Kineton stands a roadside **battle memorial** erected by Warwickshire County Council in 1949. There is another on the field of action.

In **St Peter's Church** reclines the mutilated effigy of a Royalist shot in the battle, Captain Henry Kingsmill of Kent. The broach-spired building of 1866 used materials from its predecessor on a site to the south, at the oddly named Westend, where upright tombstones border a path and only the Miller family vault remains. Westend

Clockwise from top left: Chesterton Windmill, possibly designed by Inigo Jones; Saddleback tower, St Lawrence's Church, Barton-on-the-Heath; lych gate, church of SS Peter and Paul, Long Compton; Victorian postbox at Spernall Ash – a listed building.

The Malthouse, Claverdon

All Saints' Church, Burton Dassett – "The Cathedral of the Hills"

Holy Trinity Church, Morton Bagot – escaped restoration

Nicholas Chamberlaine's Almshouses, Bedworth

Cottages, Burmington

Manor House, Arlescote: royal connections

Manor Farm House, Stoneleigh

St Leonard's Church, Charlecote – High Gothic

Abbey Fields, Kenilworth

also has a small **Primitive Methodist Chapel** of 1866.

The new church incorporated a mid 15th-century priest's effigy and a tablet, carved as drapery, to the architect **Sanderson Miller of The Grange**. Miller adapted his Elizabethan house to a Rococo Gothic style from about 1745 – some four years ahead of Horace Walpole at the better-known Strawberry Hill, Twickenham. The house was further altered in the 19th century. Its mid 17th-century owner was John Washington, great-uncle of **George Washington**, the first American president. **Field Marshal Earl Haig** also lived there. He is commemorated, with other local men who served in the First World War, on the church's lych-gate. David Richards, the Benetton Formula One chief executive, is the present owner. Miller built **Radway Tower** on Edge Hill about 1750 to mark where the King's standard was raised before the battle. A crenellated fairy-tale castle rising above the wooded hilltop, it is a small-scale replica of Guy's Tower at Warwick Castle and contains an octagonal Gothic room.

Radway Tower at The Castle Inn, Edge Hill

Since Victorian times it has been the Castle Inn. The **Stone Obelisk** of 1854, half-hidden among hillside trees, commemorates the Battle of Waterloo (1815) in which Colonel Fiennes Sanderson Miller was severely wounded. Just below, the monks of Stoneleigh Abbey – early owners of the manor – had a cell. A former barge-boarded Victorian **school**, now a house, stands by the church and the village has several thatched stone cottages. The small **Church Institute**, built as a library and reading room in 1852, has become the village hall. Until 1851, like many south Warwickshire villages, Radway had a Friends' Meeting House. The building is now **Oriel Cottage**.

RATLEY [Stratford-on-Avon]

SP3847: 4 miles (6km) SE of Kineton

The compact village shelters in a hollow east of Edge Hill, its houses built of Hornton ironstone from a nearby quarry now reclaimed for nature conservation. A former railway carried the stone north to the main line at Fenny Compton. Stone cottages, two of them thatched, descend the hillside. They include **The First Post Office** of 1882 to 1932, which was replaced by **The Old Post Office** uphill.

By a small green at the bottom of the hill stand the partly 16th-century **Rose and Crown**, the plain-featured **Church Farm** and the gabled former vicarage, refronted about 1840. Nearby is the **church of St Peter ad Vincula**, in the parish of Ratley and Upton. The unusual name (repeated at Hampton Lucy) means St Peter in Chains. Outside stands a creeper-covered preaching cross with a tall shaft, attributed to the 13th century. The building has unusual ogee-arched windows. The style is mainly Decorated.

We enter through a 17th-century stone north porch, enclosing a carved 13th-century doorway, to find a nave, south aisle and chancel. The aisle was added in the 16th century, when two chapels were linked to form it. Unusually, the pillars have no capitals and one of them carries four arches, including the chancel arch.

In a corner rests a large, intriguing carved stone, said to be an Achievement of Arms showing the armorial bearings of the Harbornes of Tackley and the Eures of Heyford Warren, both in Oxfordshire. Catherine Harborne, who inherited Tackley Manor in 1651, married Edward Walker of Ratley Manor. The first vicar is listed as Philip de Sapelton in 1251 – about the time the octagonal font was carved.

In Chapel Lane stands the stone-built **Wesleyan Chapel** of 1865, with triple and double lancets. It is now a house, as is the **school** that operated from 1887 to 1976. The **village hall** was converted from a barn in 1937.

The Mount, an overgrown motte and bailey castle site, rises outside the village, and the National Trust's **Upton House** stands to the south. Built about 1690 for Sir Rushout Cullen, a London merchant, it was purchased in 1757 by Francis Child of the Child's Bank family and passed to the earls of Jersey by marriage in the early 19th century. The elegant mansion is noted for its art, tapestries and porcelain collected by the 2nd Viscount Bearsted, who bought the house in 1927 and gave it to the Trust in 1948. A classical temple by Sanderson Miller (see RADWAY) overlooks the large Temple Pool.

The Centenary and Macmillan Ways pass through the village.

ROWINGTON [Warwick]

SP2069: 4 miles (6km) NE of Henley-in-Arden

A parish from Saxon times and the Rochintone of Domesday Book, the manor was once the property of Catherine Parr, widow of Henry VIII. At the bottom of a hill on the winding Old Warwick Road lie the **Cock Horse Inn**, (which has a half-timbered gable-end and used to include a forge), a timber-framed **barn** and a lovely black and white **cottage**.

The church, vicarage, hall and former school occupy the hilltop, which is included in the Heart of England Way. Nearby is a deep cutting of the Grand Union Canal, beside which stands the Tom o' the Wood Inn, named after a former windmill.

From a sloping graveyard with great clipped yews, **St Laurence's Church** offers a lovely outlook over rolling countryside. The nave retains a Norman north wall, the chancel is Decorated, and the west door and great window above it are Perpendicular. An unusual feature is the central placing of the tower of about 1330. Before its 1871 restoration, funded by James Dugdale (see WROXALL), the building was a near ruin.

Next door, the large mid-19th-century former **vicarage** has Dutch gables and a ha-ha. Across the road, **Rowington Hall** is stone-faced at the front but brick at the back. The former **Church of England School**, with lancet windows and a bellcote, served from 1861 until 1984. It has since been converted to housing.

Shakespeare Hall at Rowington Green is partly 16th century, with much half-timbering and several gables. It may have belonged to a branch of the poet's family, and he is reputed to have written *As You Like It* there. Most of the early records of the name Shakespeare were at or near Rowington in the 15th century.

Rowington Mill, a nearby tall, sail-less windmill, has a strange concave roof. Once known as Bouncing Bessie, it has been converted to a house. Bessie's sister mill, Grinning Jenny, is long gone.

Two outlying farms are of interest: the prominent **High Chimneys**, where 18th-century brickwork encases 16th-century timbering; and **Old Farm**, Mousley End, its late 16th-century timber-framing almost hidden behind red-brick outbuildings in unspoiled countryside threaded by narrow lanes.

ROYAL LEAMINGTON SPA [Warwick]

SP3165: 2 miles (3km) E of Warwick

The name of the gracious Regency town on the River Leam is recognisably the Lamintone of Domesday Book. The original settlement, during 400 years of ownership by Kenilworth Priory, became known as Leamington Priors. But for its spa waters, however, it would have been just another village near Warwick.

John Rous, the chantry priest at Guy's Cliffe, praised the waters in the 15th century. However, it was not until William Abbots of the Dog Inn discovered a spring on his land in 1784, and began to promote its medicinal benefits with Benjamin Satchwell, that steps were taken towards the development of a town.

Most of the major buildings were constructed in the 1820s and 1830s, which makes Leamington slightly post-Regency. Queen Victoria granted its 'Royal' prefix soon after her accession in 1837, in appreciation of a happy childhood visit, and incorporation as a borough followed in 1874.

Dr Henry Jephson was instrumental in encouraging society to take the waters. Among those who consulted him was the writer John Ruskin in 1841. Dickens used the fashionable town for a scene in *Dombey and Son*, and gave readings from his works there in 1855 and 1862.

The American authors Ambrose Bierce, Washington Irving and Nathaniel Hawthorne also made lengthy visits, the latter living at 10 Lansdowne Circus. Napoleon III of France stayed at 6 Clarendon Square whilst in exile.

The biographer **Lytton Strachey** and **Sir Frank Whittle**, inventor of the jet engine, were pupils at Leamington College for Boys. A plaque in the town hall commemorates local boxer **Randolph Turpin**, who defeated Sugar Ray Robinson to become world middleweight champion in 1951. **Sir Anthony Eden**, prime minister at the time of Suez (1956) and later the Earl of Avon, was for many years MP for Warwick and Leamington.

In The Parade, twin Italianate lodges built in 1846 flank the gates of the **Jephson Gardens**. The lovely gardens were laid out beside the Leam ten years earlier on land leased from Edward Willes. Their dedication to Dr Jephson rather than the Willes family was controversial.

Features include a fountain erected in 1968 to commemorate Free Czechoslovakian Volunteers stationed in the town during the Second World War, who died after being parachuted into their homeland.

Mill Bridge, a suspension bridge of 1903, spans the river near a curious feature – the Elephant Wash, a cobbled slipway to which elephants, kept at a house in Morton Street, were marched down The Parade for their daily ablutions.

Opposite the lodges, **The Assembly Rooms** present their colonnaded front to The Parade, with the **Royal Pump Rooms and Baths** behind them. Their architect was C.S. Smith in 1814, but they have been considerably altered. In 1999, a transformation to an art gallery, museum and library was completed.

Nearby **Victoria Bridge** was built in 1840 to replace a structure dating from 1809.

The lofty **All Saints' Church**, begun in 1843, had predecessors going back to the 11th century and is unusual in having been mainly designed by its vicar, Dr John Craig. Its length is 172ft (52m), its height 80ft (24m). The style is Continental Gothic.

The immense red-brick **town hall** of 1884, with Tudor and Baroque features, sits uneasily amidst Leamington's stuccoed classicism. Its neighbour is **The Regent Hotel**, claimed to be the largest in Europe when opened in 1819. The Prince

Regent, who was visiting at the time, granted it the right to use his name and coat of arms. The eleven-year-old Princess Victoria stayed overnight in 1830. The hotel closed in 1998 and a conversion to a department store, restaurant and café bar is planned.

Two other Parade buildings that changed uses in the late 20th century were the **Clarendon**, a hotel from 1830 to 1984, which was refurbished as offices, and the **Golden Cross Inn** of 1810, now a bank.

The oldest dwellings in Leamington are **cottages** dating from about 1600 in Church Street. Rendering conceals their timber-framework. Streets not to be missed include **Lansdowne Crescent** of 1835-38 by William Thomas, a local architect who successfully transferred his talents to Toronto, and the same designer's **Landsdowne Circus. Clarendon Square**, which proved good enough for Napoleon III, was built from 1825 to 1830.

The **Upper Parade** of 1825 was originally terraced houses, but the upper floors are now offices. Those on the east side, redeveloped in the 1960s and 1970s, have replica facades.

Leamington Art Gallery and Museum hosts exhibitions and has permanent displays of local history, which includes the fact that the world's first lawn tennis club was founded at the Manor House Hotel in 1872.

The Grand Union Canal and the Centenary Way pass through the town.

RUGBY [Rugby]

SP5075: 10½ miles (16km) E of Coventry

Rugby has been dubbed 'Butterfieldtown' (by Pevsner), because of the contribution of the Victorian architect William Butterfield to the town and public school. It lies on the River Avon and is skirted by the Oxford Canal along the 325ft contour. To the east, Watling Street, marking the Northamptonshire boundary, bisects the forest of masts at Rugby Radio Station, beyond which runs the M1.

In Domesday Book the settlement is Rocheberie, probably meaning 'rough hill'. It became a focal point for many villages in the Middle Ages, some of which have been drawn into the borough. The main growth of the old market town took place in the 19th century, especially after the railway arrived in 1838 and Rugby developed into a major junction. The wagon works and electrical engineering provided most of the employment until the labour market diversified after the Second World War.

The poet **Rupert Brooke** (1887-1915), the son of a Rugby School housemaster, was born at 5 Hillmorton Road. The Horse Shoes Hotel was the birthplace of the astronomer **Sir Norman Lockyer** (1836-1920).

A statue of **Thomas Hughes** (1822-96), author of *Tom Brown's Schooldays* and a pupil from 1834 to 1842, stands outside the **Temple Library and Art Museum** of 1878. **Dr Frederick Temple** (later Archbishop of Canterbury) was headmaster (1857-69) and was responsible for much of the school's expansion.

The **parish church of St Andrew** was rebuilt (1877-85) by Butterfield, though the 182ft (55m) spire was not completed until 1895. Parts of the original 14th-century building were retained, including the tower, as was a wheeled chest with iron scrolls from the same period.

The Catholic **St Marie's Church** was begun by A.W.N. Pugin in 1846 and enlarged (1864-67) by his son Edward. The slender steeple was added in 1872. Other churches include **St George's** from 1961-62 (applauded by Pevsner), but Sir George Gilbert Scott's Holy Trinity of 1852-54 was demolished in 1983.

Rugby School was founded in 1567 by Lawrence Sheriff (see CLIFTON-UPON-DUNSMORE) and moved to its present site in 1750. The buildings date from the early 19th to the early 20th century. Butterfield's first major contribution was the neo-Gothic New Quad for the tercentenary in 1867 – an extension of the early 19th-century Old Quad in red, yellow and black brick.

The Chapel came in 1872, its 105ft (32m) octagonal central tower topped by a pyramid roof. Dr Thomas Arnold, the school's most famous headmaster (1828-42), has a recumbent effigy, and there are memorials to his son, the poet Matthew Arnold, and to Lewis Carroll (Charles Lutwidge Dodgson), Walter Savage Landor and Rupert Brooke.

A plaque on Doctor's Wall in the Close commemorates William Webb Ellis, who 'with a fine disregard for the rules' was in 1823 the first to pick up and run with a football, 'thus originating ... the Rugby game'. The sport is also celebrated at **Rugby School Museum**, which tells the stories of the town, the school and the great game. The **James Gilbert Rugby Football Museum** displays memorabilia at the shop where rugby footballs have been made since 1842.

RYTON-ON-DUNSMORE [Rugby]

SP3874: 6½ miles (10km) NE of Kenilworth

The A45(T) dual carriageway has ruthlessly carved this mainly modern village south of the River Avon into two parts. They are linked by a pedestrian underpass, which is used by the Centenary Way.

There are two inns – the Blacksmiths Arms and the Malt Shovel, which has a gabled mansard roof and an intriguing high attic window. The large Dilke Arms on the main road, a former coaching inn named after the lord of the manor, was closed in the mid-1990s and its site used for housing. It was formerly the home of **Joseph Starley**, whose Ariel bicycle was patented in 1870.

St Leonard's Church is an early Norman building of great interest, though the tower is 14th-century Perpendicular. Its 900th anniversary was celebrated in 1980, in the presence of the Duke of Edinburgh.

Features include a Jacobean pulpit, an

Ryton-on-Dunsmore

unusually placed early 19th-century north gallery and 18th-century lunette windows above and beside a Gothic brick porch. A small church hall was added in 1975. Additions of the late 1990s include a carved stone Madonna and Child and a stained-glass window of St Leonard.

Among graves at the north-east end of the churchyard is that of Harold Claude Noel Williams (1914-1990), Provost of Coventry Cathedral from 1958 to 1981 and a prime mover in the building of the new cathedral.

Warwickshire County Council's **Ryton Pool Picnic Area**, a former sand and gravel quarry, is a pleasant place for a short walk and one of the county's most important sites for dragonflies. Towards Wolston is **Ryton Organic Gardens**, the National Centre for Organic Gardening. Peugeot Talbot cars are manufactured at Ryton.

SALFORD PRIORS [Stratford-on-Avon]

SP0751: 1½ miles (3km) W of Bidford-on-Avon

The village lies on the Stratford to Evesham road, which crosses Marriage (originally Marlridge) Hill and drops to the River Arrow at **Salford Bridge** of 1806. South of the bridge, on the Worcestershire border, the Arrow meets the broader Avon. An earlier name, from the Droitwich salt road that forded the Arrow, was Salteford Major. Nearby Abbot's Salford was Salteford Minor.

There are said to have been Roman vineyards by the present church long before King Kendred of Mercia bestowed the manor on the Benedictine monastery at Evesham early in the 8th century. Later owners included Lady Godiva and Bishop Odo of Bayeux, who had the famous tapestry made. When Geoffrey de Clinton became Lord of the Manor, he passed it to the Prior of St Mary's, Kenilworth, and the village became Salford Priors in 1122.

Valentine Green (1739-1813), mezzotint engraver to George III, was born at Salford Priors. The Bell Inn and several black and white, thatched cottages stand beside the main road.

A Georgian house faces **St Matthew's Church**. The date (1633) carved on the Norman tower tells us when Sir Simon Clarke had its height raised. The zigzag arch and fine carved tympanum of the north doorway are 12th century. The 13th-century chancel has a priest's doorway and a low (or lepers') window. On the south side of the nave, large gargoyles protrude.

An unusual feature, a semi-octagonal tower, was probably a beacon for travellers crossing the rivers and water meadows. It has a niche containing a statue of St Dubricius, the only Bishop of Warwick, purchased from All Saints', Emscote, Warwick, when that church was demolished in the 1960s. In 1873-74 St Matthew's underwent a complete restoration, including the raising of the roof.

The narrow nave, flanked by a broad south aisle, features a clear, 15th-century Decorated window of three lights in the French Flamboyant style, one of only twelve in England. Also unusual is a memorial of 1926 picturing two quaint tractors. It commemorates Harry Evershed of local agricultural machinery manufacturers Bomford and Evershed.

Memorials to the Clarkes of Broom Court include a large tablet of 1631, which shows eighteen coats of arms and a boy with a toy sword. Sir Simon Clarke's has a stone coffin lid, and that of his grandchild Margaret, who died aged three in 1640, a figure in a shell-niche, with a touching epitaph.

Sir Simon's second wife, Lady Dorothy (died 1669), was a daughter of the famous Cambridge carrier and livery-stable proprietor Thomas Hobson, whose rigid methods of hire gave us the expression 'Hobson's choice'. Her figure reclines on the chancel wall.

Along School Road, **Park Hall** of 1880 (now flats) is in an ornate Queen Anne style and was the Dower House of Ragley Hall (see ARROW). Matching modern developments are designed to harmonise.

At Abbot's Salford, named from the Abbot of Evesham, **Salford Hall Hotel and Restaurant** is Elizabethan, stone-built, with distinctive ogee-shaped gables and half-timbered outbuildings and gatehouses. It served as a nunnery from 1807 to 1838.

The Blossom Valley Inn (a name referring to the fruit-growing Vale of Evesham) was formerly the Eyston Arms, after the owners of Salford Hall, who were descended from Sir Thomas More.

Also in the parish, at Dunnington, the small, stone **school** of 1876 once doubled as a church. The **Baptist church** (1878) is large and stone-built, with lancet windows. Its neighbour, **The Manse,** is in Victorian red brick. Between school and church stands **The Old Bakehouse**.

Gabled **Bevington Hall** at Cock Bevington is 18th-century red-brick, its garden partly surrounded by a ha-ha. A linked domestic block, now a cottage annex, has rounded arches on front, back and side walls.

SAMBOURNE [Stratford-on-Avon]

SP0661: 3 miles (5km) NW of Alcester

The village lies between the prehistoric Ridgeway, just over the Worcestershire border, and Haydon Way, a section of the Roman Ryknild Street. In medieval times it was part of the Royal Forest of Feckenham, and in the 17th century became, like nearby Studley and Redditch, a centre for needle making.

Mostly up-market modern, it radiates from a lovely triangular green, overlooked by an impressive timber-framed cottage of about 1600 and the **Green Dragon Inn,** which has a 17th-century timber-framed extension. Long ago a market was held on the inn's land and it was a gathering place for carters, who proceeded in convoy to meet the perils of the forest.

In the 1940s the Green Dragon was kept by the mother and stepfather of the Birmingham-born comedian **Tony Hancock** (1924-68), who was a regular visitor.

Though a separate civil parish, Sambourne is part of the ecclesiastical parish of Coughton and has a small brick-built **chapel of ease** of 1892. Its ancient chapel probably stood near **Sambourne Hall,** a 17th-century house with square timber-framing, but mostly covered by rough-cast cement.

SECKINGTON [North Warwickshire]

SK2607: 4 miles (6km) NE of Tamworth

A tiny hamlet near the county's northern tip, it lies peacefully off the Tamworth to Ashby-de-la-Zouch road – but it was not always so. There is a hint of former aggression in its castle mound, and long ago a king was murdered here. A Civil War battle involving Charles I was fought nearby in 1647, and the road we arrive by is Hangman's Lane.

King Aethelbald ruled Mercia for 41 years in Saxon times, extending his kingdom by conquest to include Wales and all England south of the Humber. In 752, however, the West Saxons defeated him at Burford, and five years later he was slain in bed by his own thanes at Seckington.

The village was then known as Secandune. A later version of the name, used in the 14th century, was Sekyndon. The Burdett family held the manor from Henry II's reign (1154-89) until 1919, and the Washingtons (ancestors of the first US president) were here in Henry VIII's time. In 1316, Gerald de Sekyndon was joint holder of the manor. His descendants, the Seckingtons, retain links with the village.

Veiled by trees and denuded of masonry, a Norman **motte and bailey castle** comprises a steep-sided, flat-topped hill surrounded by a deep ditch and a flanking earthwork

At **All Saints' Church**, the Early English tower is capped by a Perpendicular spire, visible from afar. The doorways are ogee-shaped. Within, Robert Burdett's alabaster monument includes eight kneeling figures. He was a counsellor to Elizabeth I and died, like his Queen, in 1603.

In the churchyard stands the large tomb of the courtier's namesake, Sir Robert Burdett (1796-1880), provided by his three sisters, the name of one of whom indicates a link with the Burdett-Coutts banking family.

The neighbouring **rectory** is Georgian, with mullioned windows and a Gothic wing added. Nearby, the mainly brick-built **Seckington Old Hall** has cross-shaped windows and some old stonework. At the bottom of Church Lane stands the handsome **Church Farm** of Georgian times.

SHERBOURNE [Warwick]

SP2661: 2½ miles (4km) SW of Warwick

The Saxon name means 'clear stream', referring to the bourne, or brook, running down to the River Avon. It is the village – small, scattered and secluded – of the Smith-Rylands of Sherbourne Park, who built its distinctive bargeboarded estate houses in the mid-19th century. Samuel Ryland, of the Birmingham wire-manufacturing family, bought the estate in 1837. When his daughter Louisa Ann died in 1889, the property passed to a Smith cousin, who took the name Smith-Ryland. The Feldon Cycle Way passes through the village.

The vast, Gothic **All Saints' Church** of 1862-64 is the fourth to occupy the site. It stands at the end of a track and beside a pool fed by the brook. Designed by Sir George Gilbert Scott, the building was completed at a no-expense-spared cost of £20,000 from the purse of Lousia Ann Ryland (contrast £5000 for the substantial Ullenhall Church in 1875). Its 150ft (46m) steeple, elegant when viewed across the Avon from Barford Bridge, is stunning at close quarters.

Richly carved inside and out, the new church was built round a Ryland tomb chest of 1843, designed by A.W.N. Pugin. In the churchyard stands an ancient cross. The porch contains a useful information board.

Among mostly indecipherable tombstones east of the church is that of the wife of the Revd W. Grice, vicar for 37 years. Her second Christian name was Waterloo. It follows that she was born on 18 June 1815 – some say on the battlefield, where her father was a participant and her mother a spectator.

Sherbourne Park, the red-brick mansion of the Smith-Rylands, dates from the early 18th century. Unfitting accretions have been removed in modern times. The **school** of 1881 by John Cundall, architect of Leamington Town Hall, acts as the estate office. Nearby, **Church Farm**, a former vicarage, is 16th-century timber-framed, though refaced in the 19th century.

SHILTON [Rugby]

SP4084: 5½ miles (9km) NE of Coventry

Plundered by victorious Parliamentary Scots after the Battle of Naseby in 1645 and granted hefty compensation of £31-17s, the village was bisected two centuries later by the London North Western Railway. Along the main street, where old cottages were once occupied by weavers, are two inns, the Shilton Arms and the Old Plough.

St Andrew's Church – Perpendicular, with a tower – is noteworthy for its elaborately carved late 18th-century gravestones. A curiosity is the two north aisles, one medieval and the other by Sir George Gilbert Scott in 1865. The timber chancel screen has medieval carving.

Opposite, at **Shilton House Farm**, stands an 18th-century half-timbered and brick barn. The small **Baptist Chapel** of 1867 is unpretentious, with arched windows. Nearby, the **Church of England First School** (1849) replaced a building of 1725 sacrificed for the railway.

A mile west stands the 17th-century **Barnacle Hall**, which is timber-framed, with a stone front and mullioned windows. An earlier hall was burnt down during the Civil War. Until the 18th century its owners were the Feildings, earls of Denbigh, who lived at Newnham Paddox (see MONKS KIRBY). The hamlet of Barnacle has attractive 18th-century cottages and the Red Lion Inn.

SHIPSTON-ON-STOUR [Stratford-on-Avon]

SP2540: 10 miles (15km) SE of Stratford-upon-Avon

Shipston is a small, handsome town of mainly Georgian appearance standing west of the River Stour. The Saxon Scepwaeisctune (Sheepwashtown), it was originally part of the large Tredington parish. Mop Fairs, dating from the 13th century, are held in June and October (the latter known as the Runaway Mop). Until 1931 Shipston was in Worcestershire.

The Cotswold wool trade led to the town's development. Today it centres on a short High Street (effectively a square) and has a lively and prosperous atmosphere. **Francis Haverfield**, the archaeologist and authority on Roman Britain, was born at Shipston in 1860.

Two old coaching inns, the **Bear** and the **George Hotel** (its coach entrance filled in), face High Street, down which gazes a Victorian Italianate building that began as the rectory, was latterly council offices and is now apartments.

The long Sheep Street is lined with 18th-century buildings, some of them displaying dates. At the Georgian **Bell Inn**, the coaching entrance has also been filled in. The neighbouring **Manor House** is early Georgian, with battlemented stables of 1876. Number 21 is set back and was the police station (1874). Number 21a, **The Court House**, is the former magistrates' court and police cells from the 1880s, and was in use until 1991.

Beyond the town end of the street, a house with mullioned windows has the date 1678, though there has been Victorian tampering with the window frames. In Old Road are two pretty Gothic cottages with ogee-shaped door and window arches. A small, red-brick former **National School** at its far end has stone-framed, ogee-shaped windows.

The tall, confident-looking **Wesleyan Chapel**, now Shipston-on-Stour Methodist Church, presents a light rocky face to New Street, where a **wine merchant's shop**, with vaults, was established in 1842. Opposite stand **The Coach House** and **Tandoori Cottage**. Both have half-timbering, but the latter, now a restaurant, has been painted black and bright yellow.

In Church Street, the **Horseshoe Inn** is black and white and very picturesque. A Cotswold-stone building, with a single mullioned window and tall red-tiled roof, is the **Friends' Meeting House** of about 1690. It is still owned and used by the Quakers, but occupied mainly as the public library.

St Edmund's Church has a 15th-century tower of rough brown stone; the rest, ashlared, is an early design of G.E. Street in 1855. It looks cramped from outside, but is spacious within. A rear graveyard of worn headstones includes a railed table-tomb of George Marshall, a timber merchant of Theobald's Row, London, who died in 1748. It displays the arms of Jesus College, Oxford, patrons of the church when Shipston became an independent parish in 1719. On the south side, Thomas Waring's stone of 1714 bears the arms of the Blacksmiths' and Farriers' companies.

Memorials retained from the previous building include John Hart's of 1747 – 'A considerable Improver and Promoter of Manufacture in this his native Town'. Shipston's first rector was **William Parry** (1726-56), a skilful calligrapher whose work can be seen in Oxford's Bodleian Library. A major refurbishment of the church in 1995 saw the rotting floor replaced and various domestic offices created.

Towards the north end of the town stands the **Baptist Manse** of 1906, and down Watery Lane is the 16th-century **Black Horse Inn** – stone-built and thatched, with adjoining cottages in similar style. The brick-built classical **Workhouse**, or Shipston House, of 1837 is now offices.

The six-arched **Mill Bridge** (widened in 1826) has a brick parapet on a stone base, with the date 1698 facing the river on its north side. The white-walled **mill** is now a hotel and restaurant.

SHOTTERY [Stratford-on-Avon]

SP1854: 1 mile (2km) W of Stratford-upon-Avon

The village, part of Stratford parish, expanded after the Second World War but has many old houses dotted about. It is famous for **Anne Hathaway's Cottage**, the home of Shakespeare's bride before her marriage. Formerly The Hewlands, the thatched and half-timbered farmhouse with cruck-trusses, set in an old-fashioned English garden, contains family furniture and relics. Though the lower part is 15th century or earlier, the west section was built about 1600 and is probably post-Anne (she married in 1582).

The Shakespeare Tree Garden displays a specimen of every tree mentioned in the poet's works, except those that cannot survive in the English climate.

Behind clipped hedges, **Stratford-upon-Avon Grammar School for Girls** occupies the grey stone Manor House of the 14th or 15th century. It has a hammer-beam roof and 17th-century wooden cross-shaped windows. Nearby stands a square stone **dovecote**.

By a small green, **Tavern Lane** ('No coaches or motor vehicles') displays lovely black and white half-timbered houses, some with thatch. **Shottery Hall**, behind a tall brick wall, is of Georgian red brick. Further on, picturesque black and white thatched cottages face **St Andrew's Church** of 1871, which was brick-built in the 13th century style. It seems to have had no predecessor. **The Vicarage**, in matching red brick, stands next door.

Our Lady of Peace is a plain, modern Catholic church - long and low. **The Shottery Chapel** or Elim Pentecostal Church (by the Bell Inn) dates from about 1833. The unusual **St Andrew's School** building is a former National School, briskly opened in response to the 1870 Education Act, in a brick and timber-framed barn brought from Redditch, Worcestershire.

SHOTTESWELL [Stratford-on-Avon]

SP4245: 6½ miles (10km) SE of Kineton

The parish is a peninsula of Warwickshire thrusting deep into Oxfordshire, and the hillside village below the Warwick to Banbury road is built of local Hornton ironstone. There is no mention of Shotteswell in Domesday Book, though it may have been 'the two hides of Warmington' recorded as belonging to an unnamed knight.

Even so, the nucleus of **St Laurence's Church** then existed in the form of the present vestry, where the old altar stone still stands, and may have already undergone the first of four enlargements. The tower is 13th century and the spire was added in the 14th, but both were rebuilt to their original designs in 1807-08. A general restoration took place in 1875.

A small, 13th-century oak chest stands in the side chapel, where there are also stone wall-seats. The chancel arch is less than 2 metres wide. The Flemish reredos of about 1600 consists of eleven carved wooden panels that seem to have been collected rather than designed as a whole.

The bells had not rung a full circle for over fifty years until they were refurbished and a new steel frame installed in 1995. An additional bell was brought from the redundant church at Atherstone-on-Stour. The church clock of 1680 has no face, but strikes the hours. Its mechanism can be seen at the base of the tower. Outside, near the east end of the south aisle, is an earlier timepiece – a scratch dial for indicating when mass was due.

The earliest recorded vicar was Father Stotterwell in 1287, but there is no evidence of a vicarage until 1381. A later building east of the church, with gables and small mullions, is **The Old Vicarage**

The large, thatched **Woolgrove Cottage** in Snuff Lane is impressive. The lane rises to the former **Flying Fox Inn** – now a house but identifiable by a metal fox on its wall. The Victorian school was converted to the **village hall** in 1974, and the brick **Wesleyan church** of 1854 has become a house, The Old Chapel, with domestic windows.

The d'Arcy Dalton Way, a 65-mile trail mainly in Oxfordshire, cuts through Shotteswell.

SHREWLEY COMMON [Warwick]

SP2167: 4½ miles (7km) NW of Warwick

This small village was recorded in Domesday Book, its Saxon name meaning 'a cave' or 'pit'. Today it consists mainly of modern houses on a straight road, beneath which the horse-drawn narrow boats of the Grand Union Canal used to pass via an unusual **double tunnel**. The horses were unhitched and led through a narrow passage, still used by towpath walkers, while the men legged the boat through the waterway tunnel.

Beyond a stone railway bridge, the **Durham Ox** has 17th-century beams within a later exterior.

Scanty remains (a wall or two and a small Perpendicular doorway) of **Pinley Abbey** or Priory survive among fields to the south. The sale of the Cistercian nunnery, dating from the early 12th century, brought Henry VIII a much-needed £342-11s in 1538. The adjacent timber-framed **Pinley Abbey Farm** of about 1500 may have been the residence of the later prioresses.

SHUCKBURGH – LOWER AND UPPER [Stratford-on-Avon]

SP4862: 4½ miles (7km) E of Southam

The Sochberge of Domesday Book (possibly referring to a long-lost barrow, or burial mound), it falls into two parts – the hamlet of Lower Shuckburgh on the Leamington to Daventry road and Upper Shuckburgh, the site of a deserted medieval village on Beacon Hill.

The Oxford Canal skirts Lower Shuckburgh and the large, Georgian **Red House Farm** stands above an old metal milepost by the road, which is bordered by ridge and furrow. Arts and Crafts estate houses of 1895, with the prominent initials 'H.J.S.' (Major Henry James Shuckburgh), are named from the Second Afghan War (1878-90).

The curious **church of St John Baptist** is a lively Gothic design of 1864 by J. Croft, who has been described as 'a rogue architect'. The elaborately carved stonework, rising above clipped churchyard yews, includes a six-sided tower, each side supporting a gable overlapping the base of the spire.

A double porch leads to an interior with imitation brickwork painted on the piers and purple-gravel mosaics. It is said to have been designed to the taste, picked up in the Crimea, of George Shuckburgh. More soberly, there is a tub-shaped 13th-century font. Across the main road, the red-brick former **vicarage**, also by Croft and in course of restoration, is large and rambling, but contrastingly plain.

At Upper Shuckburgh, the home of the Shuckburgh family since the 11th century, **Shuckburgh Hall** sits on a lovely hillside below woods and above a deer park, its Victorian Renaissance front of 1844 concealing ancient timberwork. The traveller and journal writer Celia Fiennes was a visitor in 1697.

The nearby church of Hornton stone, **St John the Baptist in the Wilderness**, is not attached to a diocese and is therefore termed a peculiar. It is said to have been rebuilt in the 1660s after destruction by Cromwell's troops, but has much Victorian work. Many monuments and tablets commemorate Shuckburghs. Flaxman portrays the astronomer **Sir George Shuckburgh-Evelyn** (1804), who has a crater on the moon named after him, holding a globe and astrolabe.

Framed by exterior arches on the south and north walls are carved stones depicting, respectively, a skull and crossbones and the Tree of Life. They are said to have come from Cardinal Wolsey's palace at Esher.

Below, at the handsome 18th-century **Home Farm**, stands a pyramid-roofed **dovecote**.

SHUSTOKE [North Warwickshire]

SP2290: 2 miles (3km) NE of Coleshill

Shustoke is best known for the Severn Trent reservoirs of contrasting sizes (36.6 and 3.4 hectares (90½ and 8½ acres) that provide water for Coventry and Nuneaton, but a village has existed since Saxon times and was the Scotscote of Domesday Book.

The settlement was at Church End until plague struck in 1650, forcing a move to the present setting. There the **Plough Inn**, once two farmworkers' cottages, dates from 1790 and looks out at the old **Pound**, restored in 1975. The Centenary Way passes through.

Off the Coleshill road stands **Blyth Hall**, rebuilt by the young **William Dugdale** in 1625 and refronted in the early 18th century. The present owner-occupier, and landlord of much of the surrounding countryside, is Sir William Dugdale, descendant of the historian and former chairman of Severn Trent.

The author of *The Antiquities of Warwickshire* (1656) and *The Baronye of England* (1675) was born in 1605 at **The Old Rectory**, Church End – a long, white, single-storey house with a tiled roof. He married Margery Huntbach at 17, lived at Blyth Hall, fought on the losing side in the Civil War and forfeited his estate. Regaining it after the Restoration in 1660, Dugdale was knighted and created Garter King of Arms in 1677. He died in 1686.

His tomb-chest stands in **St Cuthbert's Church** at Church End, where it survived a lightning strike that necessitated the 1886 rebuilding, as did the impressive 14th-century red-sandstone tower and spire. A tiny Norman window was reset in the new vestry, and weathered 18th-century gravestones, some carved with cherubs' heads, line the path.

Beyond the church are former **almshouses**. The original six cottages with high roofs and dormers, built by Thomas Huntbach in the late 17th century, have been converted into three in recent years.

Church Farm has gables from the 17th and 18th centuries, one stone and one brick, and a **dovecote**. Nearby, **The Old Vicarage** was built about 1820, though its downstairs bay windows are surely Victorian. Hard against the main road is the small **Griffin Inn** of 18th-century brick, but with timber-framing inside.

Hall Farm, in Moat House Lane, was the

Shustoke Hall of Thomas Huntbach. The handsome, red-brick, 17th-century mansion, with a hipped roof and dormers, stands by an old moat.

Beside the Whitacre Heath road rise the splendid Venetian Gothic gables of **Nether Whitacre Pumping Station** (1885). Over a railway bridge and on the site of a former station in Nether Whitacre parish, **Peggs Barn** shelters among trees. Brick and timber-framed on a stone base, the 12th-century longhouse was moved from Daw Mill Colliery by Coleshill Civic Society for use as a scout hut. It was officially opened by Prince Charles in 1993 and won a Europa Nostra award.

St Cuthbert's church, Shustoke

SHUTTINGTON [North Warwickshire]

SK2505: 3 miles (5km) NE of Tamworth

Recorded in Domesday Book, Shuttington is a small hill village near the Staffordshire border. There are fine views of vast, silvery lakes in the Anker valley and across rich arable fields to Seckington's distant spire. The lakes are due to mining subsidence. The first appeared about 1900, but most were formed during the Second World War. Sloping meadows west of the village have been reclaimed from opencast mining.

The Wolferstan Arms is named from the family at Statfold Hall, in Staffordshire. The small **St Matthew's Church** commands a magnificent panorama. Stone-built in Norman times (though the windows are neo-Norman), it was originally a chapel of Alvecote Priory. Features include a weather-boarded bellcote and a great Norman doorway brought uphill from the priory ruins. The plastered interior and the pulpit are 18th century.

From the same period is the tombstone of a man claimed to have been the fattest in England. Thomas Spooner weighed 40 stone 9lbs (258kg), measured 4ft 3in (1.3m) across the shoulders and could only get about in a trap. He survived a stabbing because the fat prevented the blade from reaching a vital organ.

In 1551, when the young Edward VI's Council ordered that 'such churche plate as remaineth be emplaced unto His Highness's Use', Shuttington was among several Warwickshire churches to report that theirs had been conveniently stolen.

Founded in 1159 by William Burdet, **Alvecote Priory** is now a county council picnic area. The small Benedictine foundation was originally a cell to a larger one at Great Malvern in Worcestershire. Most of its buildings were pulled down about 1700, but the lower walls of the church remain. There is a good late 14th-century doorway and a square, stone-built, 13th-century **dovecote**.

Across the Coventry Canal is Warwickshire Wildlife Trust's 225-hectare (555-acre) **Alvecote Pools Nature Reserve**, an SSSI since 1955. The pools attract many birds for breeding and passage, and the reserve is noted for sphagnums, bladderwort and marsh orchids. A public footpath passes through.

The tiny former mining village of **Alvecote** consists of a line of terraced houses and a post office store facing the Trent Valley railway line.

SNITTERFIELD [Stratford-on-Avon]

SP2160: 3 miles (5km) N of Stratford-upon-Avon

The glorious view from the village's strikingly situated **war memorial** on White Horse Hill includes the Welcombe Obelisk, Stratford and the Cotswolds. The memorial stands beside King's Lane, where **Charles II**, disguised as Jane Lane's servant, rode when escaping south after defeat at the Battle of Worcester in 1651.

The village's name is of Saxon origin (Snytenfeld – 'place of snipe'), though from earlier days a Roman urn has been unearthed near the church. In Victorian times, brick making was a local industry. William Shakespeare's father John was a Snitterfield man. His father, Richard, farmed land rented from John Arden of Wilmcote, whose daughter John Shakespeare married.

For about a century from 1816, the Philips family (see STRATFORD-UPON-AVON) were lords of the manor. They built estate houses, showing a predilection for Gothic windows and bargeboards, and from the 1950s there was further expansion.

The **church of St James the Great** stands in a large, green churchyard. Its tower and nave are 14th century, but the ragstone chancel is mostly a rebuilding of 1858. There are Philips family memorials in the chancel and four Saxon bishops of Worcester are pictured in the east window. Two fine stall fronts and stall ends date from about 1530.

Among the incumbents was the poet **Richard Jago** (see ULLENHALL), who became curate in 1737 and vicar in 1754. In his day, the church was in the Worcester diocese.

A nearby brick wall leading to **Park Cottages** (of about 1700, with old brickwork, dormers and high chimneys) surrounded the former Snitterfield Manor, where the earls of Coventry succeeded the Hales family. In Church Road, **The Dower House** is large, plain and of red brick. A long, white, stuccoed **house** displays an impressive Gothic repertoire of half-timbered end wall, stone tower (with a door and filled-in window, both ogee-headed), quaint windows and bargeboards.

Opposite the church, **The Old Vicarage** has gables and decorative tall chimneys. Hutton says Jago's daughters planted silver birches in the garden. Downhill, an ancient brick **barn** with unpainted timbering and small windows is believed to have been part of the Shakespeare property.

From a green, where **Park House** stands behind red-brick former stables capped by a dome, Smiths Lane descends past thatched **Fern Cottage**, which has a gable-end of cruck construction. At the bottom are a small inn, the Foxhunter, and the red-brick **Snitterfield Methodist Church**, with lancets and a tall, pointed bellcote. Beyond, again in red brick, stand the school of 1884 (in memory of Robert N. Philips), the modern village hall and the tall Snitterfield Arms.

To the north-east, in village-less Fulbrook parish, a Victorian farmhouse at **Northbrook** (or Norbrook) occupies the site of a moated manor where some of the escaping Gunpowder Plotters sheltered on the night after their failed attempt to blow up Parliament.

SOUTHAM [Stratford-on-Avon]

SP4161: 6½ miles (10km) SE of Royal Leamington Spa

The small town stands on the modern

Leamington to Daventry road and on the ancient Welsh Road used by Cambrian drovers bound for London's Smithfield Market. The River Stowe flows through to join the Itchen. Roman coins have been found in the churchyard, and a charter granted by King Ethelred the Unready exists from 998. Recorded in Domesday Book as Sucham, the town had a weekly market from 1227.

Southam still holds an October Mop Fair, though its Runaway (or Draffletrail) Mop, at which dissatisfied servants and those who had not obtained a situation were given a second chance, was long ago discontinued.

In the 1540s, John Leland found it 'a modest market town of a single street' and crossed 'a small bridge on the road to Banbury', which Banbury Road now bypasses. Known as **Brown's Bridge**, it retains a parapet of old stone.

Visiting Southam in 1641, Charles I, annoyed by the town's failure to ring the bells, had his men lock the church door until a fine was paid. Nevertheless, two nights before the Battle of Edge Hill in October 1642, he returned to sleep at the Manor House. One of the Civil War's first skirmishes took place about a mile west of Southam on 23 August 1642 – the day after Charles raised his standard at Nottingham.

A disastrous fire in 1741 means that there are few buildings earlier than that, but several coaching inns recall the time when Southam was on the London – Warwick – Birmingham route. One of them, the **Black Dog**, has a galloping black knight on its sign – a reminder that Edward II's favourite, Piers Gaveston (see LEEK WOOTTON), called the Earl of Warwick 'the Black Dog of Arden'.

Another, the 16th-century grey stone and mullioned **Old Mint**, is noted for its collection of antique armoury. It is said to owe its name to Charles I having retreated there after Edge Hill and melted down locally commandeered silverware to pay his soldiers. This seems doubtful because the King made for Oxford after the battle, but tokens may have been minted on the premises.

The Manor House of Elizabethan times, with carved gables, is now a pharmacy. A long **National School** of 1816, in polychromatic brick, has a pedimented central part. By the Gothic-windowed **Stoneythorpe Hotel**, a pillar topped by an urn marks the site of Britain's first provident dispensary, established in 1823.

An avenue of limes planted in the year of Waterloo (1815) leads past long lines of old headstones to **St James's Church**. The building replaced an earlier church in the 14th century. Its broach spire, with four clock faces, was added a century later and soars 126ft (38m) above the ground.

The nave is as tall as it is broad (53ft) and its timber roof is supported by decorative wooden bosses. The pulpit, which is probably Jacobean, was lost for many years and found in a barn at Wormleighton.

Fragments of lettering on the tower wall were discovered when a 17th-century gallery was removed in 1919, and the arms of Charles I were presented in 1936 by the Tailors' Hall at Bristol. Among the memorials are several to the Chamberlaynes of Stoneythorpe Hall. Augustine Barnhere, who was briefly rector in 1566, courageously gave time, money and comfort to Protestant martyrs under Mary Tudor and happily survived those dreadful years.

According to Alfred Watkins' *The Old Straight Track*, the church is set on a ley linking it to Warwick Castle. A fieldpath from the church leads to a **Holy Well**, where the cold water (now nearly dried up) was considered a remedy for eye infections.

The Old House Retreat, an early 17th-century town house, was acquired by the Sisters of the Poor Child Jesus in 1876 and restored in 1988-89. Behind it, the Catholic church of **Our Lady and St Wulstan** (tall and brick-built in 1925) adjoins **The Convent of Our Lady** (brick and Gothic of 1892). Also Gothic, the white-fronted **Congregational church** dates from 1839.

Stoneythorpe Hall stands by the River Itchen and was home to the Chamberlaynes for 350 years. They traced their descent from John, Comte de Tancarville, Lord Chamberlain to William the Conqueror. The lovely, gabled, stone house, with great mullioned windows, dates from the early 17th century, though there were many additions and changes over the next 200 years. A Chamberlayne lived in the West Wing until the 1990s.

In the dining room, a stained-glass window records a tradition that Sir Thomas Chamberlayne of Princethorpe, Ambassador to the Emperor Charles V and to Philip II of Spain, introduced both watches and coaches to England in the 16th century.

SPERNALL [Stratford-on-Avon]

SP0862: 3 miles (5km) N of Alcester

This medieval village just off the Roman Ryknild Street was depopulated by the Black Death in the 1340s. Today there is no more than a redundant church, a former rectory and a few farms. Brisk but shallow, the River Arrow skims the former **St Leonard's Church**, which stands, concealed by trees, off a farm drive and is in the care of the Ancient Monuments Society.

Neo-Norman of 1844, its most striking feature is a rose window at the east end. An earlier building was a chapel of Studley Priory, from which the small, grey stone, red-roofed church retains a late 13th-century west window and a north door with panels of about 1535. There are monuments to the Chambers family of Gorcot Hall (see MAPPLEBOROUGH GREEN).

Incumbents included **Henry Teonge** (1621-89), who went roving as a naval chaplain in his mid-fifties and recorded the experience in lively diaries published in 1825. The Georgian **rectory** presents its workaday rear brickwork and tall chimneys to the church, but is seen as smart and classically stuccoed from the north.

At Spernall Ash on Alcester Road, in Sambourne parish, a Victorian **postbox**, restored in 1997, has listed building status.

STOCKINGFORD [Nuneaton]

SP3391: 2 miles (3km) W of Nuneaton

Stockingford became part of Nuneaton in 1639 and is a western suburb of the town. It was recorded in 1155 as Stoccingford, meaning 'a ford near an enclosure' (in the Forest of Arden). In the 19th century, mining and brickyards were the main industries.

St Paul's is a red-brick Georgian church of 1822-23, with round windows in the upper tower and a balustrade. The chancel was added in 1897. A tablet commemorates the Reverend J.E. Jones, who appears in George Eliot's *Scenes of Clerical Life*. **George Eliot** (Mary Ann Evans, 1819-80) was born nearby at South Farm on the Arbury Hall estate.

Arbury Hall, the home of the Newdegate family since 1586, is perhaps the finest example in England of the early Gothic Revival style. Earlier buildings on the site were an Augustinian priory and an Elizabethan mansion, of which features remain.

Richard Newdigate (the spelling has varied from time to time) added the classical stables and the chapel in the 1670s and Sir Roger Newdigate Gothicised the house from 1750. Sir Roger also founded the Newdigate prize for verse at Oxford and was portrayed by George Eliot as Sir Christopher Cheverel of Cheverel Manor, which he transformed 'from ugliness into beauty'. The present owner of the hall is Viscount Daventry, Lord Lieutenant of Warwickshire, a collateral descendant of Richard Newdigate.

STOCKTON [Stratford-on-Avon]

SP4363: 2 miles (3km) NE of Southam

The name, first recorded in 1272, means 'a

fenced enclosure'. We see today a former industrial village that developed near the Nelson Cement Works from the early 19th century. Using the local blue lias clay and aided by the Grand Union Canal, the works contributed to many major developments, including London's Victoria Embankment. Though Nelsons closed long ago, a large cement works is still active a mile away at Long Itchington.

In 1898, the Stockton workers found an almost perfect ichthyosaurus fossil, some 20 million years old and over 19ft (6m) long, which went to the Natural History Museum.

After leaving the cement works with heart problems in the 1940s, a local craftsman, Charles Gardner, achieved a world-wide reputation as a woodturner. The Neal family have long carried on the tradition of making chairs in the Gimson style learned from Edward Gardiner (see PRIORS MARSTON).

When the nave and chancel of **St Michael's and All Angels Church** were built of the local blue lias in 1863-73, the Perpendicular red-sandstone tower and the ancient base of the porch were retained from the medieval church. Except for its medieval chancel arch, the interior is thoroughly Victorian. Above an old four-wheeled bier, sculptured heads support the rafters, on which are carved the heads of four bishops.

The most notable rector of Stockton was Archdeacon Colley, in the early 20th century, who kept a glass-topped coffin in his study, ready for the day he would be called. He wore his mitre and gown at all times and blew a cornet at the gate to announce the Sunday service.

Behind the church stands the tall, red-brick **Manor Farm** – the old manor house from the 17th century, though altered in the 18th. The white-walled Barley Mow faces the speckled-brick **School House** of 1843, behind which the present school dates from 1906. The same year saw the red-brick **Stockton Methodist Church** built in Post Office Lane. The parallel High Street has the small Crown Inn, brick-built and ivy-covered, the Neals' workshop (formerly the Co-op) and (set on a tiny green by an old water pump) an **erratic boulder** moved from Mount Sorrel in Leicestershire during the Ice Age.

In Victoria Terrace, rows of former cement workers' cottages, built by Nelsons in the late 19th century, lead to the village hall of the same era and the Working Mens' Club of 1914, which retains the name of the Nelson works.

Out on the Southam to Rugby road, brick-built **Stockton House** was the home of the Nelson family.

STONELEIGH [Warwick]

SP3372: 3 miles (5km) E of Kenilworth

The Stanlei of Domesday Book and one of Warwickshire's loveliest villages, Stoneleigh lies where the little River Sowe flows past Motslow Hill to join the Avon and is a highlight of the Centenary Way. The hill's name derives from the Moot, or hundred court, formerly held on a mound raised there. During a Civil War skirmish, Roundheads are said to have fired at the church below while the parson was in his pulpit.

The Sowe is crossed by **Stoneleigh (or Rennie) Bridge**, designed by Sir John Rennie in 1840, with eight stone arches. Further south, on the River Avon and now bypassed, are the nine arches and cutwaters of the 14th-century **Stare Bridge**, which takes its name from tiny Stareton nearby.

The riverside meadows belong to a preservation trust set up in 1982. Overlooking them is the red-sandstone **church of St Mary the Virgin**. It dates from Norman times, though the Perpendicular belfry was added later. A quaint verse carved on a stone outside the south wall commemorates Humphrey How, porter to Lord Leigh, who died in 1669.

In the north wall is a large filled-in Norman arch, and carved snakes and dragons gnaw their tails above the north door. The richly decorated chancel arch is one of the county's finest. The font is Norman too, from about 1300. It came from Maxstoke Priory after lying amongst the ruins for 250 years. Early 19th-century fittings include box pews and the pulpit. The organ is 18th century, rebuilt and enlarged in 1968.

In the chancel is a monument to Alice, Duchess Dudley (1578-1668), and her daughter Alicia. Alice Leigh of Stoneleigh married Sir Robert Dudley, an illegitimate son of Elizabeth I's Earl of Leicester, but he ran away to Italy, accompanied by a 'page' who turned out to be the beautiful Elizabeth Southwell. Alice was granted his father's estates by the Crown, and in 1645 Charles I created her a duchess in her own right.

Her mother (also Alice) built the long row of stone **almshouses** by the village green in 1594. Another stone row across the road, now **The Village Club**, was originally a gaol and later a coach house used by the Leighs when attending church.

Further along, the superb black and white **Manor Farm House** has three gables, two from the 16th century and one from the 17th. Early occupiers seem to have been unpopular. Richard Hopkins (1566) 'made dunghills in the street to the annoyance of neighbours' and in 1600 Thomas Dunton provoked an innkeeper, William Winsmore, to strike him on the head with a fork handle – the fine was three shillings and four pence.

Today Stoneleigh has no inn. Winsmore's Three Swans was demolished long before Lord Leigh closed the 16th-century Stoneleigh Arms in the early 1890s – because cyclists were beginning to call and, worse, to whistle at his daughter Cordelia. The premises are now cottages – 19 and 20 Birmingham Road.

Near the church gate stand the 18th-century **parsonage**, gabled and ivy-covered, and **The Cruck Cottage**, a name indicating its method of timber construction. On the green, a still-active **smithy** has the date 1851 in its brickwork. A map of 1597 shows a smithy there.

The history of **Stoneleigh Abbey**, Warwickshire's finest Georgian house, began in 1154 when Henry I granted the land to Cistercian monks, but came to a temporary halt when it was suppressed in the 1530s by Henry VIII. Survivals from that period include the beautiful 14th-century gatehouse and a dormitory undercroft.

Sir Thomas Leigh, a Lord Mayor of London and the Duchess's father, built an Elizabethan house. Francis Smith of Warwick designed the superb Baroque west wing (1714-26), and there were further 18th- and 19th-century additions. A disastrous fire in 1960 caused damage not fully restored for 24 years.

The Leighs came in 1561, but Lord Leigh no longer lives at the house, which has been converted to luxury apartments and is managed by the Stoneleigh Abbey Preservation Trust. Charles I and Queen Victoria were entertained at the Abbey, as was Jane Austen, whose mother was a Leigh. She took the house as her model for Sotherton Court in *Mansfield Park*, describing it as having 'an alarming number of rooms'. The site of the Royal Agricultural Show has occupied part of the grounds since 1963.

At Stareton, Stoneleigh Deer Park is a Massey Ferguson training centre. **Tantara Lodge**, the gatehouse on its eastern side, which has a carving of a two-headed eagle, is impressive.

STRATFORD-UPON-AVON [Stratford-on-Avon]

SP2054: 8 miles (13km) SW of Warwick

Though Stratford is The Birthplace, it is in its own right a large, attractive country town with an extensive central area of buildings dating from Georgian times and much earlier. The medieval street layout is unchanged and Stratford's ancient Mop

Fair is still held annually in October. Non-Shakespearean attractions include the Brass Rubbing Centre, the Teddy Bear Museum and the Butterfly Farm.

William Shakespeare was born at Stratford in 1564 and died in the town in 1616. Though he lived in London from about 1585, he retained his hometown links, bought land locally and retired there some five years before his death. The Shakespeare Birthplace Trust has three properties within the town (the Birthplace, Nash's House and Hall Croft), plus Anne Hathaway's Cottage at Shottery and Mary Arden's House at Wilmcote.

Shakespeare's Birthplace, in Henley Street, dates from the 16th century and was originally two houses. The birth probably occurred in the western part. The buildings were subsequently much altered and were restored in 1858 to match a drawing of 1769. The house is half-timbered and boldly gabled, its furnishings contemporary with Shakespeare.

Next door stands the **Shakespeare Centre**, opened in 1964 for the 400th anniversary of the poet's birth. It houses the offices of the Birthplace Trust, a library, a study centre and a local history archive. The Bard retired to New Place in Chapel Street, but the house was later rebuilt and finally demolished in 1759.

An **Elizabethan knot garden** occupies the site, next door to **Nash's House**, the home of Shakespeare's grand-daughter Elizabeth, whose first husband was Thomas Nash. It contains outstanding period furniture and a museum of Stratford's history. Further west, in Old Town, stands **Hall's Croft**, where Shakespeare's daughter Susanna lived with her husband Dr John Hall. A timber-framed late 16th-century building, it includes a 17th-century dispensary and has Tudor and Jacobean furniture.

Shakespeare is commemorated by the **Gower Memorial** in Bancroft Gardens, created by Lord Ronald Gower in 1888, and by Jethro Cossins' Gothic **American Fountain** in Rother Street, dedicated by the actor Sir Henry Irving in Queen Victoria's Golden Jubilee Year of 1887.

A bust of a rather puffy-looking Bard, with a real quill pen in his hand, is placed above his grave in **Holy Trinty Church**. Impressive when seen from across the Avon, the church is in the Early English and Perpendicular styles, though the central spire was rebuilt by William Hiorn of Warwick in 1763 and restorations were carried out between 1888 and 1898. A variety of diverting misericords were carved about 1500 and there is an original hammerbeam roof. The earliest of several monuments is the large tomb-chest of Dean Balshall (1491), its brass missing.

St James's Church in Guild Street is Victorian Decorated (1853-55). The tower and spire were added in 1875 and 1893. **St Gregory's Roman Catholic Church** in Warwick Road, with an apse and thin lancets, dates from 1866, and the pedimented **Baptist Chapel** in Payton Street from 1835.

A long row of vertically timbered **almshouses** in Chapel Street were built about 1427 by the Guild of the Holy Cross, which was established before 1269. The **Guild Chapel** stands nearby, its nave and tower of the late 15th century, but the chancel somewhat earlier.

The 18th-century **Masons' Croft** in Church Street (now the University of Birmingham's Shakespeare Institute) was the home from 1901 until her death of the once-popular novelist **Marie Corelli** (Mary MacKay, 1855-1924), who is buried in Stratford Cemetery. She took a lively interest in local matters and was instrumental in the renovation of the timber-framed **Harvard House** in High Street. The house was built in 1596 by Thomas Rogers, whose daughter Katherine was the grandmother of **John Harvard**, founder of Harvard University in the USA.

The neighbouring **Garrick Inn** is named after the great Shakespearean actor **David**

Garrick (1717-79), though the building is much earlier – late 16th century. Garrick presented the bust of Shakespeare, in lead, on the front of the handsome Palladian **town hall** of 1767.

The Royal Shakespeare Theatre is an undemonstrative brick building of 1932 overlooking the river. A forerunner of modern architecture in England, it replaced the theatre financed (1874-79) by the local brewer Charles Edward Flower, which (though burnt-out in 1926) partly survives as the rounded **Swan Theatre**, opened in 1986.

The Avon is crossed by the 14-arched **Clopton Bridge**, built by Sir Hugh Clopton (later Lord Mayor of London) in the 1480s, to which the tollhouse was added in 1814, and by the 9-arched **Tramway Bridge** of 1823. The 16-mile horse-drawn tramway ran to Moreton-in-Marsh (see DARLINGSCOTE). In the 1540s John Leland found Clopton Bridge 'very smalle and ille, and at high waters very harde to passe by'.

The **Stratford-upon-Avon Canal** was opened from Birmingham to Hockley Heath in 1798, but the rest of it only in 1816. After falling into disuse, it was re-opened by its then owners, the National Trust, in 1964. It has since reverted to British Waterways.

North of the town, **Clopton House** is 17th century (early and late), but greatly altered in 1830 and now converted to flats. The materials are stone, timber and brick, and there is a freestanding polygonal tower and a lodge. The house was connected with the Gunpowder Plot of 1605, being then rented by one of the conspirators, Ambrose Rokewood. The local militia raided it and took away items used in the Catholic mass. In 1999, Stratford District Council purchaed 30 hectares (74 acres) at nearby Clopton Fields for recreational use.

A hill in the adjoining **Welcombe Hills Country Park** is capped by the 120ft **Welcombe Obelisk** of 1876. It commemorates Mark Philips, Manchester's first MP after the 1832 Reform Act. His father Robert, a cotton manufacturer, became Lord of the Manor of Snitterfield in 1816.

In 1867 Mark Philips built a vast Jacobean-gabled mansion, now the **Welcombe Hotel**. The writer and statesman **Sir George Otto Trevelyan** inherited it through his wife. Their son, the historian **G.M. Trevelyan**, was born there in 1876. It became a hotel in 1931 under the LMS Railway Company.

On the Welcombe Hills in 1643 Parliamentarian soldiers under Lord Brooke of Warwick Castle put to flight a Royalist horse troop occupying Stratford.

STRETTON-ON-DUNSMORE [Rugby]

SP4072: 7 miles (12km) NE of Leamington Spa

The village stands on the Fosse Way, a channelled stream running through its pleasant centre and small green. Further out, there has been much modern development. There are two inns – the central Oak and Black Dog, and, to the south, the Shoulder of Mutton.

In 1795 **Joseph Elkington** of Stretton was awarded £1000 by the government for a new land drainage system, first employed at nearby Princethorpe in 1764. The money was used to found the family firm of Elkingtons, the silversmiths. In the centre, **Moor Farm** is a medieval twin-gabled house of unpainted half-timbering on a stone base.

On high ground, the ashlar-walled **All Saints'** of 1835-37 by Rickman is a large impressive Commissioners' church. From its small medieval predecessor, the outlines of which can be seen in the churchyard, the present building incorporates a 17th-century chancel window of Christ at Emmaus and a tablet to a vicar, the Revd William D. Clark, who died in 1817 and 'provided for the reconstruction of the church'. The churchyard also has an old stone pillar capped by a metal sundial.

Across the road, **Stretton House**, of Georgian chequered brick, was the vicarage. Its neighbour is the **Manor House**, partly of the 16th century.

On a traffic island on the now tamed Dunsmore Heath, a large Portland stone memorial stands 'Where Telford's Coaching Road from London to Holyhead Is crossed by the Roman Fosse Way'. Unveiled on Empire Day (May 25) 1921, it marks the spot where George V reviewed 'the Immortal XXIX Division, Shortly before they embarked for Active Service in Gallipoli'.

To the west, on Knightlow Hill, just within Ryton-on-Dunsmore parish and within yards of the busy dual carriageway, is the hollow base of an ancient **cross**. It marks the meeting place of the Manor Court, where at sunrise on St Martin's Day (November 11) the agent of the Duke of Buccleuch, Lord of the Manor, still collects the Wroth Silver from representatives of the 25 parishes in Knighlow Hundred. The ceremony is understood to date back to about 1190 and may have been an early form of road tax.

STRETTON-ON-FOSSE [Stratford-on-Avon]

SP2238: 3 miles (4km) SW of Shipston-on-Stour

A quiet village off the Fosse Way and near the Gloucestershire border. There was a village here in Saxon times and a priest in residence when the Domesday survey was made. The horse tramway from Stratford to Moreton-in-Marsh – opened in 1826 and later part of the Great Western Railway – ran nearby. The track was taken up in 1961. On the county boundary is the site of the deserted medieval village of **Ditchford Frary**.

Stretton's older buildings occupy high ground. The stone-built Plough Inn lies at the bottom of the hill and midway stands **St Peter's Church** – an 1841 rebuilding with a fine hammerbeam roof. The graveyard has several splendid monuments, including Edward Gibbes's table-tomb of 1748 with impressive sculptures at each end.

Table-tomb, Stretton-on-Fosse

Next door stands the **Court House**, which is late Georgian but with a 17th-century wing. Across the road is the stone **Glebe Cottage**. Behind it, **The Old Rectory** of 1690 hides from prying eyes. Of a cluster of cottages uphill, two are stone-built and thatched, and **The Malthouse** has mullioned windows asymmetrically set in ancient stone walls.

The Manor House, built in the Cotswold style in 1836, incorporates a row of older cottages alongside the tall, gabled main block, behind which stretches brick and half-timberwork.

STRETTON-UNDER-FOSSE [Rugby]

SP4581: 5 miles (8km) N of Rugby

The village, its Main Street lined with lovely old cottages, lies just off the ancient

Fosse Way and the modern M6. A brick-built inn (the Union Jack, but formerly the Farriers) has the date 1895 under a wooden central gable. Opposite, behind a brick outer wall thickly coated with ivy, **The Manor House** is of stone with timber gables.

A large corner house (**number 27**) is black and white half-timbered, its upper floor partly overhanging. A former **Congregational Chapel** of 1780-81 (brick, with a pyramid roof) hides behind other buildings.

Nearby **Newbold Revel**, a grand mansion built in 1716 for Sir Fulwar Skipwith on the site of an earlier manor house, is attributed to Francis Smith of Warwick as architect. Now a prison officers' college, it was substantial and impressive even before the 'Cricketers' Wing' was added about 1900 to accommodate visiting teams. Outbuildings include stables, chapel and assembly hall.

The greater fame of Newbold Revel, however, is as the home of **Sir Thomas Malory** (died 1471), who inherited the manor house about 1433 and is generally considered to be the author of *Le Morte D'Arthur*. Published by William Caxton in 1485, the classic retelling of the Arthurian legends was written while the author was in prison for offences that included armed assault and rape.

STUDLEY [Stratford-on-Avon]

SP0763: 4 miles (6km) N of Alcester

This large village beside the little River Arrow and on the Roman Ryknild Street is recorded in Domesday Book, its name meaning 'horse-pasture'. Its prosperity, like that of Redditch across the Worcestershire border, was based on the manufacture of needles and fishing tackle, a local industry first mentioned in 1695. The main population growth occurred after 1800, when James Pardow, the first to apply steam power to needle making, opened a mill in Castle Road.

Studley is not scenic, but has features of interest. Alcester Road (on the line of Ryknild Street) and High Street meet at the long, red-roofed and white-walled **Old Barley Mow**. Until converted to an inn for the benefit of travellers by the monks of Studley Priory in 1534, the building was probably their granary and salt store.

It faces a substantial **house** with square half-timbering, now in commercial use. Round a corner, the **Shakespeare Inn** has an entrance from coaching days, and down Alcester Road the **Duke of Marlborough** is a grand Victorian inn. All this is unfortunately dominated by a hideous and aggressively gabled supermarket of about 1990.

Nearby **Priory Farm** incorporates parts of the Augustinian priory founded by Peter de Corbuson about 1150. The date 1539 on a chimney stack refers to its conversion to a house by Sir Edmund Knightley of Fawsley three years after the monastery was dissolved.

On Alcester Road, **Studley Methodist Church** of 1872 is an odd concept, its square-pillared stone portico with leafy capitals fitting uneasily onto the red-brick nave. Further along, **St Mary's Roman Catholic Church** (1853) by J.A. Hansom (of the Victorian cabs) is a large, bellcoted and buttressed building of grey stone. A gabled white presbytery adjoins it.

The **Manor House**, a handsome brick mansion with tall flanking Ionic pilasters and a Tuscan doorway, was built about 1680 for Thomas Chambers. Now renamed Mountbatten House, it has been the Commonwealth Headquarters of the Royal Life Saving Society since 1980. Off Toms Town Lane, stands a **Baptist Chapel** of 1847 – in brick, but classical and pedimented.

Three major buildings lie outside the village. The **church of the Nativity of the Blessed Virgin Mary** was built about 1105 on a Saxon foundation. Its Norman features include the north wall of the nave and the north doorway, which has a hood-mould and a well-preserved zigzag arch, the latter not necessarily original. Above it, time has smoothed away the features of a small, carved head.

The south doorway is Early English and the windows on that side 14th century. The tower and west windows are Perpendicular. Restorations took place in 1888 and 1935. Within are monuments to the Chambers and Dewes of Gorcott and Mappleborough Green, and a large 13th-century coffin lid with a foliated cross.

Prominent in the churchyard is the vault of the family of the splendidly named Sir Francis Lyttelton Holyoake-Goodricke, MP, who built Studley Castle in 1834 and died in reduced circumstances in 1865. On a weathered table-tomb, with carved draperies, cherubs and coats of arms, 'John Knottesforde' and '1781' can be made out. The Knottesfordes inherited the priory from Sir Edmund Knightley and remained until 1791.

William Jaffray, 2nd Baronet of Skilts (1852-1914, see MAPPLEBOROUGH GREEN) lies with his wife, Mabel Augusta, in a large, low, railed tomb.

Beside the church stands **The Old Castle**, a lovely half-timbered and gabled early Tudor building on a site first used by the Normans. There is evidence of a moat or earthwork beside the lane.

Prominent on a hilltop, **Studley Castle** (1834) is a Gothic fantasy with a large octagonal stone keep and lesser turrets below it. From 1903 it was a college, founded by Frances, Countess of Warwick, for women 'in the higher branches of agriculture', and is currently a marketing centre for Rover Cars.

SUTTON-UNDER-BRAILES [Stratford-on-Avon]

SP2937: 3 miles (5km) SE of Shipston-on-Stour

Beneath Brailes Hill, scattered 17th-century stone cottages and a farmhouse surround a vast green dotted with trees and a small railed war memorial. At its edge, like a pale, carved Gothic pillar, stands a thick dead oak.

The tiny village is pre-Domesday Book and was until 1840 an island of Gloucestershire within Warwickshire, the result of its having been a possession of the Saxon monastery at Deerhurst. The young River Stour separates the village from Cherington and Stourton.

Brailes Hill House, overlooking the green, has old mullions and a later ashlared and rounded wing. Its neighbour, veiled by trees, is Regency.

In the **Church of St Thomas à Becket**, primitive carvings of Mary and the infant Jesus surmount the arch of the graceful 13th-century chancel. There are no aisles and the interior walls are of bare stone, having been scraped in 1879, when the west wall was rebuilt and the tall, narrow Norman north doorway rediscovered.

Soberingly, the verse on the memorial to William Wilkes, who died aged 42 in 1803, begins, *'In perfect Health I went from home, Not thinking that my Glafs was run.'* In the porch beneath the 14th-century tower are several benefactors' boards, the last dated 1907. A Perpendicular nave window is quaintly bowed and the table-tomb of Thomas Billing (1675) has a splendid carved cornucopia.

By the church, the small, stone **school** of 1852 is now a cottage. Down the lane lies **The Moat House**, a long stone-built and thatched cottage. The **Manor House** stands along the Brailes road and the disused **Sutton Mill** out among fields by Sutton Brook.

TANWORTH-IN-ARDEN [Stratford-on-Avon]

SP1170: 4 miles (6km) NW of Henley-in-Arden

A tree-lined village green leads towards a

large, spired church, beyond which the land drops to the little River Alne and the Birmingham to Stratford railway line. Though dating from Saxon times, the settlement does not appear in Domesday Book because it was, in Dugdale's words, 'antiently a member of Brailes' in the south of the county.

In the 19th century, Tanworth became '-in-Arden' to avoid confusion with Staffordshire's Tamworth. Properties on the north side of the main street used to be in Tanworth parish and those opposite in Wootton Wawen. The civil parish boundary was moved in 1895, but the ecclesiastical one remains the same.

The earls of Warwick were lords of the manor until the death of the Kingmaker in 1471. He was succeeded by the Duke of Clarence (brother of Edward IV and Richard III, and said to have been drowned in a butt of malmsey), then by the Throckmortons, the Archers and the Muntzes.

The Tanworth Association for the Prosecution of Felons, founded in 1784, is one of the few surviving pre-Victorian law enforcement agencies. Its functions, traditionally chaired by a member of the Burman family, are now purely social.

A St George's Day cattle fair and a Michaelmas Day mop, or hiring fair, used to be held on The Green, where the Bell Inn was kept for many years by former British welterweight champion boxer **Jack Hood**.

Several shops and businesses survive, and the former uses of some cottages, such as The Old Boot Shop, are identifiable by their names or windows. Danzey Green windmill, which stood to the south, is now in working order at the Avoncroft Museum of Buildings, near Bromsgrove, Worcestershire.

In the Age of Chivalry, when nearby Aspley was a separate parish, the famous knight **Sir Walter Manny** of Hainault held it. A hero of the *Chronicles* of the French historian Froissart, he founded the Carthusian monastery of the Charterhouse in London.

As befits one of the county's biggest parishes, the early 14th-century **church of St Mary Magdalene** is large. In 1790 it underwent a disastrous rebuilding, ironically during the long incumbency (1780-1829) of the Reverend Phillip Wren, grandson of the architect Sir Christopher Wren – whether he was villain or victim is uncertain. In 1880, when an attempt was made to put things right, many old features were rediscovered. There are monuments to the Archers of Umberslade and a 13th-century wooden chest.

An unobtrusive gravestone beside the path reads '**Nick Drake**, 1948-1974', to which the names and dates of his parents have been added. Nick, a brother of the actress Gabrielle Drake, was a gifted singer, guitarist and songwriter whose short life was marred by depression. The verdict on his death from an overdose of prescribed drugs was suicide. Though not great sellers in his lifetime, when reissued on CD in the 1990s his albums attracted a younger generation of pop artists and a cult grew up. A biography appeared in 1997.

Near the church is the ivy-covered **Aspley House**, built in 1808 by John Burman, a banker and member of a distinguished Warwickshire family. His business premises, the Regency **Bank House**, stand just along the street. Arched sash windows are features of another building that proclaims its former use, **Doctor's House** on Doctor's Hill. At **Whalebone Cottage**, Vicarage Hill, a whalebone acts as a gateway arch.

The Mile Walk, a right-of-way from Tanworth to **Umberslade Park**, was used by the Archers when driving to and from church. Andrew Archer built Umberslade about 1695 on the site of an earlier hall. Though his brother Thomas was an architect, the hall was probably the work of Francis or William Smith. Thomas Archer designed St Philip's Cathedral in Birmingham, using stone quarried at Umberslade.

The Archers could trace their line from the late 12th century until it became extinct in 1778. Lord Plymouth, a relative, succeeded them. In 1852, when Dr Edward Johnstone of Birmingham was using the hall as a nursing home, the poet Tennyson became a patient. Soon after, the Birmingham MP G.F. Muntz lived there as tenant. His son of the same name bought the property in 1859, and the family remained until recent years. Umberslade is now divided into luxury flats.

Nearby, above the busy M42, stands an **obelisk** built in 1747 by Thomas, Baron Archer of Umberslade – seemingly as one of the pieces of landscape furniture then popular. At Obelisk Farm is a small **mortuary chapel** of 1834, perhaps occupying the site of a chapel mentioned in 1218, and of another built in 1567 but in ruins by 1730.

North of the M42 are the **Earlswood Lakes**. The three wooded pools (34 hectares) were constructed in 1821 on the site of Earlswood Common as feeders for the Stratford-upon-Avon Canal. Together with Warwickshire Wildlife Trust's **Clowes Wood Nature Reserve** and New Fallings Coppice, they form a designated SSSI.

Down a tree-lined avenue at Nuthurst, near Hockley Heath, is the splendid **Umberslade Baptist Church** of 1877. The pale Gothic appearance, tall slender spire and remote setting are all unusual for its denomination.

TEMPLE GRAFTON [Stratford-on-Avon)]

SP1254: 2½ miles (4km) SE of Alcester

A small village at a minor crossroads, its infertile soil made it the 'Hungry Grafton' of the rhyme (see BIDFORD-ON-AVON). By the mid-19th century, large-scale quarrying had damaged the landscape, but the scars healed long ago. The village narrowly escaped disaster in 1944 when a Flying Fortress crashed nearby after its crew had bailed out.

Top Farm is a charming Queen Anne house. Otherwise, much of what we see was built by James William Carlisle, Lord of the Manor from 1862 to 1892. First came **The Old Vicarage** in 1867, of red brick and gabled. The **Church of England Primary School** (Gothic, with massive timber-framing at the gable-ends), sprang up across the road in 1874. A year later the large **St Andrew's Church** replaced a building of the Knights Templars (from whom the village took its name) and Knights Hospitalers. There is documentary evidence of a Saxon church in 710, when it belonged to Evesham Abbey. The new church was built in early 14th-century style, with a nave, north aisle and chancel, and is capped by a timber-framed belfry.

The fact that in 1582 a licence was issued for the marriage of a William Shakespeare to Anne Whateley has led to speculation that 'Whateley' was an error for 'Hathaway' and that the Bard was wed at St Andrew's. It is possible that his wife-to-be, Anne Hathaway, was Anne Whateley's servant at the nearby 16th-century **Hillborough Manor**, where a more recent occupier was **John Barton**, distinguished as a producer at Stratford's Royal Shakespeare Theatre. An ancient, circular, stone **dovecote** stands nearby. This is the 'Haunted Hillborough' of the rhyme.

To the south, Carlisle's timber-framed **Grafton Court** of 1876-79 is in the Arts and Crafts style. It has stained-glass windows depicting scenes from Chaucer and Shakespeare. Along the road, the hamlet of **Ardens Grafton** begins with the thatched **Grafton Cottage** – brick on a stone base. **The Chapel House**, also thatched, is black and white, and the names of the stone-built **Malt House Cottage** and the brick **Post Office Cottage** indicate their former uses. Beyond the latter stand the delightful brick and stone cottages of **Little Britain**.

Warwickshire Wildlife Trust's **Grove Hill Nature Reserve** lies off Exhall Road.

THURLASTON [Rugby]

SP4671: 3½ miles (5km) SW of Rugby

The only road in or out of the secluded village leaves the Dunchurch to Coventry highway and bridges the M45 before winding past modern houses. On a small green at the north end of the broad Main Street are the two-seater **stocks**. Further down, **The Old Forge** is heavily thatched, as is **Rose Cottage** in Church Lane. A tall, brick-built **tower-mill**, without sails, has been converted to domestic use.

St Edmund's Church, an unusual red-brick building of 1849, has served as both church and school. The interior is large and impressively timber-roofed. Its substantial tower, capped by a bellcote, is the private Church House, built for the schoolmaster.

Below is Draycote Water, at 8.75 hectares (21½ acres) the county's largest reservoir, which attracts much birdlife. The small **Draycote Water Country Park** has waterside walks, picnic places and an adventure playground. Permits can be obtained from Severn Trent to visit other parts of the shore.

TIDDINGTON [Stratford-on-Avon]

SP2255: 1½ miles (2km) NE of Stratford-upon-Avon

Mainly modern, the village is part of Stratford-upon-Avon parish. The River Avon borders it to the north and is accessible via School Lane, where there was once a sheep-wash. The former **school**, now a fine art auctioneers, is a striking Victorian building in polychromatic brick, its large gable topped by a clock turret. From it, red-brick houses stretch away eastwards, where the Catholic **St Joseph's Chapel** (also red-brick) has pepper pot turrets.

Tiddington's major building is the long, pale **National Farmers' Mutual and Avon Insurance Group head office**, in Bath stone. Opened in 1984, it was hailed by *The Architects' Journal* as 'a masterpiece' and 'the first large-scale realisation in Britain of the taste for neo-classicism'. It also mixes in modernism and Art Deco, and enjoys distant views towards the obelisk-capped Welcombe Hills. A less enthusiastic description was 'straight out of the Third Reich'.

Beside it and now part of the complex, **The Oaks**, a three-storeyed Georgian farmhouse with a large white-pillared porch, accommodates NFU visitors. The company has grown from an enterprise formed in Stratford by seven local farmers in 1910.

The village inn is The Crown, of red brick and gabled. 'D' Company Home Guard Club, a thriving survival from the Second World War, has some 600 members.

TIDMINGTON [Stratford-on-Avon]

SP2638: 1½ miles (2km) S of Shipston-on-Stour

Tidmington's few buildings stand along the Stratford to Oxford road, which crosses the infant River Stour via a **bridge** of mainly 18th-century construction, though one of its arches was recorded in 1615. A mile to the west, a narrow **packhorse bridge** spans Knee Brook.

The handsome gabled front of **Tidmington House** – an 18th-century updating of a building of about 1600 – faces the road across a ha-ha. Close beside it, veiled by trees supporting a rookery, is a small **church** (dedication uncertain, but possibly The Ascension). Severe carved faces peer from its pyramid-capped 13th-century tower, and in the churchyard a tree has grown inside an unusual double-barrelled table-tomb.

Enter through a Norman arch within a later stone porch. The nave was Norman too, and the chancel 16th century, but they were heavily restored in 1874-75. The bare-walled chancel has a small

13th-century piscina, and over its arch are the arms of George III. The tower arch, supported by glum-faced carved heads, is original, and the broad-based font, with its well-preserved carving of Christ triumphant, may be late Saxon. Ancient carved bench ends include a panelled one in Perpendicular style.

By the river, a large, early 19th-century, stone-built **mill** of four floors, with a central gable, has become the Green Hill Christian Centre. The adjacent **mill house** is mid-18th century. At a road junction **The Granary**, in stone, has been converted to a house. Attached is a former brick-built **mill**.

TREDINGTON [Stratford-on-Avon]

SP2543: 2 miles (3km) N of Shipston-on-Stour

A Stour valley village, identifiable from afar by its tall church spire, Tredington lies on the Stratford to Oxford road, just south of a crossing with the Fosse Way. The earliest known reference, as Tredinctun, is in 757. The Centenary Way passes by.

Though a big parish, Tredington was even larger before Shipston and Tidmington were separated in 1719 and Newbold and Talton in 1833. Until the county boundary was changed in 1931, the area was in Worcestershire. In the 13th century, the parish was granted a Peculiar Court, under which the rector sat in judgement on matters that would normally have gone before the diocesan ecclesiastical court.

Tredington Rectory was the birthplace in 1713 of **Vice-Admiral Sir Hyde Parker**, Commander of the Fleet at the First Battle of Copenhagen in 1801, where he sent the order to which Nelson turned his famous blind eye. He was related to the Parkers of Honington Hall (see HONINGTON).

The main road neatly divides the old from the modern, except for **The White Lion Inn** – partly half-timbered and thatched, but mainly ivy-covered stone – which stands west of it.

In the picturesque eastern part, grass verges front old cottages and the 15th-century spire of **St Gregory's Church**, set on a tower built a century earlier, rises 210ft above the churchyard. The building's many points of interest include the filled-in outlines of Anglo-Danish doors and windows above the nave arches. They date from the Saxon church, reputedly of 961, which was probably used as a refuge against Danish invaders and entered via ladders.

Civil War bullets lodged in the 14th-century north door are thought to have been fired by Roundheads who took part in the skirmish at Halford Bridge in 1644. A Perpendicular porch containing a priest's room shelters the door. The larger, Norman-arched south doorway dates from about 1200, though its zigzag pattern is 19th century. A sundial is set above.

The Norman doorway at St Gregory's church, Tredington

St Gregory's underwent a very necessary and sensitive restoration of 1896-1900. The nave is spacious, with two aisles and rounded Norman pillars, but the 14th-century chancel, which has low stone benches along the walls, is taller. From the outside it looks very much an afterthought.

The reading desk is pre-Reformation, the bench ends and pew fronts 15th century, and the pulpit Jacobean. Artefacts include a houseling table formerly used for kneeling at Communion, but a 17th-century book of Homilies has been removed for safe keeping.

Well-preserved wall brasses of 1427 and 1482 commemorate two rectors of Tredington: Richard Cassey, Chaplain to Henry V, and Henry Sampson, Provost of Oriel College, Oxford, who built the vestry. In the south aisle floor is a brass of 1568 to Alice Barnes. A plaque records that two livery pots given in 1631 by the then rector, William Smith, were sold in 1971 for £30,000. The proceeds went to a fund for the upkeep of the church.

Manor Farm, a restored early 17th-century farmhouse, has a **dovecote**. **Old Tythe Barn**, a stone building with a black and white gable, was originally twice its present size. A former **school** of 1840 occupies the site of the Bear and Bacchus Inn. Though heavily domesticated, it retains its bell in a tall gable-end.

A vast 15th-century rectory built by Henry Sampson was torn down in the 1840s because the Reverend Charles Watling wanted something more modern. In 1954 a new rectory was provided, but the 19th-century building, now **Tredington House**, which incorporated parts of the original, stands beside it.

Domesday Book recorded three mills at Tredington. Two survive, though not as working mills. Behind the church is an 18th-century brick **mill** and a large mill house, and the stone-built former Tredington Town Mill stands by **Mill House** at the north end of the village. Both are three-storeyed.

TYSOE [Stratford-on-Avon]

SP3344: 4½ miles (7km) S of Kineton

The long village lies in the Vale of the Red Horse, at the foot of the South Warwickshire hills. It consists of three parts, all recorded in Domesday Book – Lower Tysoe, detached to the north, and the Middle and Upper Tysoes, which have grown together. To the east, the parish and county boundaries follow an ancient hill road, Sugarswell Lane, the name of which is derived from the Saxon words for 'robbers' and 'well'.

The vale takes its namè from the great figure of a horse (origin unknown) cut at Lower Tysoe and obliterated when the fields were enclosed in 1798. Lower Tysoe, where stone cottages and farms stand back from the road, was earlier called Temple Tysoe because of an association with the Knights Templars, who owned the three manors.

At Middle (or Church) Tysoe, Main Street is lined with brownstone cottages. There are several shops (though 'H. Heritage, Est. 1833' is sadly empty) and the Peacock Inn has a large sign standing as proud as that magnificent bird. A Methodist church is modern (1970) and the large village hall was built in 1929. Tysoe had its own fire station until 1998.

Saddledon Street is named from a Civil War incident when a troop of Royalist cavalry, riding to Edge Hill, unsaddled and helped themselves to bread, beer and cider. Near the junction stands an old metal drinking trough.

Handsome thatched stone cottages face the war memorial on a small green, and against a wall is the stone arch of an old fountain. Others are found opposite the inn and the church.

The **church of the Assumption of the Blessed Virgin Mary** (its name a rare

Church of the Assumption of the Blessed Virgin Mary, Middle Tysoe

pre-Reformation survival) stands in a large churchyard, with ivy-covered table-tombs and a tall 15th-century cross. Unusually for a towered church, it has a bellcote, added in the 17th century.

Above the north doorway is set a strange medieval stone frieze containing heads of a man and woman flanked by angels holding scrolls. Begun in the 11th century, the church has a nave, two aisles and a chancel. The interior stone walls have been scraped. It is believed to occupy the site of a Romano-Celtic temple that may have been linked with the red horse. A vicar is mentioned in Domesday Book, but the first named one is Richard de Lyndon in 1278.

The impressive Norman south doorway is 12th century. Above it, a Lamb and Cross are flanked by a probably older mask and beakhead. Monuments include a founder's tomb, with a 14th-century stone coffin, and the reclining effigy of William Clark (died 1618), a former patron. There are wall-brasses to Jane Gibbs and Tomizane Browne, wives of Nicholas Browne, who died in 1598 and 1611 respectively, and to a priest, Thomas Mastrupe (1463).

The splendid 14th-century octagonal font, a picture carved on each face, is capped by a tall, suspended wooden lid. The pews are variously Elizabethan, Jacobean and Victorian, and there is a 17th-century churchwardens' chest. A four-wheeled bier survives as a relic of distant funerals.

Sir George Gilbert Scott, who also designed the neighbouring substantial stone **primary school** in 1856 and added to it in 1872, restored the church in the 1850s.

Undistinguished 20th-century houses lead south to **Upper Tysoe**, where old, stone cottages and farms border the Shipston road and the gabled medieval **Manor House** has additions from the 17th century and 1932-33.

The neighbouring parish of Compton Wynyates has no village – its inhabitants were expelled in the early 16th century so that Sir William Compton could rebuild his manor house in greater splendour. The result was his descendant the Marquis of Northampton's mellow brick (and 'Strictly Private') **Compton Wynyates**, the ultimate castellated Tudor showcase.

Nearby stands a stone **chapel** built about 1665 to replace a building damaged in the Civil War. It has unusual twin naves containing Compton monuments and great hatchments of about 1700.

On hills to the north and south stand, respectively, a **tower windmill**, with sails, and **Compton Pike**, a brick pyramid built as a beacon at the time of the Spanish Armada (1588).

UFTON [Stratford-on-Avon]

SP3762: 2½ miles (4km) W of Southam

A small village poised where the Southam to Leamington road drops to the Leam Valley – as does Ridgeway Lane, a rutted prehistoric track used by the Centenary Way. It was Ulchetone in Domesday Book and Ulfetune a little earlier, when Earl Leofric

The preaching cross at St Michael's church, Ufton

granted the land to the monks of Coventry, who held it until the Dissolution.

Later lords of the manor included Thomas, Lord Wriothesley (Lord Chancellor to Henry VIII and the subject of a portrait by Holbein), Sir John Spencer of Althorpe and his younger son Thomas Spencer (see CLAVERDON). In 1679 John Snell left it to Balliol College, Oxford, for the support of Scottish scholars.

By the gateway to **St Michael's Church** stands a tall, 14th-century preaching cross with a worn, carved head. The building is mainly 13th century, with a Perpendicular tower and a Decorated priest's doorway.

A brass of 1587 depicts Richard Woddomes, 'Parson and Pattron and Vossioner of the Churche and Parishe of Oufton in the Countie of Warrike', with his wife and seven children.

An inscription to Richard Field, 'a faithful labourer', tells us that he gained two prizes from the Royal Agricultural Society and was crushed by a steam windlass in 1878.

In White Hart Lane are the village **stocks** (a two-seater) and the stone-built inn from which the road is named. A **windlass** survives above a filled-in well. **The Old Rectory**, gabled and in lias, and **School House**, in brick stand nearby. The school closed in the early 1970s.

Across the main road, the brick front of a large Georgian **house** retains outlines of demolished gables. **Colbourne House** in Ufton Fields, with its Georgian front and old stonework at the rear, is a mixture of periods. The stone-fronted, vandal-proof bus shelter was built by local volunteers in 1975 as the first in a series of community projects.

South of the village, Warwickshire Wildlife Trust's **Ufton Fields Local Nature Reserve**, established in 1972, is an SSSI on a site where lower lias limestone was quarried from 1952 to 1954. The 30-hectare (77-acre) area consists of pools, grassed-over ridges and woodland. It is noted for orchids, hairstreak butterflies and numerous bird species.

ULLENHALL [Stratford-on-Avon]

SP1267: 2 miles (3km) W of Henley-in-Arden

The village has gradually climbed Main Street from its centre by the pub and the war memorial. An earlier centre probably lay to the east, near the Old Chapel. The move from this area is likely to have been due to plague. Ullenhall was created an ecclesiastical parish in 1861, having previously been part of Wootton Wawen. Its most ancient relic is **Hobditch Causeway** at Dean's Green, identified as a Roman road in 1964.

South of it is Warwickshire Wildlife Trust's **Dean's Green Nature Reserve**, with old ridge and furrow meadows, rich in wildflowers and good for butterflies.

The village inn, the **Winged Spur**, takes its name from the emblem of the Knight family of Barrells Hall, though it is first recorded in 1772 as the Catherlough Arms. Opposite is a **school** of 1876, built by the Knights' successors, the Newtons. It closed in 1987 and is now residences. Nearby cottages can be identified by their names as the former post office, forge and central stores. There were other businesses too, but none exists today.

Three local charities are administered. St Mark's draws an income from cottage and land rents, splitting it between the Parochial Church Council and the Parish Council while the Agar and Herring Aid in Sickness Charity divides its proceeds between neighbouring parishes. The Francis Brittain Charity provides for the purchase of a gown and petticoat for each of six poor women of the parish – out of an income of £3 per year!

The Old Chapel (originally St Mary's) is simply the chancel of a 13th-century church. When the rest was demolished in 1875, a porch and bellcote were added and the building was used as a mortuary chapel. The interior has Jacobean panelling, a wrought-iron communion rail of 1735 and early 19th-century commandment boards. The chapel was restored in 1962. A low, half-timbered cottage stands near the gate and there is a fine view over the Alne valley.

A long inscription on a memorial of 1617 to Francis Throckmorton, 'borne in the Citie of Mantua in Italy', curiously turns into a potted biography of his father, Michael, but fails to mention that he fled abroad after intriguing against the Protestant government. The Knight family vault lies beneath the chapel. Some of those interred were shifted from Wootton Wawen church to a mausoleum at Barrells Hall and thence to their present resting place.

The chapel's replacement, the **church of St Mary the Virgin**, was built in 1875, conveniently near the hall, whose then inhabitants, the Newtons, bore the £5000 cost. Its style is Early English, with a touch of Romanesque about the apse, and the interior is broad and wagon-roofed.

Crowleys Farm, at the top of Main Street, occupies a moated site and has a 1000-year-old oak in its grounds. **Barrells Hall** (visible from the Henley road) has been falling into ruin since it was abandoned after a fire in 1933. Building began in 1580, but the original farmhouse (later the manor house) was extended by Robert Knight, who bought it in 1730. He became Viscount Barrells and was granted the Irish titles of Baron Luxborough of Shannon and the Earl of Catherlough.

Knight's father, cashier to the South Sea Company, fled abroad with £2000 on his head when the South Sea Bubble burst in 1721. William Newton, a Birmingham industrialist, purchased the property in 1856.

Barrells is best remembered for the coterie of friends and minor poets, including Shenstone, Somerville, Jago and Richard Graves, who gathered there in Henrietta, Lady Luxborough's time. A half-French aristocrat, born in 1699, and half-sister of Queen Anne's minister Viscount Bolingbroke, she was retired to the hall on £500 a year by her husband in 1736, 'upon a gallantry she had with Dalton', a clergyman. Forbidden to go within 20 miles of London, or to leave England, she died in 1756 and lies in the chapel.

Meanwhile, Catherlough fell in love with Jane Davies of Moat House Farm. She bore him four illegitimate children, the eldest of whom inherited the estate and married into the Dormer family of Grove Park (see BUDBROOKE).

In 1808 William Booth of Perry Barr, Birmingham, was found not guilty of beating his brother John to death with a shovel at **Hall End Farm**. The jury decided that the deceased had been kicked by a horse. Four years later the same accused was condemned to death for forgery, but his execution at Stafford Gaol was bizarre. Only at the third attempt did the hangman succeed in dispatching him.

WALTON [Stratford-on-Avon]

SP2852: 2 miles (3km) S of Wellesbourne

Scattered stone-built Victorian estate cottages form this hamlet on a quiet lane by the River Dene, north of Walton Hall and in Wellesbourne parish. In the 12th century the hamlet was Walton Mauduit. A separate village of Walton d'Eivile lay in Town Field, just south of the present hall, where a manor house stood. Roman remains are said to have been found there in the 19th century.

Walton Hall was designed (1858-62) by Sir George Gilbert Scott for Sir Charles Mordaunt, whose family had acquired the estate by marriage in Elizabeth I's time (1558-1603). The Mordaunt baronetcy lasted from 1611 until 1934.

The great stone house, with its five-storeyed tower, is in the style of about 1400. Best seen across a lake crossed by the triple-arched, ornamental Gog Bridge, it is now a time-share hotel and country club, the 18th-century stables and other outbuildings having been converted for holiday use. For some years from 1963 the hall was a girls' school, St Vincent's, and in the early 1980s its owner was the entertainer **Danny la Rue**.

Beside the hall stands **St James's**

Walton Hall

Church (1750), built in a simple classical style by an earlier Sir Charles Mordaunt. Of the previous church only the font remains, unearthed from a shrubbery in 1842. The gentleman architect Sanderson Miller (see RADWAY) may have advised his friend Sir Charles on the design. Features include a Tuscan porch, a bellcote and a Venetian east window, and there is a gallery on wooden pillars. A crumbling Mordaunt grave stands beside the building.

In 1842, when the church was lengthened, **The Old Rectory** (originally the Parsonage House) was built near the village.

WAPPENBURY [Warwick]

SP3769: 4½ miles (7km) NE of Royal Leamington Spa

The hamlet lies above the winding River Leam and within the boundaries of an Iron Age earthwork. Pottery, kilns and the remains of a hut have been found from Romano-British times. Finds were scattered over 8 hectares of fields east of the village. We even know the names of some local potters: G. Atius Marinus, Erucanus and Coertutinus.

The site was again occupied in medieval times, but abandoned after the Black Death in 1349.

The **church of St John Baptist** is of uncommon interest for the men of distinction buried there. In the churchyard is the base of an ancient cross.

A tall, richly carved Celtic cross of 1898 marks the grave of the 6th Earl of Clonmel, and Samuel Shepheard (see EATHORPE) lies in his family vault. More modest graves hold the remains of the cycle-pump manufacturer **Frank Henry Bluemel** and **Sir William Lyons** (1901-85), founder of Jaguar Cars. The Vyner family vaults lie east of the building and there are tombs of the Umbers of Weston Hall at Weston-under-Wetherley.

Samuel Shepheard is also remembered inside the church, on one of several plaques moved to the base of the oddly placed 15th-century tower during the wholesale restoration of 1886. The largest is 'sacred to the memory of Mr Tho. Umbers, ... a zealous and scientific agriculuralist.'

William Vyner, who purchased the Eathorpe Estate and died in 1639, was belatedly commemorated by a Victorian memorial. It tells us that the estate remained in the possession of his direct descendants until 1858. Beyond a Victorian arch is an Early English chancel.

Unobtrusively placed between the parish church and the Leam, **St Anne's** is a small, plain Catholic chapel of 1849, with lancet windows. Possibly designed by A.W.N. Pugin, it is built onto a cottage overlooking the river valley. This was given to the church by the Clifford family in 1734 and is now the presbytery. The cottage had been used for secret celebrations of the Mass when the Catholic Morgans were lords of the manor.

Wappenbury Hall, a large mansion of Cotswold appearance built on the site of the manor house, was the home of Sir William Lyons (see above).

Wappenbury Wood is a Warwickshire Wildlife Trust nature reserve. The trees are mainly birch, oak, ash and hazel. The soil, varying from sandy to heavy clay, produces a diversity of flora. There are noteworthy moth and bird populations, plus badgers and muntjac deer.

WARMINGTON [Stratford-on-Avon]

SP4147: 5 miles (8km) SE of Kineton

A sentinel church tower on a ridge traversed by the Warwick to Banbury road indicates the delightful village lying below on the Oxfordshire border. It has been there since Saxon times. Pre-Reformation lords of the manor included the earls of Warwick, Preaux Abbey in Normandy and the Carthusian Wytham Abbey in Somerset. The monastic connections ex-

St Michael's church, Warmington

plain the discovery of the foundations of a small priory when Court Close was built in the 1950s.

The old houses are mostly of Hornton stone, some clustering round the spacious green, where the lily-flagged Town Pool has a sheep-wash. The green is overlooked by several fine buildings, of which the **Manor House** (stone-built, gabled and divided by a central chimney breast) dates from about 1600.

Its neighbours include **The Rectory** (red-brick, early 18th century) and, just off the green, the 17th-century **Grove Farm House**, with cross-windows and a hipped roof. Uphill stands the Plough Inn. Chapel Street leads past the roughcast **Wesleyan Chapel** of 1811 to School Lane, which has thatched stone cottages and a large, mullion-windowed **mill** dated 1539.

Despite the Norman arches in its broad nave, **St Michael's Church** is mainly 14th century. An ogee-shaped doorway in the chancel leads to the vestry of about 1340. Above, a medieval priest's room has a small window for observing the altar, and there were such contemporary mod cons as fireplace and garderobe. The church, restored between 1867 and 1871, retains a four-wheeled wooden bier.

Among weather-worn gravestones near the porch is that of Alexander Gourdin, a Scottish captain killed at the Battle of Edge Hill in 1642. A cottage on the green has taken his surname. Also buried, according to the eccentrically written parish register, were Richard Sannes, 'Captaine of Foot companie a gentleman of Worcestershire ... and Seven other ... whose name I know not'.

WARTON [North Warwickshire]

SP2803: 2 miles (3km) NE of Polesworth

Part of Polesworth civil parish on the Leicestershire border, the villages of Warton (or Waverton) and Little Warton – the first high and the second low – have grown into one. There is no mention of them in Domesday Book, but they may have been included in the estate at Orton-on-the-Hill, across the county boundary. From the early 12th century until the Dissolution, the nuns of Polesworth held the lordship.

Warton has two inns side by side, the Boot and the Hatter's Arms, the first of which is dated 1871. At Little Warton is the older Fox and Dogs. A few old buildings survive. At the top of Church Road, half-timbering can be seen within the brickwork of a derelict **cottage**, and **14 Austrey Road** (1775) is Tuscan-styled, with a portico.

The **Parish Room** is dated 1909 and the old brick walls of **Hillcrest Farmhouse** have an intriguing variety of windows scattered over them. **The Old School** and the **Master's House** of 1857 still stand, having replaced a cottage school of 1832. Though enlarged in 1895 and 1905, the school was superseded by modern boxes in 1975.

There used to be Baptist and Primitive Methodist chapels, but the first was demolished in 1971 and the other is now a garage in Austrey Road. **Holy Trinity Church** was built in the 1840s, when a separate ecclesiastical parish was formed, and was restored in 1857. Its style is Early English. It is built of stone, with a classical, aisle-less interior and a bellcote. In a 1998 renovation the pews were transformed into cupboards. The Hull family gravestones are a reminder that cholera ravaged the village in the 1850s.

WARWICK [Warwick]

SP2865: 9 miles (15km) S of Coventry

The most significant dates in the long history of the county town are 914 and 1694. The first was the year in which Ethelflaeda, daughter of Alfred the Great and holder of the title Lady of the Mercians, moved the Saxon settlement uphill to protect it from the Danes; the second that of the disastrous fire, which destroyed much of the central area. The fire started at the west end of High Street and spread as far as the present Lord Leicester Hotel. It destroyed 460 buildings and left 250 families homeless – all within five hours.

Another important change occurred about 1790, when the Earl of Warwick, tired of the bustling traffic at his gate and wishing to extend the castle grounds, closed the 14th-century bridge over the Avon and built the present **Castle Bridge** upstream. Though the old bridge was later swept away, its abutments remain.

Castle Bridge gives an outstanding view of **Warwick Castle**, which, despite its immense size, fails to dominate the town. William the Conqueror began it in 1068 with a Norman motte and bailey – the motte survives, and is inaccurately known as Ethelflaeda's Mound. Stone replaced the timberwork a century later, but the walls were razed by Simon de Montfort in 1264, during the Barons' War against Henry III.

When the Beauchamps took over in 1268, they began a long period of expan-

St Mary's Church and Shire Hall, Northgate Street, Warwick

sion, during which the lofty Caesar's and Guy's towers were constructed and the Gatehouse rebuilt. In 1604, Sir Fulke Greville, 1st Lord Brooke, was granted the dilapidated castle (though not the earldom, which the Grevilles later received from George III). He added the domestic ranges, and the castle became a Roundhead stronghold during the Civil War. Despite a Royalist siege, the only real damage the fortification has suffered was from a fire in 1871, after which the Great Hall was rebuilt.

In the 18th century, Capabilty Brown landscaped the 279 hectares (690 acres) of parkland. The castle ceased to be an Englishman's home in 1978, when Lord Brooke, 8th Earl of Warwick, sold it to the Tussaud's Group. Much costly restoration, plus the Tussaud expertise in mounting realistic tableaux, has since made the castle one of Britain's most popular tourist attractions.

The slender tower of **St Mary's Church**, a landmark for miles around, is 174ft (53m) tall, including pinnacles. The building retains a Norman crypt, and the late 14th-century chancel is truly Perpendicular, with almost unique flying ribs in the vaulting.

The superb Beauchamp Chapel, in Perpendicular Gothic, commemorates Richard Beauchamp, Earl of Warwick, who died in 1439. Its later tombs include Ambrose Dudley, Earl of Warwick, and his brother Robert, Earl of Leicester – Queen Elizabeth's favourite. Sir Fulke Greville lies in the Chapter House.

The great fire destroyed the nave, aisles, transepts and tower. They were rebuilt by 1704, but the new tower began to crack before it was completed, and had to be taken down and moved west, where it juts into the street. The nave is tall and spacious, but has very odd windows.

Another Norman church disappeared when **St Nicholas's** was rebuilt in 1780, its ancient tower having been replaced by a steeple in 1748. The style is Gothic Revival – very early in the case of the tower. A brass commemorates Robert Willardsey, a vicar who died in 1425.

The East and West Gates have chapels above them. **St James's** (at the West Gate, where the passage is cut through rock) is mentioned in 1123. By the late 16th century it was a near ruin and had to be repaired. Falling into decline again, it was rescued by Sir George Gilbert Scott's restoration of 1863-65.

At the East Gate, the 15th-century **St Peter's Chapel** was rebuilt in 1788 by a local architect, Francis Hiorn, in the Strawberry Hill Gothic manner, and is part of the Girls' High School. At the East and West Gates stand two of the oldest pillar boxes in Britain, dating back to 1856.

The Friends' Meeting House was rebuilt in 1695, its predecessor having been destroyed in the great fire. A modest, cottage-like building, extended west in the 18th century, it has a gallery and some 18th-century panelling, and retains its original cross-mullioned windows.

Opposite, the superb half-timbered and gabled buildings of **The Lord Leycester Hospital**, dating from the 15th and 16th centuries, rise above the West Gate. Robert Dudley, Earl of Leicester, founded the hospital in 1571 as a rest home for old soldiers. Round the corner, in Bowling Green Street, is one of the few surviving sections of the medieval **town wall**.

Oken's House in Castle Street, dating from about 1500, escaped the great fire and has survived to become Warwick Doll Museum. Its one-time occupant, Thomas Oken, was a wealthy mercer and benefactor of the town.

At nearby crossroads, the classical **Court House** was the work of another local architect, Francis Smith, in 1724. The town council meets there, in the former magistrates' court, and the building houses the

Warwickshire Yeomanry Museum. The Mayor's Parlour has become the Tourist Information Centre.

In the Market Place, the **Market Hall** of 1670 escaped the fire and is the County Museum. The gentleman architect Sanderson Miller of Radway designed the pedimented **Shire Hall** (1753) in Northgate Street, used by the Crown Court. Alongside is the former **gaol** of 1779 and a prison cell rebuilt in 1695.

Landor House, beyond the East Gate, was built in 1692. It is named after the poet and essayist **Walter Savage Landor** (1775-1864), who was born there. Further out, the large **St John's House**, with ogee-shaped gables, is an extension of the County Museum. It also houses the Museum of the Royal Warwickshire Regiment, opened by Field Marshal Viscount Montgomery in 1961. Built in 1626, on the site of the 12th-century St John's Hospital, the house was extensively altered in the 1660s.

Mill Street and **Bridge End**, once busy roads linked by the medieval bridge, were transformed by its closure into quiet and charming backwaters.

At Saltisford, a 14th-century stone **chapel** (the only surviving part of the medieval St Michael's Hospital) has undergone restoration. The adjacent **Master's House**, a timber-framed building of the 15th to 17th centuries, is in dire need of it. Nearby, the **gasworks** of 1822 is cunningly disguised as a stuccoed Regency building, flanked by turreted octagonal gasholders.

At Warwick Racecourse, part of the central grandstand dates from 1809. With 25 meetings annually the course is Britain's busiest, but occupies common land where the public may walk freely on non-racing days.

The Grand Union Canal passes through the town, which is also on the Centenary Way route.

WASPERTON [Warwick]

SP2658: 4 miles (6km) S of Warwick

When John Leland rode from Warwick to Charlecote on one of his 'Itineries' in the 1540s, he noted 'a priory of Maturins, also known as the Order of the Holy Trinity, which held very few possessions'. The Lucys of Charlecote, he wrote, had founded it and several of them were buried there. Today the site lies in a field beside the Warwick to Wellesbourne road at Thelsford Brook. Hutton says that the sanctus bell was moved to Wasperton church.

Nearby, down a winding no through road, stands the small village of Wasperton. The name is unique and means 'muddy pear-tree town'. Earl Leofric, husband of Lady Godiva, was Lord of the Manor before the Conquest, and some time after the Dissolution it became the property of St John's College, Oxford.

At the end of the road, **Manor Farm** is encased in 18th-century brickwork concealing an early 14th-century aisled hall with a spere-truss. A decaying stone dovecote at its rear was demolished about 1970.

Though the bellcoted **church of St John Baptist** was remodelled in 1843 by Sir George Gilbert Scott in 14th-century Gothic-style and has an east window reputed to be Pugin's last design, the building is basically of 1736. A wall brass of 1664 has a long rhyming verse commemorating 'Honest Henry Collins'. Near the porch, the grave of the architect **Thomas Garner** of Wasperton Hill, who died in 1880, and his wife, lies among other Garner tombs.

The neighbouring **Cedar House** of about 1840 – red-brick, gabled and bargeboarded – was originally the vicarage, and a small building of 1843 with patterned brickwork was once a **school**.

WATER ORTON [North Warwickshire]

SP1791: 2 miles (3km) NW of Coleshill

A Birmingham dormitory, islanded by the

River Tame, the M6 and the M42, the village expanded after the railway came in 1842 – the station now occupies a towered Edwardian building. Its original name of Overton ('settlement above the water') was corrupted to Orton, and became Water Orton in the 16th century.

There are two hostelries, one small and the other large – The Dog of 1722 and the Digby Hotel, which, though built about 1860, is of earlier appearance and has a coach entrance. The Digbys lived at Coleshill Hall and several of them lie buried at Coleshill church.

The truncated look of the brick-built **church of St Peter and St Paul** (1879) is due to the removal of its crumbling spire in 1987.

An overgrown **graveyard** in Old Church Road was the site of the former church, established in 1347 as a chapel of ease to Aston (now part of Birmingham). Water Orton became a separate ecclesiastical parish in 1871. The graveyard contains the base and shaft of a 15th-century **cross**, from which the Sutton Coldfield-born Bishop Vesey of Exeter and many itinerant preachers are said to have addressed the villagers.

Across the road stand **The Chestnuts**, a timber-framed house, and the black and white **Wakefield House**, from the 15th and 16th centuries respectively. Pottery dating back to the 13th century has been dug up in the Wakefield garden.

Further out, the road crosses the River Tame by a six-arched former **packhorse bridge** of about 1550, reputedly built by Bishop Vesey. In 1926 a headless stone figure, believed to be the Archangel Gabriel, was moved from the bridge to Curdworth church.

The small **Methodist church** was built in 1868. 'Captain Greenacre of Durban, South Africa' laid one of its two foundation stones, it baldly and intriguingly declares. **Overton House** (part timber-framed, part Georgian brick, and named from the original village) is passed on the way to the green, which is overlooked by a gabled **school** of 1878.

WEDDINGTON [Nuneaton]

SP3693: 1 mile (2km) N of Nuneaton

Watling Street, the busy modern A5(T), buzzes to the north, marking the Leicestershire boundary. To the west, the River Anker hems in the village, now a Nuneaton suburb.

The medieval **St James's Church** was destroyed in the 18th century, probably by fire, except for the 14th-century north transept. Its successor was rebuilt (1881) in orange brick and with a pyramid-roofed tower, but contains a Norman font and a monument of 1639 to the Humphrey Adderleys, father and son. The elder was Gentleman of the Wardrobe to four monarchs – Henry VIII, Edward VI, Mary and Elizabeth I.

WEETHLEY [Stratford-on-Avon]

SP0555: 2½ miles (4km) SW of Alcester

This tiny settlement is the most westerly in the county, lying only half a mile from where Weethley Wood marks the Worcestershire border. The Saxon name meant 'withy clearing', or 'withy wood'. King Kendred of Mercia gave it to Evesham Abbey in 708, and in 1877 it became part of the Marquis of Hertford's Ragley Estate.

By a small pool at Weethley Hamlet, its churchyard offering a panoramic view over Worcestershire, stands the bellcote-capped **St James's**. Built (1857-58) in late 13th-century style, using local lias stone, it consists of nave, chancel and apse. Carved flowers and fruit decorate the chancel arch brackets.

Neighbours include **The Manor** – 17th-century brick, with timber and stone features, gables and a tiled roof. Where the main road angles at Weethley Gate, the partly thatched **Turnpike Cottages** stand opposite a former **toll-house**.

WELFORD-ON-AVON [Stratford-on-Avon]

SP1452: 4 miles (6km) SW of Stratford-upon-Avon

The straggling village, which has many black and white cottages and lies in a great loop of the Avon, was part of Gloucestershire until 1931. It was then linked to Warwickshire by Binton Bridges, which span the divided river by the **Four Alls Inn**, whose sign illustrates the functions of the soldier, king, parson and farmer: 'Fight all', 'Rule all', 'Pray all' and 'Pay all'. At opposite ends of High Street are two other inns. The Bell (which has a large bell hung outside) and The Shakespeare each stand by a green, forming a focal point, of which the village has three.

The third is the slim-towered, blue-lias **St Peter's Church**, which had a 14th-century lych-gate, claimed to be the oldest in England until it was replaced by a replica about 1970. The font bowl is believed to be Saxon, though set on Elizabethan supports, and there is much Norman work, including the lower tower, south doorway, filled-in north doorway and nave arcades.

The carved heads of Henry VI and Margaret of Anjou ('the she-wolf of France') are included in the Perpendicular aisle windows, and the east window is from the 1920s by Christopher Webb. In acknowledgement of an early link with the Saxon priory of Deerhurst in Gloucestershire, which was a cell of the Abbey of St Denis in Paris, it includes the saint holding the French fleur-de-lys.

Sir George Gilbert Scott restored the building in 1866-67. The Reverend James Davenport, who served first as curate then as vicar from 1847 to 1904, was prominent in the Tractarian Movement (see WILMCOTE).

Lovely thatched cottages are gathered near the church, behind which stands a Georgian **rectory** of classical appearance. A nearby small, handsome house of 1713, **Cleavers**, had a reproduction period porch added in the 1950s.

By a rushing weir, **Welford Mill**, a white-painted private house, retains two undershot waterwheels. Welford's famous red, white and blue **maypole**, topped by a running fox weathervane, rises 65ft (20m) from the green by the Shakespeare Inn. The present metal pole is modern, but Welford has had a maypole since at least the 14th century.

WELLESBOURNE [Stratford-on-Avon]

SP2755: 5 miles (8km) E of Stratford-upon-Avon

The large, expanding village is divided by the River Dene, which meets the Avon at nearby Charlecote, and stands just off the Warwick to Stow-on-the-Wold road. The part east of the river was originally Wellesbourne Hastings and that to the west Wellesbourne Mountford.

Its name was recorded in 862 as Wallesburam, held by King Burgred of Mercia. Domesday Book has Waleborne, and the Lord of the Manor was by then a Norman knight, Henri de Newburgh. Nearby places of interest include **Wellesbourne Wartime Museum** on Wellesbourne Airfield, and **Wellesbourne Watermill**, off the Kineton road. The Warwickshire Feldon Cycle Way passes through.

Behind the King's Head stands **St Peter's Church**, where Henri de Newburgh began building on a Saxon site. The Perpendicular tower of about 1400, the fine Norman chancel arch (reset to the north), and the south aisle's 14th-century west window survive from the medieval church. Most of the rest was rebuilt in 1847-48.

In the chancel floor is Sir Thomas le Straunge's brass (1426) and on the wall a 17th-century tablet to Paul Aylworth and his wife Isabella, with an Achievement of Arms above. There are also memorials to the Granvilles of Wellesbourne Hall. A large Aylworth table-tomb in the churchyard, said to bear the date 1670 and a carved skull and bones, is almost totally smothered in ivy.

The Old Vicarage of 1698-99 has a hipped roof and dormers. Its neighbour, the ivy-covered **Church House**, is Georgian. Down a drive by the church, **The Old Malthouse** is also ivy-covered, with cross-windows. The Church Street cottages are brick and have bargeboarded end-gables.

Across the river, Chestnut Square is a delight. The **Stag's Head**, thatched and half-timbered, is small and domestic looking. The misnamed **Little House**, in brick, is dated 1699, and the Georgian, creeper-covered and pedimented **Red House** was the home of the later Aylworths.

An unusual memorial is the bus shelter built in 1952 by the National Union of Agricultural Workers to commemorate Joseph Arch (see BARFORD), whose historic public meeting at Wellesbourne in 1872 led to the establishment of the first agricultural trade union. The square is named from the chestnut tree, replaced in 1949, under which Arch spoke.

Off it, Church Walk has lovely cottages, some of which are thatched. **Buckle House**'s 18th-century brick frontage conceals a much older building. In Chapel Street stand **Coopers** (a former butcher's, with patterned glazing and bargeboards), an old-fashioned, bow-windowed shop, **Old School House** and tall, polychromatic cottages.

The Old Dispensary in Stratford Road is now a library. It faces **Wellesbourne Hall** (1697-1700), built for the Granvilles. Mary Granville (Mrs Delany), who made two of the hall's shell-work fireplaces in the 18th century, has many examples of her pictures of flowers, pieced together from innumerable tiny pieces of paper, in the British Museum.

The **Manor House** (originally of the Venours and standing sideways on to Bridge Street) is gabled and faced with brick.

WESTON-ON-AVON [Stratford-on-Avon]

SP1551: 3½ miles (5km) SW of Stratford-upon-Avon

The small, no-through-road village stands beside the River Avon and was part of Gloucestershire until 1931. Its long, battlemented church, **All Saints'**, is unusual in being of one period (the late 15th century) and remarkable for its fenestration. On the south side, two great windows with pointed arches were originally the bays of the demolished St Anne's Chapel. The north wall is lined with 15th-century Perpendicular windows containing old glass.

Gargoyles lean out above them and from the corners of the tower. Below, the medieval churchyard cross has lost its shaft, but its carved head has been placed on the base. Inside is a roundel of 15th-century heraldic floor-tiles.

Wall-panelling and a bier survive from the 17th century, and 16th-century brasses depict the armour-clad Sir John and Sir Edward Greville of the old Milcote Hall (see MILCOTE). The Adkins family, of the later hall, have Greek Revival monuments. An 18th-century vicar, Joseph Green, is notable for having discovered Shakespeare's will.

Nearby, a former railway line has become **The Greenway**, a walking/cycling route and nature trail linking Stratford with Long Marston.

WESTON-UNDER-WETHERLEY [Warwick]

SP3669: 3½ miles (5km) NE of Leamington Spa

A small village on the Leamington Spa to

Rugby road, it consists of a church, a few cottages (their thatch removed), some modern houses, including a small estate built on a former hospital site in 1997, and the Bull Inn. The hospital was constructed about 1840 as a reformatory and latterly used as a sanatorium.

Sir Edward Belknap, the absentee landlord who depopulated the Burton Dassett Hills in favour of sheep lived at Weston-under-Wetherley. The name of one of the cottages, **The Old Forge**, indicates its purpose in the pre-motoring era.

St Michael's Church, in soft red sandstone, rises boldly above the road, its chancel dating from Norman times and its single aisle 13th century. The chancel has a blocked window on each side. Four bells, one of 1583, hang in the 14th-century tower, though they can no longer be rung. The irregularly shaped font is also 14th century. A Perpendicular chapel on the north side was added in the 16th century.

There are memorials to the Umbers family of nearby Weston Hall and to Margaret and Mary Morgan, who died as infants in 1568. A small brass plaque of 1497, one of the county's earliest memorials, commemorates Anne Danet. Another (in Latin, with an English verse) tells us that Joyce Tomer, who died in 1566, 'had of physic skill'. Joyce seems to have been a man.

WHATCOTE [Stratford-on-Avon]

SP2944: 3½ miles (5km) NE of Shipston-on-Stour

A small remote village where quiet lanes meet in the Vale of the Red Horse (see TYSOE), it was perhaps busier in Roman times as the crossing place of two secondary roads. Today the Centenary Way passes through.

Not much is old, but some of it is very old. The stone-built and ivy-covered **Royal Oak** is said to be Warwickshire's longest established inn, having begun as a shelter for the 12th-century workmen who rebuilt the church. The Royalist Dugdale wrote that 'Cromwell and his men quenched their thirst and filled their bellies' there following the Battle of Edge Hill in 1642, but like the many other Royal Oaks, it was renamed in honour of Charles II after the Restoration.

The Norman **St Peter's Church** presents

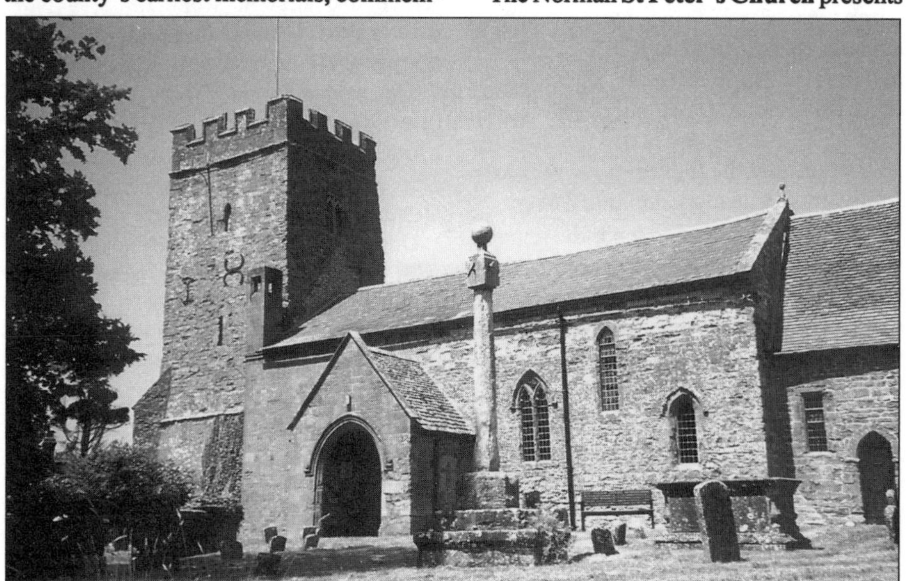

St Peter's church and medieval churchyard cross, Whatcote

an attractive modern east wall of grey and brown stone to the churchyard gate. The explanation is that a German bomb struck the building in 1940, causing great damage.

There are two churchyard crosses. A tall medieval one supports a later sundial top, and the other was built in 1997 to commemorate the fiftieth anniversary of the rededication after repair of the war damage. Stone from the damaged church forms its base and the cross came from the rector's former church of St George at Salford, Greater Manchester, now demolished. The oldest gravestone is that of William Hickes, who died in 1634.

The north wall has a simple round-headed Norman doorway and Norman windows. Evidence suggests that the doorway was carved by a mason who also worked on Halford church. High on the tower, above the church roof, is a stone coat of arms of former lords of the manor, the earls of Stafford, who sold to the Northamptons about 1520.

Within the white-walled, aisle-less nave, look for the 18th-century graffiti scratched on the 13th-century tower door jamb and note the tub font, skilfully restored after the bomb damage, which may have come from a Saxon church on the site. There are wall memorials to former rectors, including the remarkable John Davenport, who served from 1597 to 1668 and died aged 101. His gravestone is in the chancel floor, as is John Audlyngton's headless brass of 1486.

Set in a chancel window are the remains of the pre-bombing stained glass. It is dedicated to William Sanderson Miller (a descendant of Sanderson Miller the architect), who became rector in 1888 and was the last of the Miller squires of Radway when he died in 1909.

Furnishings include three early 16th-century pew ends and two pews from the **Wesleyan Chapel** of 1905. Closed in 1988, the small brick chapel is sadly becoming derelict.

The L-shaped and stone-built **Old Rectory Cottage** (from the 17th century and originally three houses) was used as a temporary rectory in the 1880s, when the **Old Rectory** to the south was out of use during restoration.

WHICHFORD [Stratford-on-Avon]

SP3134: 5 miles (8km) SE of Shipston-on-Stour

Away from main roads, the village lies in a valley and near the extensive Whichford Wood. It existed when the Domesday surveyors called, and retains a **moat** on the site of the old manor house of the de Mohuns. A large green is overlooked by the brick-built Norman Knight Inn (the name refers to the de Mohans) and **The Old School**, of unusual drystone walling.

Whichford Pottery, opened in 1983, has a 19th-century filter-press from Stoke-on-Trent.

Beyond the splendid, but never completed, former **rectory** of ochre-coloured stone (dating from about 1700), **St Michael's Church** is approached along a path bordered by weathered headstones. Tomb-chests cluster near the porch, within which are ancient stone seats, a Norman-arched doorway and a faintly carved tympanum.

The tower is early 14th century, the priest's doorway and piscina a century older. The tomb of John Merton, a 16th-century rector, has a book and spectacles carved on its west end.

Other monuments include a coffin lid with the de Mohun arms – perhaps of Sir John de Mohun, who died in Scotland about 1323 and was one of the barons responsible for beheading Piers Gaveston (see LEEK WOOTTON). A later Sir John (died 1376) was among the original Knights of the Garter.

The church was restored in 1845, when the Gothic pews were added. Advice for bellringers, believed to date from 1717, was found in the belfry in 1975. Among other things, ringers were assured,

*''tis houlfum, hanfum and a comly thing
to caft your cloaths of when you comes to
ring.'*

North of the village, a large stone cottage called **The Old Rectory** is considered more likely to have been a farmhouse. The nearby hamlet of Ascott has the 18th-century **Ascott House** and a number of Cotswold-style cottages.

WHITCHURCH [Stratford-on-Avon]

SP2248: 4 miles (7km) SE of Stratford-upon-Avon

There is no Whitchurch village, its inhabitants having been removed in 1498 by Sir Edward Belknap (see BURTON DASSETT) to make way for sheep, but the parish includes the hamlets of Crimscote and Wimpstone.

The Saxon Alwin, who held Witcerce before the Conquest, was soon replaced by the Norman bigwig, Robert de Beaumont, Comte de Montes and Viscount D'Ivry. Later lords of the manor were the earls of Warwick, the de Montforts and the Wests of Alscot Park (see PRESTON-ON-STOUR).

Cottages and former estate houses of Alscot Park border the lane at Wimpstone, where a late 18th-century red-brick **rectory** has stone quoins, a hipped roof and Doric pilasters. At Crimscote stands a 17th-century **dovecote** of coursed stone.

Between the hamlets, the **church of St Mary the Virgin**, Whitchurch, is rendered remote by the River Stour, which separates it from nearby Alderminster on the Stratford to Oxford road. Reached via a farm track and a fieldpath, it adjoins the site of the depopulated village. An unusually placed Norman doorway at its south-west corner is a result of the building's west end having been demolished in 1670. Above is a late 12th-century carved Lamb and Cross.

The stone church is believed to have been built about 1020 to replace a wood and thatch structure erected by the monks of Deerhurst in Gloucestershire. It has early herringbone masonry on the north wall and large Perpendicular windows in the chancel, where William Smyth, a rector who died in 1442, rests in an incised tomb-chest.

The pulpit is Jacobean and the lectern was moved in 1976 from a redundant church at Wispington, Lincolnshire, where it was carved by a rector, Charles Terrot (1848-1931). Reset on the west wall is an Anglo-Danish carved panel and on the nave wall are two replicas of medieval women's heads from a ruined cottage at Crimscote. A piscina in the chancel probably came from the long-gone medieval chapel there.

There is a rare survival of a houseling table, and the Royal arms of Charles I apparently remained untouched, despite the Commonwealth, until Charles's 'XR' was amended to 'GR' for one of the Georges. A Whitchurch rector, J. Harvey Bloom, was the father of the novelist **Ursula Bloom.**

WHITNASH [Warwick]

SP3263: 1 mile (2km) S of Royal Leamington Spa

Though part of the Warwick and Leamington conurbation, Whitnash has its own town council and appointed its first mayor in 1992. It stands two miles from the Fosse Way and is a much older settlement than Leamington. Domesday Book recorded it as Witenas and by 1327 it had become Whitenasshe ('white ash'). Despite vast 20th-century development, some ancient cottages remain. To the south, the Leamington and County Golf Club has restrained expansion since 1908.

The mound on which **St Margaret's Church** stands may have been a pagan site and, according to Alfred Watkins's *The Old Straight Track*, is set on a ley running from Southam church to Warwick Castle. The tower is probably Perpendicular, but much of the rest was rebuilt between 1855 and 1880 to designs by Sir George Gilbert

St Mary's church, Wibtoft

Scott. The expense was borne by the energetic rector for 38 years, Canon James Reynolds Young, who is commemorated by a brass plaque.

A much-praised feature of the broad interior is the rich stone carving of the capitals, altar and pulpit by Agnes Bonham, a local young lady of Irish family. The west window (1876) was designed by Ruth Young, daughter of the Canon.

The old is represented by the piscina and sedile, and by the narrow priest's door, all salvaged from the medieval church; the new by the north transept and octagonal Chapter House added in 1989.

Facing each other across the chancel are brasses to Richard Bennet (rector 1492-1534) and to a Lord of the Manor, Benedict Medley (died 1503) and his wife. Medley, Clerk of the Signet to Henry VII, probably built the church tower. Nicholas Greenhill (rector 1609-50) was appointed as the first headmaster of Rugby School in 1602, when he was aged 21. His tablet has an inscription in Latin.

Later lords included the Willes family (see ROYAL LEAMINGTON SPA) and Henry Landor, father of the author and poet **Walter Savage Landor** (1775-1864). The brick-built school, donated by Henry Eyres Landor in 1860, became a **Church Centre** in 1964. A half-timbered cottage, **Elderfield**, is the former 17th-century Homestead Farmhouse. Reassuringly, the black and white **Plough and Harrow** still fulfils its original function as an inn. The oldest part dates from the 17th century.

Anderson Drive, a road built in 1984, commemorates 2nd Lieutenant Jean Anderson of the US Air Force, killed when he stayed at the controls of his doomed bomber to avoid it crashing on Whitnash in 1945.

WIBTOFT [Rugby]

SP4787: 7 miles (12km) E of Bedworth

The hamlet stands against the Leicestershire border, near the crossing of Watling Street and the Fosse Way at High Cross (see COPSTON MAGNA). It is a rarity in Warwickshire in having a name of Danish origin.

Dugdale records that it occupies the site

of a Roman city, Cleychester, and that Roman stonework and coins 'have been frequently discovered'. A meadow of pronounced **ridge and furrow** slopes down to Watling Street from **St Mary's Church** – an attractive setting, but marred by the drone of traffic.

The small, plain building is a mixture of periods. It has a stone medieval west wall and more medieval stonework to the south, but the east and north walls are of brick on a stone base. The bellcote was added about 1890 and there are broad, pointed Gothic windows.

WILLEY [Rugby]

SP4984: 8½ miles (14km) E of Bedworth

The small village lies just off the ruler-straight Watling Street, which marks the Leicestershire border, and beside the dismantled Rugby to Leicester railway line.

St Leonard's Church has a slim, Perpendicular tower with gargoyles and there are carved heads on the battlemented nave. The Early English south doorway is flanked by carved shields. Houseling tables have survived, probably from the 17th century, and an early 14th-century monument is unusual in that the effigy is seen through quatrefoil openings. Robert Beresford Podmore, rector for 40 years, is commemorated in the Gothic Revival style.

The name of the village pub, the Sarah Mansfield, was changed from the Plough in the 1970s by the then licensee, in memory of his grandmother.

WILLOUGHBY [RUGBY]

SP5167: 5 miles (8km) S of Rugby

The village lies just off the Coventry to Daventry trunk road and within half a mile of the Northamptonshire boundary. The Oxford Canal passes nearby, as, until 1969, did the Great Central Railway (later the LNER) from London Marylebone to Yorkshire via Rugby. In 1900 it was the last main line to be opened in England. The name, meaning 'village in the willows', is probably a mixture of Saxon and Danish, which would indicate a Norse settlement.

A 16th-century inn, **The Rose**, is stone-built and thatched, with a later brick extension. Four crosses depicted on a panel on an outside chimney of a large red-brick **house** facing the main road show that it was once the Four Crosses Inn. Originally The Three Crosses, it reputedly owed its change of name to the satirist **Jonathan Swift** (1667-1745), who, after losing an altercation with the landlord's wife, engraved on a window-pane:

'You have three crosses
On your door.
Hang up your wife
And she'll make four.'

In Main Street stand a **Wesleyan Chapel** of 1898, with patterned brick work over lancet windows, and a large, stone house, **The Smithy**. **Vale House**, in Lower Street and probably the village's oldest residence, has a roughcast front, red roof, gables and a balustraded 17th-century wooden porch said to have come from the demolished manor house. **The Old Vicarage** is Regency, with a hipped roof, and the Georgian **Northcote House** faces the village pond.

The grey stone **St Nicholas's Church**, first recorded in 1215, has a Decorated tower and a nave with Perpendicular arches and windows. Its ashlared chancel, set on an older stone base, was probably added, with no attempt at harmony, in the early 19th century. The north porch, its outer doorway replaced by a window, has been converted to a small chapel.

The cauldron-shaped font has a crude Early English carving of two men and an unidentifiable creature, and the arms of George III are painted on canvas. The turret clock came from Southam in 1724 and was restored in 1983, largely at the expense of the Willoughby Charities. Its carillon plays five tunes.

John and Margaret Hayward established the Willoughby Charities in 1437, and John Brook, whose name is commemorated by the modern Brook's Close, made a charitable bequest in 1535.

WILMCOTE [Stratford-on-Avon]

SP1658: 3 miles (5km) NW of Stratford-upon-Avon

The village is a mixture of some old and many new buildings, but has an attractive core centring on a lane junction. Until 1863 it was part of Aston Cantlow parish. The Stratford-upon-Avon Canal skirts it and there is a railway station on the Birmingham to Stratford line. Two hostelries – the Mary Arden Inn (a mid-1990s change of name from the Swan House Hotel) and the stone-built Masons Arms – serve the village and its many visitors.

They come to see **Mary Arden's House**, the childhood home of Shakespeare's mother, who is said to have inherited it before John Shakespeare came courting. It acquired its present name in the late 18th century.

The early 16th-century house is pleasingly picturesque, with unpainted half-timbering bulging like reflections in a distorting mirror. Furnishings include a monks' bench of about 1480. Among stone outbuildings is a **dovecote** for 3000 birds. With neighbouring **Glebe Farm**, the property forms the Shakespeare Countryside Museum, run by the Shakespeare Birthplace Trust.

The bellcoted **St Andrew's Church**, built in 1841, played an important role in the history of the Church of England. Attributed to William Butterfield, it is a Gothic Revival building designed for the High Church practices introduced by the Tractarian (or Oxford) Movement, and is said to have been the first at which Anglo-Catholic services were routinely held.

It is a tall building in blue lias, with pews spreading across the side-aisles – the south ones, originally reserved for men, have fittings underneath for hanging top hats. The short but richly decorated chancel has stepped lancets and on the side walls are stencilled murals by a former vicar. The west wall contains a Flemish relief of about 1520.

So popular was St Andrew's among Tractarians that Butterfield designed a stone **guest house** adjoining the churchyard to accommodate retreatants. Visitors included the great leaders of the Movement, such as Newman and Manning. The house later became the vicarage and passed into private ownership in the 1970s.

A grey stone **school** by Butterfield also borders the churchyard and is still used, though with modern extensions. A red-brick former chapel is now **Chapel House**.

WINDERTON [Stratford-on-Avon]

SP3240: 1 mile (1.5km) NE of Brailes

Folded within hills, the hamlet has the fine Gothic Revival former **church of St Peter and St Paul**. Built of Hornton stone in 1879 by Canon E. Thoyts in memory of his parents, it was closed and deconsecrated in 1976 and is used for community purposes and the occasional service.

The 90-foot (27m) tower is capped by a pyramid roof. Inside, the effect of the great rounded apse of red and white stone is marred by the erection of a stage and curtains. A gravestone of 1938 near the path is inscribed 'in memory of my dear husband Mister Maycock'. Mister is said to have been the deceased's Christian name.

WISHAW [North Warwickshire]

SP1794: 4 miles (6km) SE of Sutton Coldfield

Though a parish of Wishaw exists, dotted with houses, there is no village. The main settlement comprises the Cock Inn and its neighbours at Over Green on the county boundary, and by far the biggest development is the internationally known Belfry

Hotel and Golf Course, the European Headquarters of the Professional Golfers' Association.

It occupies the site of Old Moxhull Hall, the home of the Ryland family, Birmingham industrialists. The unfortunate deaths of several family members giving rise to a superstition about the building, the Rylands demolished it early in the 20th century and built New Moxhull Hall (now Moxhull Hall Hotel) a mile away.

Wishaw is recorded in Domesday Book as Witscaga ('Wita's grove'). Together with Moxhull, it was a manor of the Knights Templars before being granted to Walter de Beresford in 1257. His descendants lived locally into the 20th century.

The dedication of the small **St Chad's Church** is to a 7th-century bishop of Lichfield. (It was a Wishaw man, John Hackett, Bishop of Lichfield, who restored the Cathedral after the ravages of the Civil War in the 1640s.) Said to occupy the site of a Roman church, it has 13th- and 14th-century arcades. A lepers' squint enabled the sacrament to be observed from outside. The Gothic tower of about 1700 probably replaced a spire.

In Church Lane, the First World War **memorial hall** of 1923 stands beside the former **workhouse**, now cottages. At Over Green, **The Cock** was a coaching inn reputed to have been used as a refuge by Dick Turpin. **The Grove**, brick-built and gabled, is noted for its fine interior cruck-trusses. Other neighbours include the Regency **Old Rectory** and a **tithe barn**.

Wiggins Hill Farm has a Dutch gable. Nearby stand a renovated half-timbered barn and **The Cottage**, a former Quaker Meeting House of 1724. **Cuttle Mill**, now a fishery, is a mid-19th-century watermill with most of its machinery intact.

WITHYBROOK [Rugby]

SP4384: 5 miles (8km) SE of Bedworth

The small village lies just off the Fosse Way and near the Oxford Canal. From a long plain inn, The Pheasant, a byway beside a stream leads to **All Saints' Church**, where the graveyard contains unusual 18th-century triple-arched headstones. Trinity College, Cambridge, was patron of the living of Withybrook and Monks Kirby from 1546 until the late 20th century.

The Perpendicular nave and chancel were built in the 14th century (the first incumbent was William de Leone in 1313), replacing a chapelry of Monks Kirby, and the Decorated north-west tower was added a century later. A major restoration took place in 1995.

Entering through a large porch with side and upper windows (above which was formerly a room for the priest), we find a nave of scraped stone, with broad aisles. Well-preserved carved heads, including a bear and a lady wearing a wimple, cap the pillars. A modern shaft supports a late 12th-century font.

The main item of interest is the Easter sepulchre, set between the chancel and the chapel, which was found hidden by plaster in 1848. It consists of a hollow tomb-chest, with carvings of soldiers and an angel. In the dark chapel stands the table-tomb of Sir Christopher Wright, topped by a round-headed alabaster panel. He died in 1602, and was thus spared the distress of knowing that relatives, Christopher and John Wright, were to be involved in the Gunpowder Plot three years later.

The Arnolds of 'Comb Fields' and Hopstone are commemorated by 18th-century tablets, and a stone in the wall reads 'Cristofar Watkin Philip Hartley Chvrchwardens Anno Dom. 1632'.

In a field beside the church, grassy mounds indicate village earthworks abandoned centuries ago, and a mile west is the deserted medieval site of **Hopsford village**.

WIXFORD [Stratford-on-Avon]

SP0854: 2 miles (3km) S of Alcester

The tiny village lies where the Roman Icknield Street crossed the little River Arrow. It is a civil parish in its own right, but part of the ecclesiastical parish of Exhall. There are two inns: the Fish, overlooking the river, and the Three Horseshoes to the east, where a blacksmith's forge once stood. The humpbacked red-brick **bridge** is 18th century. It stands where travellers waded through a ford until the first bridge was built in 1566.

The village is the 'Papist Wixford' of the well-known rhyme (see BIDFORD-ON-AVON) – probably because of the Catholic Throckmortons of Coughton Court, who were lords of the manor from the mid-16th until the early 20th century. A line of lovely black and white cottages raised above the road near The Fish are former **almshouses**, built by the Throckmortons in 1709.

The 11th-century **St Milburga's Church** (one of only five with this dedication) stands to the north. It is small, with light grey stonework and a red roof, but has a south chapel. There are Norman doorways on both north and south sides, the former filled in and the latter flanked by pillars. The plain north wall has small lancet windows, two of them curiously set side-by-side. The large wooden bellcote is from an 1881 restoration. Mass-dials can be seen on the south wall.

A yew tree of great antiquity spreads low branches across the churchyard. In 1669 villagers showed themselves to be early conservationists by complaining to the registrar of the diocese when they believed the rector had plans to fell it. Perhaps the same incumbent built the small thatched shed by the gate, said to be a 17th-century stable for use by the rector's horse when he rode over from Exhall.

The large base of a 15th-century cross and the remnant of its pillar also stand in the churchyard. Its head is in the church, as are an ancient dug-out parish chest and two of the county's finest brasses, which adorn the tomb of Thomas de Cruwe and his wife (1411). Other brasses commemorate Rise (or Rhys) Griffin, who was 'but three-quarters old' when he died in 1597, and Jane Alline and her ten children.

Among the village's listed buildings is a traditional red telephone kiosk.

WOLFHAMPCOTE [Rugby]

SP5265: 7½ miles (12km) NE of Southam

This tiniest of hamlets, depopulated for sheep grazing in 1501, stands at the Northamptonshire border and at the end of a long, metalled lane from Flecknoe. Domesday Book has Ulfelmescote (a Norman scribe's version of the Saxon Wulfhelmescote), to which Dugdale adds that it was 'vulgarly called Ovencote'.

Wolfhampcote was the crossing point of two railway lines – the Grand Central (see WILLOUGHBY) and the Leamington to Daventry line, both now dismantled. The Oxford Canal skirts it and the infant River Leam flows by. In Elizabeth I's reign (1558-1603) her courtier (and possibly lover) Sir Christopher Hatton was Lord of the Manor.

Isolated **St Peter's Church** is no longer used for regular worship, but remains a consecrated building and is maintained by the Churches' Conservation Trust. Long, low and built of grey stone, it has a broad, squat, 13th-century tower and a north aisle of the same period. The ancient font may be Saxon.

To the east stands the 18th-century Gothic mausoleum of the Tibbits and to the west is the classical **manor house** from the late 17th century. North of the church there is evidence of the deserted village. An excavation in 1955 revealed over 2000 items of early medieval pottery and a rare Viking barrel padlock.

WOLSTON [Rugby]

SP4175: 5 miles (8km) E of Coventry

A large village just off the Fosse Way, with a long Main Street leading towards Brandon, its antiquity is emphasised by a small, tree-capped **round barrow** on Lammas Hill.

Until the link was broken in the 14th century by the Hundred Years' War, the Abbey of St Pierre-sur-Dive in Normandy had a cell at Wolston. Beyond a housing estate, **Wolston Priory**, a mid-16th-century house, occupies the Benedictine site. Built of red sandstone and lias, it has mullioned and transomed windows, gables and a three-storeyed porch. In 1589 it became one of the houses at which the Martin Marprelate texts were printed (see HASELEY).

At the south end of Main Street, a **Baptist church** with classical touches faces the handsome Georgian **Manor House** of red brick, which has a hipped roof and dormers. A stream flows beside the street, passing cottages and two of Wolston's three inns.

The Old Post Office stands near the war memorial, from which a long church drive runs parallel to the road. The stream continues through the green area between them, where cattle graze. The road passes **Brandon and Wolston Village Hall**, which still proclaims its former use as an Oddfellows Hall of 1890, though a modern ground-floor front has been added.

A long line of Regency cottages leads to a narrow **bridge** of four 18th-century sandstone arches and brick parapets spanning the young River Avon, which marks the boundary with Brandon. The bridge belonged to the original manor house that stood by the church until demolished in 1926.

The spaciously set **St Margaret's Church** has a squat, pyramid-topped central tower built to replace a steeple that collapsed in 1759. The church is Saxon in origin and has a Norman south doorway. The crossing below the tower is also Norman. Beside the path stand 18th-century headstones, and ivy-fringed 19th-century slate tombstones line a wall.

WOLVERTON [Warwick]

SP2062: 4½ miles (7km) N of Stratford-upon-Avon

A small village on a quiet lane, it was Wolverdington until the name was abbreviated in the 19th century. Domesday Book recorded the settlement, and lords of the manor have included the earls of Warwick, the Chapter of St Mary's, Warwick, and Clement Throckmorton (see HASELEY).

The **church of St Mary the Virgin** claims the date 1208 on its notice board and was consecrated in 1316. The building, concealed by trees planted by the Reverend Arthur Campion (rector 1909-21), is reached by climbing a tarmac path from the village. Its red-tiled roof, on walls of grey stone, is capped by a squat wooden belfry, which replaced 'a tin spire' believed to have been destroyed by 1858.

The large wooden porch has the framed advice, '*That thou injure no man, dovelike be, And serpentlike that none may injure thee.*' The circular door-handle may have been designed for fugitives to grasp when seeking sanctuary.

The 13th-century nave is narrow and aisle-less, and beyond a tall, delicately carved, modern screen, the chancel has a reset 14th-century tomb recess into which the organ has been slotted. The choir stalls have modern misericords. There is an old priest's door, blocked by a 16th-century parish chest and a small 17th-century credence table for the Eucharist. Set in the east window are fragments of a 14th-century Doom. Mrs Margaret Mayhew's memorial window is by William Morris.

The Old Rectory, with bargeboarded gables and Gothic windows, was converted in early Victorian times from a timber-framed cottage.

Wolverton Court began as a low 16th-century building with square half-timbering. A taller three-storeyed stone house was raised behind it in the 17th or 18th century and the two were linked in 1912 by Clough Williams-Ellis of Portmeirion, in Queen Anne mood.

WOLVEY [Rugby]

SP4287: 5 miles (8km) SE of Nuneaton

A Saxon settlement, near the source of the River Anker and centreing on a spacious crossroads, the village briefly entered history in 1469 during the Wars of the Roses, when Warwick the Kingmaker surprised and arrested Edward IV on Wolvey Heath. A link with those dangerous times survives in the name of the older of its two inns, the Blue Pig, a disrespectful allusion to the Blue Boar emblem of the Lancastrian Earl of Oxford.

The heath was also the scene of the burning at the stake of Dorothy, Lady Smythe, for the murder of her elderly husband, Sir Walter, in 1555 – there was a young lover involved, of course. It is said that a messenger bearing a reprieve got lost and arrived too late. In 1566, Elizabeth I, during one of her royal progresses, was welcomed in style at Wolvey by the mayor of Coventry.

Wolvey's other inn, the Bull's Head, has been rebuilt in modern times. Its predecessor was the venue for an apparently riotous Harvest Home at which Joseph Rowley was stabbed to death in 1853. His gravestone lies near the north-east corner of the church.

Knitting and milling brought wealth to the village in the Middle Ages, when there were no fewer than 27 windmills. None have survived, but several lovely thatched cottages remain.

The church of **St John Baptist** stands high above the Hinckley road, on the site of a Saxon building. Though mainly 14th century, its lower tower is 200 years older. The Norman south doorway is decorated with both zigzag and floral motifs. The north wall was rebuilt after the roof collapsed in 1620. One of its vicars, Hugh Hughes, was the model for Mr Crew in George Eliot's *Scenes of Clerical Life*.

Tucked away down School Lane is a plain Italianate **Baptist Chapel**, with long, narrow side windows. **Wolvey Hall**, to the north, was built by Thomas Astley in 1677 and extended in 1889. An earlier hall of about 1250 was destroyed by Civil War action in the 1640s.

WOOTTON WAWEN [Stratford-on-Avon]

SP1563: 2 miles (3km) S of Henley-in-Arden

With the Birmingham to Stratford road and rail routes, the Stratford-upon-Avon Canal and the River Alne all converging within half a mile of each other at Wootton Wawen, the small village occupies a strategic position.

It was a Saxon settlement ('the farm by the wood'), founded in the mid-8th century by Earl Aethelric, who was granted land by King Aethelbald of Mercia for a monastery. Some 300 years later, Wegen was its lord, thus accounting for the suffix to the common name of Wootton.

A Benedictine priory was established about 1100, but had fallen into ruin by the mid-15th century. The first church was of wood, but a stone building replaced it in the 10th century and has grown into the present **St Peter's**, one of the county's finest and most interesting churches, strikingly situated at a bend in the main road.

Between the nave and chancel, and flanked by the Lady Chapel, the base of the Saxon tower remains. It encloses the Saxon Sanctuary, which has an arch in each of its four walls, the eastern one blocked by an altar. Thus it is necessary to deviate through the Lady Chapel to reach the chancel from the nave.

The 14th-century Lady Chapel is the glory of St Peter's. It is as large as many a village church, though since 1959 some of its space has been taken for vestries. Its memorials include a marble tablet to Henry Knight of Barrels Hall, son of 'Henrietta S. John', the fascinating Lady Luxborough (see ULLENHALL). In 1898 a brass tablet was installed to commemorate her friend, the poet **William Somerville** (1675-1742) of Edstone Hall (see BEARLEY).

Against the east window is a great urn in memory of Robert Knight, the disgraced cashier behind the South Sea Bubble fiasco of 1721. Nearby, in a large, pillared memorial, Francis Smith, Lord of the Manor, has lain awkwardly on his side since 1605. The mechanism of an 18th-century clock, replaced in 1954, also stands in the chapel.

A rare 17th-century book desk contains the parish library of nine chained books, including a 'Breeches Bible' and John Calvin's *Institution of Christian Religion,* given by George Dunscombe (vicar 1642-52) who autographed most of them.

In the chancel is a tomb-chest (1505) with brasses of John Harewell, his wife and their children, though his wife outlived him, remarried and is buried elsewhere. An earlier John Harewell, who died in 1428, reclines in armour, his feet on an alert-looking dog. The family originated at Harwell, Oxfordshire.

Beside the church stands the classical **Wootton Hall** of 1687. It was the home of Mrs Maria Fitzherbert, whom the Prince of Wales (later the Prince Regent) secretly married in 1785. Built onto its rear is a former Catholic **chapel** of 1813, outwardly in plain brickwork but with a Doric interior. The buildings are now a country club, with a mobile home park and the village post office behind them.

A milestone of 1806 on the river bridge announces 'To London 100 miles'. Beyond are the white-faced **School House** (formerly a Catholic School) and a tall, red-brick **mill** of about 1800, divided into flats.

A neighbouring Roman Catholic churchyard has a simple **cross** of 1852 by A.W.N. Pugin, one of his last works.

The splendid black and white **Bull's Head** is early 17th century with tall, brick chimneys. Another inn, The Navigation, lies below a **canal aqueduct** of 1813.

Further out, against Austy Wood, is the high-chimneyed and gabled **Austy Manor**, once the home of the Fieldhouses and now the headquarters of the British Pregnancy Advisory Service.

At a corner near the railway station is the Gothic **Tollgate Cottage**, and on the Aston Cantlow road stands the Catholic **church of Our Lady and St Benedict**, built in 1905. A brick gable-end, with lancets and a modern porch, is twinned with a gable of the adjoining presbytery. Its stained glass, and a marble altar made in Rome, are early 19th century and came from the chapel at the hall.

Former mill, Wootton Wawen

WORMLEIGHTON [Stratford-on-Avon]

SP4453: 5½ miles (8km) S of Southam

A small village of great interest, it lies at the south end of a vast depopulated plain stretching more than five miles to Southam and measuring some three miles in width. No metalled roads cross it, but the Oxford Canal meanders through and makes a dog-legged detour round Wormleighton Hill. In fields north-west of the church is the site of the deserted medieval village of Wormleighton.

The landlords' desire to graze their enormous herds of sheep led to the clearances, which began about 1450. Most prominent among them were the Spencers of Wormleighton, ancestors of the late Diana, Princess of Wales. John Spencer, a livestock farmer, bought the Wormleighton estate from William Cope, Cofferer to Henry VII, in 1506. A century later, Baron Spencer of Wormleighton was considered the wealthiest man in the kingdom after James I.

The decline of the wool trade led to the Spencers leasing out some of their land in 1634. In 1924, death duties forced the sale of part of it, but Earl Spencer of Althorp, in Northamptonshire, is still a major landowner. There is also a link with the first president of the USA, George Washington (1789-97), whose great-great-grand-uncle Robert Washington married at Wormleighton in 1596.

The village stands at a junction of lanes, a mile east of the Southam to Banbury road. We enter via a no through road and see an impressive, round-arched, ironstone **gatehouse** ahead. A tower flanking it has a chiming clock without a face. The Spencer coat of arms above the arch has the date 1513 and the arms of the dukes of Marlborough are also there, indicating the family link between the Spencers and the Churchills.

Prince Rupert rode out of the gatehouse to the Battle of Edge Hill in 1642. We walk in and see to our right **The Manor House** (also with coats of arms) – the remains of the building that John Spencer obtained a Royal licence to crenellate in 1512. It was fashionably built in brick, though stone was the natural local material. The far side of the house is crenellated and has mullioned windows.

Elizabeth I visited in 1572 and her courtier Robert Dudley, Earl of Leicester (see KENILWORTH), and minister Lord Burghley (to both of whom the Spencers sold sheep) stayed on other occasions.

In 1645 the house was partly destroyed by Royalists to prevent it from falling into parliamentary hands. It was never rebuilt, because the Spencers lived mainly at Althorp. On a nearby green, a tree has been planted in memory of 'Lady Diana Spencer, Princess of Wales, 1961-1997'.

Gatehouse and tower, Wormleighton

A lovely path leads to **St Peter's Church**, in golden Hornton stone. The plain-topped tower, from which small worn heads look down, is unchanged from the 13th century, when most of the building was completed.

The high-roofed interior is rather short and broad, with aisles. Small congregations having led to the chancel being adapted for services, a curtain separates it from the nave. A fine 17th-century wooden screen, which includes a figure wearing spectacles, was originally at Southam church, but was removed to Wormleighton Manor for safe-keeping during the Civil War.

Seats in the chancel have ancient carved end-figures and a large tablet to John Spencer is of interest for its reference to a difference in dates between continental Europe and the British Isles. It tells us that he 'departed this life at Blois in France the Sixt of August after the computation of the Church of England and the sixteenth after the new computation in the year of our Lord Christ 1610, being 19 years old, 8 months, and odd days.' Between 1582 and 1752, the Gregorian calendar operating on the Continent was ahead of the old Julian one used in the British Isles.

Rather gruesomely, a 17th-century round stone near the altar rail says, 'Here lyeth the bowells of Robert, Lord Spencer'. The rest of him was buried at Brington, near Althorp.

By the gatehouse stand the ashlared former **vicarage**, a private house since 1955, and **Church Farm** (tall-chimneyed, with small but aggressive gables), which may have been the bakehouse of the manor. The **school** of 1839, which closed in 1949, is used as a village hall. A cottage next door was the mistress's house.

Ten **estate houses** of 1848, with gables and Gothic windows, possibly occupy the site of the Spencers' wool-yard and great barn. They are known locally as 'The Ten Commandments'.

WROXALL [Warwick]

SP2271: 4 miles (6km) W of Kenilworth

The tiny village at a junction on the Birmingham to Warwick road consists of a few estate cottages and a school, all built in polychromatic brick by James Dugdale in the 1860s, when the road was still a turnpike. The inn, south of the abbey, has a curious name with legal connotations – Case is Altered.

There was a Saxon village, but it is not mentioned in Domesday Book because it was 'a Member of Hatton juxta Haseley' (Dugdale). James Dugdale – who, like his namesake the historian, traced his ancestry to Clitheroe, Lancashire – bought the Wroxall Abbey estate in 1861 and rebuilt practically everything. The previous owners were the Wren family, the architect Sir Christopher Wren having purchased the estate and Elizabethan house for his son in 1713, when he was 80.

Sir Hewe de Hatton founded **Wroxall Abbey**, possibly in 1141. The story goes that, after being imprisoned in the Holy Land for seven years during the Crusades, he had a vision of St Leonard, the patron saint of prisoners, who instantly beamed him home to 'Wrocheshale'. Though at first unrecognised by his wife, he proved his identity by showing her part of a ring they had divided, and founded the priory for nuns of St Benedict in thanks. The abbey was for many years a girls' school, but is now a conference and leisure centre.

Dugdale's hall of 1866 is of red brick and grimly Gothic; the turreted school buildings are severe and unadorned. A garden wall of curved bays, possibly designed by Wren, has plain 20th-century iron gates by Clough Williams-Ellis of Portmeirion.

The grey stone, battlemented **St Leonard's Church**, in Decorated style, is simply the north aisle of the former abbey, with a brick tower of 1663-4 added. It contains monuments of five Christopher Wrens, descendants of the architect, and much medieval glass.

Bibliography

General

Allen, Geoff and Roberts, John. *Warwickshire's Centenary Way*. (1996)

Andrews, William (ed). *Bygone Warwickshire*. (1893, 1969)

Bird, Vivian. *A Short History of Warwickshire and Birmingham*. (1977)

Warwickshire. (1973)

Burgess, J Tom. *Historic Warwickshire*. (1875, 1893)

Burman, John. *In the Forest of Arden*. (1948)

Cave, Lyndon F. *Warwickshire Villages*. (1976)

Chandler, John. *John Leland's Itinerary - Travels in Tudor England* (Edited and in modern English, 1993)

Dugdale, Sir William. *The antiquities of Warwickshire illustrated*. (1656, 1730)

Duignan, W.H. *Warwickshire Place Names* (1912)

Fraser, Antonia. *The Gunpowder Plot – Terror and Faith in 1605*. (1996)

Garner, Lawrence. *The Visitor's Guide to the Severn and Avon*. (1986)

Hannett, John. *The Forest of Arden*. (1863, 1894)

Hickman, Douglas. *Warwickshire – A Shell Guide*. (1979)

Hill, Susan. *Shakespeare Country*. (1987)

Hutton, W.H. *Highways and Byways in Shakespeare's Country*. (1914, 1995)

James, Peter. *Harrison's Warwickshire – A Collection of Photographs of the County, 1890-1908, by William Jerome Harrison*. (1992)

Kelsall, Dennis. *Discovery Walks in Warwickshire*. (1998)

Lawrence, Gerald. *Warwickshire Villages Trail*. (1998)

McCulla, Dorothy H. and Hampson, Martin. *Victorian and Edwardian Warwickshire from Old Photographs*. (1976)

Mee, Arthur. *Warwickshire – Shakespeare's Country*. (The King's England, 1936, 1991)

Miller, George. *Rambles Round the Edge Hills*. (1896, 1967)

Morris, J. *Domesday Book - Warwickshire* (Edited, 1976)

Newbold, E.B. *Warwickshire History Makers*. (1975)

Parsons, Harold. *History, People and Places in Warwickshire*. (1975)

Pevsner, Nikolaus and Wedgwood, Alexandra. *The Buildings of England: Warwickshire*. (1966)

Roberts, John. *The Heart of England Way*. (Fifth edition, 1995)

Sale, Richard. *The Heart of England Way*. (1998)

Showell, Charles. *Shakespeare's Avon from Source to Severn*. (1901, 1985)

Shurey, Richard. *Shakespeare's Avon from Source to Severn*. (1981)

Slater, Terry. *A History of Warwickshire.* (1981, 1997)

Taylor, Joe and Cook, Chas. *Walks in Shakespeare Country.* (1989)

Thomson, J.A. *Salford Priors – The Tower in the Vineyard.* (c1975)

Tyack, Geoffrey. *Warwickshire Country Houses in the Age of Classicism, 1650-1800.* (1980)

Warwickshire Federation of Women's Institutes: *The Warwickshire Village Book.* (1988)

The Victoria History of the County of Warwick. (8 volumes, 1904-65)

Towns and Villages

Bland, John, Callwood, Rita and Hayfield, Colin. *Whitacre Remembered.* (1986)

Bland, John and Hayfield, Colin. *Arley Remembered.* 1987)

Drew, John H. *The Book of Royal Leamington Spa.* (1978)

Kenilworth – A Manor of the King. (1971)

Remember Kenilworth. (1984)

Feeney, Margaret. *Ullenhall – Life after Lady Luxborough.* (1993)

Field, Jean. *Beneath the Great Elms – An Illustrated History of Whitnash in Warwickshire.* (1993)

Gilbert, Audrey V. *Walking around Stoneleigh in Arden – A Village.* (c1990)

Hall, Michael. *Stratford-upon-Avon and the Cotswolds.* (revised 1993)

Hudson, Robert. *Memorials of a Warwickshire Parish.* (Lapworth, 1904)

Kingsbury History Society: *Kingsbury Remembered – Photographic Memories of the Old Parish of Kingsbury.* (1992)

Moore, Susan K. (compiled by): *I Remember Strawberries & Sewage – A Collection of Twenty Biographies, Reminiscences and Photographs of Everyday Life in the North Warwickshire Village of Fillongley.* (1989)

Morris, Richard K. and Hoverd, Ken. *The Buildings of Warwick.* (1994)

Payne, Archibald. *Portrait of a Parish – Long Itchington.* (1968)

Saville, G. Edward. *King's Coughton – A Warwickshire Hamlet.* (1973)

Saville, G. Edward (edited by). *Alcester— A History* (1986)

Scott, Helen and Storey, Richard. *A Kenilworth Collection.* (1986)

Smith, Betty. *Oxhill.* (1989)

Timmins, E.W. *Rugby – A Pictorial History.* (1990)

Woodall, Joy. *Portrait of Lapworth.* (1986)

Index

D

Also of interest from: 

BEST TEA SHOP WALKS IN WARWICKSHIRE

Julie Meech

The 25 walks in this book lead you through the beautiful Warwickshire countryside in search of tea and scones - but you'll find much more besides: medieval castles stand alongside Norman churches and hillsides are crossed by ancient trackways. All the walks can be done using public transport and shun the more obvious, over-walked routes. "This is a book which lovers of Warwickshire would be delighted to receive" SELECT MAGAZINE (Birmingham)

£6.95

LITERARY STROLLS IN AND AROUND THE COTSWOLDS

Gordon Ottewell

A collection of 40 delightful short strolls with special appeal to lovers of literature and landscape. All less than three miles in length, the routes spread right across the delightful Cotswold countryside and encourage strollers to find out more about the area through the discovery of its many-faceted literary associations. An original approach to walking which will appeal equally to lovers of literature and landscape.

£6.95